To

Out of Birmingham

George Dixon (1820-98),
'Father of free education'

Dixon Family Tree

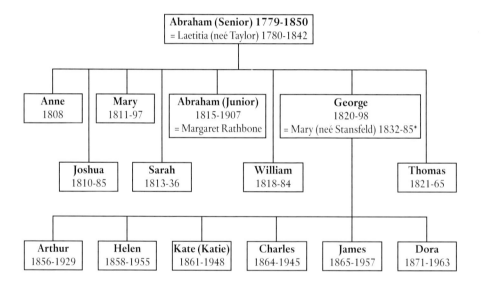

Abraham (Senior) 1779-1850
= Laetitia (neé Taylor) 1780-1842

Anne
1808

Mary
1811-97

Abraham (Junior)
1815-1907
= Margaret Rathbone

George
1820-98
= Mary (neé Stansfeld) 1832-85*

Joshua
1810-85

Sarah
1813-36

William
1818-84

Thomas
1821-65

Arthur
1856-1929

Helen
1858-1955

Kate (Katie)
1861-1948

Charles
1864-1945

James
1865-1957

Dora
1871-1963

*Sister of Sir James Stansfeld 1820-98.

For the sake of clarity, not all family members are shown.

Out of Birmingham

George Dixon (1820-98),
'Father of free education'

JAMES DIXON

BREWIN BOOKS

BREWIN BOOKS
56 Alcester Road,
Studley,
Warwickshire,
B80 7LG
www.brewinbooks.com

Published by Brewin Books 2013

A CIP catalogue record for this book is available from the British Library.

Front cover/jacket image: Birmingham Town Hall.

ISBN: 978-1-85858-504-8 (paperback)
ISBN: 978-1-85858-505-5 (hardback)

Printed and bound in Great Britain
by Gomer Press Limited.

Contents

George Dixon

Preface

THE WRITING OF this book has been an enjoyable lifetime adventure. Looking back, my curiosity in the subject-matter was first aroused in childhood days in the 1950s when my grandfather, George Dixon's grandson, would sit glued in front of the television set late on a Saturday afternoon, watching *Dixon of Dock Green*[1]. Popular though that crime series may have been at the time, his devotion inexplicably went way beyond that of most other people. On some other occasion, I learned that his grandfather was also called George. And he had been an MP, representing Birmingham. At that time, that was about the sum total of my knowledge of family history.

At school at Lancing, I was fortunate to have the truly inspirational Robin Reeve as my history master, who awakened my interest in people and things Victorian and who hinted that perhaps the life of Dixon might merit further investigation. Proceeding to Corpus Christi College, Oxford, I was again most fortunate in having Brian Harrison as my tutor. Having submitted a paper on Dixon as an entry for the Matthew Arnold Prize, Brian has continued to encourage me to take my researches one stage further and to write a book. There the matter rested for more than a quarter of a century. I entered the world of chartered accountancy.

As part of my history lessons at school, I had always been fascinated by the work of nineteenth century Royal Commissions in investigating major issues of the day, and I had this vague enthusiasm to become involved in something similar at some stage in my career. Chartered accountancy was held out to be

---

1 See also Chapter 8, p. 234.

the passport to all manner of openings, but it quickly became clear that Royal Commissions were a thing of the past. Becoming one of the country's first specialists in giving VAT advice not long after the tax was introduced was an intriguing substitute, requiring detailed analysis of the facts and advice on the way forward.

Precisely 25 years after signing articles with Barton Mayhew & Co as it then was (now Ernst & Young) I tendered my resignation to the senior partner. I had no clear idea what I was going to do next. Perhaps serendipity would step in? And indeed it has done ever since.

Seated beside Sir Stephen Tumim, HM Chief Inspector of Prisons, over dinner shortly before retirement, he asked me what I intended to do next. Replying that I had no idea, he responded with the suggestion that I should become the Honorary Treasurer of the Prisoners' Education Trust, of which he was a patron. I had never heard of it. But just a few days later, as a driver volunteering for the charity Contact the Elderly, dressed as Father Christmas and about to hand out presents, I was standing in the kitchen of the hostess of the month, Ann Grieves, when she asked me exactly the same question. So I accepted the invitation. The coincidence was extraordinary. In the scheme of things, this was obviously intended. With a turnover of just £12,000 per year when I started, this figure had increased to almost £250,000 in the six years that followed. I can claim no credit for this achievement. I was simply performing many administrative tasks which liberated the other trustees so that they could engage in far more important fund-raising activities. Today that figure is in excess of £1,000,000 per year, and the charity has national standing.

Meantime a distant relative, Bob Walker, had collated a substantial quantity of papers and diaries, most of them written by Dixon's daughter, Katie Rathbone, which were published as *The Dales,* the house in Augustus Road, Edgbaston, where the family lived for much of the second half of the nineteenth century. He suggested that this could provide the foundation for a proper biography, which has indeed turned out to be the case. However, we both bemoaned the fact that a German bomb in 1941 had destroyed all the family archives and these subsequent reminiscences were all that remained. Also active in the 1970s was Geoffrey Hayward in Leatherhead who, entirely independently and unbeknown to me, was working on the life of Abraham Dixon, George's elder brother. I was in my late thirties before I even became aware that he had constructed his substantial house, Cherkley Court, later owned by Lord Beaverbrook, standing in hundreds of acres of grounds overlooking the Mole Valley.

How was I going to set about writing Dixon's biography? At this stage John Ramsden, a contemporary at Corpus, suggested that I should take a PhD course as in no way would I achieve the desired result without a structured approach. What sound advice, and how sad it is that he is no longer alive to read the final product. As a descendant of Dixon, I wished to prevent this work from becoming a mere hagiography. By the same token, I wished to avoid the reverse, and become over-critical. A university environment would provide the correct balance, an intellectual stimulus and excellent research facilities.

Living in London, there is a wonderful choice of universities at which to study, but Royal Holloway with its great friendliness and remarkable Victorian architecture had no rival. An MA course preceded the PhD course, but as I had no ambition to obtain a doctorate, which would have required the writing of a thesis as well as the subsequent book, the Registrar Phil McGeevor kindly gave dispensation to continue.

Throughout these years, I have had the benefit of tremendous support from Penelope Corfield as my supervisor. Penelope has remained good-humoured throughout many years whilst I have slowly but surely unravelled many a strange mystery. Her contribution has been enormous, and her name deserves to have appeared on the front page alongside my own. I can not thank her enough.

There are also very many other people to whom I am hugely indebted. I would start with my late mother, who also did not live to read the final product but who unfailingly expressed interest in all I was doing. This on occasion extended to doing some research herself and I vividly recall a visit to the Grand Hotel in Eastbourne to check the visitors' book, to see whether Sir John Hall (one-time Prime Minister of New Zealand) had been staying there at the same time as Dixon, when their wives had both been seriously ill.

Greg Claeys, also at Royal Holloway, for providing a very useful summary of Victorian history. Valerie Chancellor, for an insight into her work on writing Dixon's entry in the Oxford Dictionary of National Biography. Colin Campbell and my brother Peter for advice on how to keep my computer doing what I wanted it to do, and Simon Trafford at the Institute of Historical Research for guidance on how to maximise the benefits of on-line searching. Peter Marsh, Joseph Chamberlain's biographer, for highly relevant guidance on sources. Judy Lloyd, working in parallel on a biography of a Lloyd family member. A whole host of most helpful archivists, willingly prepared to answer my questions and, thinking outside the box, even those I ought to have asked, but did not. Sarah Aitchison and Claire Drinkwater at the Institute of Education; Richard Wragg and Hannah Thomas at Royal Holloway College; Karyn Stuckey at Kew Gardens; Karen Simpson at Lloyds Banking Group; Fiona Tait at Birmingham Central Library; Simon Blundell at the Reform Club; Helga Hughes at the Red House Museum in Gomersal; Phil Parkinson at the Alexander Turnbull Library in Wellington, NZ; Jane Teal at Christ's College in Christchurch, NZ; Dawn Smith at Nelson Provincial Museum, NZ; and Sarah Laycock of the Brontë Society. Ann Morton was also most helpful in seeking to locate material at National Archives.

A very enthusiastic group of people in New Zealand, including Garth Cant at the University of Canterbury; Jean Garner at Lincoln University; Michael Vance of *The Press* in Christchurch; Binney Lock of the Christchurch Local History Society; and above all Kate Foster at Hororata Station, Sir John Hall's former residence, where is kept a wealth of papers hardly known outside the country.

A number of people connected with the Leatherhead and District Local History Society, especially Linda Heath, Roddy Clube and Geoffrey Hayward. Alex Windscheffel and Matthew Grimley at Royal Holloway for probing my skills at an early stage of my researches. Michael Rhodes in Munich, formerly with Rabone & Petersen, and quite possibly the last UK salesman working in Cuba after Castro assumed power, for an insight into the merchanting trade. The *Birmingham Evening Mail* and Peter Craven, George Orton, Jill Wood, Eric Brown, Frank Jones, Joan Myring, Christopher Midgley and Hazel Holley, all former employees of Rabone & Petersen.

Marcus Dixon for a never-ending flow of background family details, and the production of one of the largest family trees imaginable of which a very small portion is reproduced in this book. Hugh Lohan for a range of contemporary photographic material. Sarah Willis for some assistance with proof-reading.

Roger Ward and Gillian Sutherland for probing my researches at a later stage in the writing of this book, and Roger in particular for a number of insights into Birmingham local history. Susannah Wright for sight of her helpful thesis on moral education. John Avery Jones for guidance on late nineteenth century taxation aspects. Philip Walker for production of the family tree in this book. Philip Fisher of the Birmingham and Midland Institute for help with material held there. Harlan Walker, Miles Taylor and Roland Quinault for reading a draft of this book, and giving some most helpful guidance.

I have also benefited hugely from the fellowship of colleagues over the years at two seminars organised under the auspices of the Institute of Historical Research: British History in the Long Eighteenth Century, and Modern British History. It has also been a joy to attend the annual Gladstone Umbrellas at Hawarden, to meet fellow enthusiasts for the period.

I am very grateful to Asa Briggs for writing the Introduction. Over the years, his writings and enthusiasm have been an inspiration to all those who seek a firm grasp of the Victorian age. Alan and Alistair Brewin have both worked very hard indeed in producing such a magnificent-looking publication, quite in keeping with the style of which they are justifiably proud. They have also coped admirably with my various foibles in a work which, with its numerous footnotes, is a relatively complicated creation. I am also indebted to Catherine Hall for the preparation of the index.

I wish to thank the following for permission to use material in this book: Brontë Parsonage Museum, Lloyds Banking Group Archives, Birmingham

Special Collections, Joe Holyoak, Terrace Station Archives at Hororata, New Zealand, Archives and Heritage Collections, Birmingham Central Library.

If I have failed to mention anyone specifically by name, please forgive me. It has been a pleasure to have been engaged in this project. If there are any mistakes, they are mine and mine alone.

Despite the fact that I am directly descended from the subject of this book, it is a matter of pure coincidence that as Honorary Treasurer of the Prisoners' Education Trust more than ten years ago, I was saying the same things as Dixon was in 1869 when he was campaigning for compulsory and free education: Crime Costs. That is not just a chartered accountant speaking. There are huge personal and social implications, and better education can go some way to mitigating the effects. Accordingly, I am mandating the royalties from this work to the Prisoners' Education Trust and hope that it will benefit substantially as a consequence.

_____

James Dixon, Putney. July 2013.

Introduction

I T IS A pleasure and a privilege to write a brief introduction to what to me is a fascinating book. This is not just because it is a major contribution to the remarkable history of Victorian Birmingham but because it brings in many other people and places with which I have had personal connections. I wish that I had been able to read it before I published my book *Special Relationships, People and Places* in 2012.

Sixty years before that, my *History of Birmingham from 1865 to 1938*, the second volume in a history sponsored by the city in the centenary year of its incorporation as a borough in 1838, at last appeared. In writing it I became aware of the role of George Dixon, a liberal and ecumenical Anglican, in the formation of a new kind of Liberal party, governed by a caucus as it came to be called. I became aware too of his still bigger part in the evolution of the National Educational League and in the complicated politics leading up to and succeeding the landmark Education Act of 1870. I followed too the story of the Birmingham School Board which went through various phases. In 1973 I wrote a long introduction to a new Brighton edition of Francis Adams's *History of the Elementary School Contest in England*, first published in 1882.

What I did not know until I read James Dixon's book was of George Dixon's family history and of his links with other families that I had studied in other contexts. He was born at Gomersal in the West Riding of Yorkshire and educated at Leeds Grammar School. He had connections with the Brontës, hitherto never studied in detail. I was for a time President of the Brontë Society, and when I was Professor of Modern History at Leeds University from 1955 to 1962 I lived at first in a house not far from Leeds Grammar School.

George got a good education in Leeds before moving to Birmingham in 1838 in the wake of his elder brother Abraham when he joined him in a well-established business to be known as Rabone Bros., which was to play a major part in Birmingham's growing gun trade. James Dixon notes carefully the various steps in George's life as a businessman and as a philanthropist. He was by no means involved exclusively in education, although he always attached prior importance to it as an issue.

He notes also, as many others have done before him, how much the growing borough, incorporated in 1838, the year when George arrived, depended on immigrants from outside. Most attention has been focussed on Joseph Chamberlain, born in Camberwell, London in 1836, who moved to Birmingham also at the age of 18. His relationship with George was always complex and never settled and requires the kind of analysis that his descendant employs in this book.

To call Birmingham Chamberlain's 'grand duchy', as one historian, Michael Hurst, has done, is not quite the right description. Chamberlain was politically far more ruthless and ambitious than Dixon ever was. Yet Dixon preceded him not only as an MP for Birmingham, which he represented from 1867 to 1876, but as Mayor, from 1866 to 1867. He never used the term 'civic gospel' as Chamberlain did. Nor, however, did he make much mention of education in his electoral address when he won the contested by-election of 1867. Later in his life, when Birmingham was no longer a three-member constituency and in 1885 was divided into seven separate single member constituencies, he was returned as first MP for Edgbaston, in terms of wealth second only in the country to Kensington. It was a constituency with a future as fascinating as the lives of George and Joseph Chamberlain had been.

There is no space in this introduction to consider the split in Gladstone's Liberal party on the issue of home rule. They are investigated, not exhaustively, in this book. Nor is there the place in it for George Dawson or John Morley, whose role in local and national politics deserves further attention from historians. There is a prominent place, nonetheless, for his brother Abraham's wife, a Rathbone with far-reaching associations, and George's own wife, Mary Stansfeld, a Unitarian, born in Halifax. There is a place too for his travels to countries as far away as New Zealand and Australia. There is no statue to George Dixon in Birmingham – but he would not have wanted one.

Asa Briggs

CHAPTER ONE

Origins: Into Birmingham

O
UT OF BIRMINGHAM came many men and movements. One of those men, in the nineteenth century, was an apparently unassuming entrepreneur named George Dixon. He was the quiet reformer, standing alongside the nationwide reputation of John Bright,[1] and the much more showy talents of Joseph Chamberlain.[2]

Dixon was however Birmingham's Third Man in late Victorian times. For far too long his story has lain hidden in the shadows. In part this has been due to his self-effacing, if not self-deprecating character.

He would have opposed any suggestion that a statue should ever have been erected in his honour, in an era when such construction was very much in fashion. He resisted to the last months of his life the conferring of any honour. He was lacking any great oratorical skills and never made any memorable states-manlike pronouncements. Indeed, it was almost as if history wanted to forget him, for a German bomb in 1941 destroyed all his family and business records.

Dixon's main claim to fame is essentially one of advancing the cause of educational reform in England, not only in pressurising the government to assume far greater responsibilities for elementary education but, through his own example, extending that responsibility into what later became known as secondary education.

---

1 For John Bright (1811-89), see K. Robbins, *John Bright* (1979); and *ODNB-online*.
2 For Joseph Chamberlain (1836-1914), see P.T. Marsh, *Joseph Chamberlain: Entrepreneur in Politics* (New Haven, 1994); and *ODNB-online*.

During his lifetime he was to be involved in many causes with which Liberals of the day were concerned, always conscious of the needs of those less fortunate than himself, including those connected with the formation of agricultural trade unions, and those keen to make a better life for themselves overseas, especially New Zealand.

Birmingham attracted strangers, and its two most notable representatives in Parliament in the second half of the century (Bright, 1857-89, and Chamberlain, 1876-1914), both eminent radicals and Nonconformists, were neither born nor bred in the town. Indeed, John Bright never even acquired a property in the town, which he seldom visited more than once a year.

Like Bright and Chamberlain, George Dixon arrived as a visitor to the town. Unlike them, he was an ecumenical Christian, an Anglican of the broadest inclination. This breadth was to stand him in good stead as he fought many of the causes which Nonconformists espoused, but was able to bridge sectarian arguments. Divisions were most obvious in the field of educational reform, where there had long been a craving for advance, but where changes had so often been impeded by religious discord.

In this era, there were many great improvements in the physical condition of the town, with reforms led almost continuously by a Liberal grouping in municipal politics, a significant majority of whom were Nonconformists. Birmingham acquired city status in 1889 and a Lord Mayor (as opposed to Mayor) in 1896.[3] The first Anglican Bishop of Birmingham was ordained in 1905 when St Philip's Church became a cathedral.

The great urban giant of the West Midlands was immensely proud of its status and its claims. Known as the 'city of a thousand trades', it lay at the heart of the Black Country's flourishing metal-manufacturing region, making an immense variety of precision-tooled goods – from buttons, nails and screws, to jewellery, toys and ornaments, and on to firearms and sporting guns. Its industrial reputation certainly lacked the worldly glamour of resorts such as the city of Bath. Thus Jane Austen had famously allowed one of her characters, the snobbish and ill-bred Mrs Elton, to detect in the name of Birmingham 'something direful in the sound'.[4] But such condescension was inappropriate even as it was satirised. Arthur Young had already extolled Birmingham in 1788 as 'the first manufacturing town in the world'.[5] And by the mid-nineteenth-century it was not only an industrial giant but also a dynamic centre of cultural life and political debate.

The pressures on those who governed were enormous, for the population of Birmingham and the local area was rising rapidly. Whilst the rate of increase expressed in percentage terms was not as fast as it had been in earlier years,

3 V. Bird, *Portrait of Birmingham* (1970), p. 146.
4 J. Austen, *Emma* (1816; in Penguin edn 1969), p. 310.
5 Cited in E. Hopkins, *Birmingham: The First Manufacturing Town in the World, 1760-1840* (1989), p. 26.

nonetheless in absolute terms the increase was substantial: from 232,638 in 1851 to 400,774 in 1881, for example.[6] By 1901, Birmingham had become the fourth city in England, in terms of sheer numbers[7] – although for provincial civic leadership it always vied on equal terms with its close rival, Manchester, the Lancashire 'Cottonopolis'.

Within Birmingham, Bright was revered and respected for his part in the Repeal of the Corn Laws and the granting of the vote to a proportion of the urban working-class in the Second Reform Act of 1867. Chamberlain was admired, amongst many other things, for his period in office as Mayor from 1873 to 1876 when he improved gas and water supplies, and implemented new policies of slum clearance. Dixon, however, was hugely popular in a different sort of way. Often it was said of him that he had no enemies. In the world of politics that was both a great strength but also a weakness. Indeed, upon closer analysis it became apparent that Dixon and Chamberlain were not always on the best of terms. But the ultimate litmus test of Dixon's local reputation was the School Board election of 1888 in which Dixon declared that he was not standing again, and sailed away to New Zealand for almost six months. In his absence, the two opposing factions in Birmingham both nominated him as one of their own candidates. The ballot papers mentioned his name as one of the candidates, but connected to no party. The election duly took place, and upon his return Dixon once more resumed the chairmanship, victorious.

It was a feat with few parallels. In the wider world, it was not earth-shaking. But in the context of Birmingham's tense political scene, it spoke volumes.

* * * * *

George Dixon was born on 21 July 1820,[8] the seventh of eight children of Abraham[9] and Laetitia Dixon (née Taylor).

His parents were living in Yorkshire at the time, his place of birth being recorded as Gomersal, and he was baptised into the Anglican Church at Kirkheaton on 15 October 1821.[10]

For a family of not especially notable background, a surprisingly large amount is known about their circumstances, helped in good measure by the fact that, through the Taylor family, the Dixons were for a while close friends of Charlotte Brontë. Indeed, several members of the Taylor family were

---

6 Census figures.

7 B.R. Mitchell, *Abstract of British Historical Statistics* (Cambridge, 1971), p. 25.

8 Gravestone. A number of authorities incorrectly quote the date as being 1 July 1820.

9 The fifth child was also called Abraham, with whom George had very close connections throughout his life. Where there is any possibility of confusion, they are designated 'Senior' and 'Junior' respectively.

10 Family records held by the author.

prototypes for characters in her novel *Shirley*.[11] Laetitia's brother Joshua, and thus George Dixon's uncle, was the prototype of Hiram Yorke.

Abraham Dixon Senior came from Cumberland, and was known to be an inventor connected with the woollen industry. He lived in a variety of places, including London for a while, and travelled much on the continent in his efforts to sell his ideas in northern France and to the Belgian government and Belgian woollen manufacturers. George Dixon, however, was born in Gomersal,[12] to the south-east of Bradford and south-west of Leeds, being thus readily accessible to the whole of the West Riding woollen district.

The Taylor family came from Yorkshire and lived in the Red House, Gomersal, now preserved as a Museum. In *Shirley*, the building featured as Briarmains. The family has been described as 'anti-establishment', since, despite being successful in business, they were excluded from political power by the local gentry.[13] This attitude spilled over into their religious beliefs: the Church of England was rejected, and the family instead built its own chapel.

Charlotte Brontë described Hiram Yorke [in reality, Joshua Taylor, George Dixon's uncle] as follows:

> a Yorkshire gentleman he was par excellence. His hair was silver white, his forehead was broad, his face fresh and hale; the harshness of the North was seen in his features as it was heard in his voice. Every trait was thoroughly English, not a Norman line anywhere; it was an inelegant, unclassic, unaristocratic mould of visage.[14]

It is impossible to determine the impact Uncle Joshua had on his nephew, but they had much in common. Almost as soon as Brontë introduces Hiram Yorke, then he is offering hospitality;[15] their respective houses had taste; there was music; they liked wine;[16] they both suffered from 'want of veneration ...: kings and nobles and priests, dynasties and parliaments and establishments ... were to him an abomination'.[17] Moreover, there was a hint of Dixon's religious stance in Hiram Yorke, too: 'He was not irreligious, though a member of no sect, but his religion could not be that of one who knows how to venerate. He believed in God and heaven, but his God and heaven were those of a man in whom awe, imagination, and tenderness lack'. Both believed in equality, and both were benevolent to all who were beneath them.

---

11 See T.J. Wise and J.A. Symington (eds), *The Brontës: Their Lives, Friendships and Correspondence in Four Volumes* (Oxford, 1932), Vol. 1, p. 222.
12 *The Times*, 25 Jan. 1898.
13 Anon., *Red House Museum: A Guide* (Kirklees, n.d.).
14 H. Ashwell Cadman, *Gomersal Past and Present* (Leeds, 1930), p. 58.
15 C. Brontë, *Shirley* (1849), p. 42.
16 Ibid., p. 43.
17 Ibid., p. 47.

Joshua Taylor's business was that of cloth manufacturing, but he was also a merchant, and a banker issuing his own notes. Unfortunately, Joshua Taylor & Sons failed in the general financial crisis of 1826, but it was to the credit of the family that nearly 30 years later, the total amount of the bank's obligations to the depositors had been repaid. Joshua Taylor travelled widely, and was fluent in both French and Italian, seldom returning home without bringing with him paintings or other artistic objects.

Many of these characteristics were also to manifest themselves in George Dixon's future career.

No less auspicious was the school which he attended from the age of eight: Leeds Grammar School.[18] The school had a history of being involved in one of the longest-running litigious suits of the period. As far back as 1777 the governing body, representative of local mercantile interests, had been trying to broaden the curriculum, only to be met with the flat opposition of the Master. In 1795 the dispute was taken to the Court of Chancery. The governors' case was that Leeds 'had a very extensive foreign trade' and that the teaching of subjects 'usually considered to form the basis of a mercantile and commercial education' would be useful to the inhabitants and would increase the number of scholars.

By contrast, the judgment of the ultra-conservative Lord Chancellor, Lord Eldon, when it finally came in 1805, was based on a legalistic interpretation of the founder's intent, namely the provision of a free grammar school in which the learned languages were grammatically taught. How the poor would have benefited from a knowledge of Latin or Greek was not explained, but on the other hand the parents of potential 'poor' scholars were not at that time in a position to act as an articulate pressure group.[19]

There was however a rider to Eldon's judgment, and in 1807 the teaching of sciences was permitted so long as a boy at the same time 'pursued also Classical Learning'.[20] In 1817, the boys themselves petitioned for the introduction of mathematics, and by 1820 the core curriculum appeared to comprise divinity, classics, mathematics and English. Some ancient history, geography and other subjects were also taught.[21]

For the eight or so years between 1829 and 1837 when the young Dixon was at the school, there was a period of consolidation, the number of pupils varying between 78 and 123.[22] Around the end of his career there, an examiner spoke highly of the school's education being of 'a very happy medium between an over-anxious attention to minutiae and that loose, vague, and multifarious

18 George Dixon (1820-98), see *ODNB-online*.
19 B. Simon, *Studies in the History of Education, 1780-1870* (1960), p. 105.
20 A.C. Price, *A History of the Leeds Grammar School from its Foundation to the End of 1918* (1919), p. 145.
21 Ibid., p. 161.
22 Ibid., p. 179.

reading which tends to dissipate rather than to strengthen the mind'.[23] At the time of his death sixty years later, nobody would ever deny that he had benefited enormously from an appropriate grasp of the importance of attention to detail.

Just before Dixon started at Leeds Grammar School, his elder brother Abraham had moved to Birmingham to start work with the old-established firm of export merchants, Rabone Bros.

Founded in 1765, the original Rabone business was the importation of wines from Spain and Portugal. In those early days, problems were often encountered with making payment, until it came to be appreciated that settlement could be most easily effected through the exchange of products, such as jewellery, in which the Birmingham area specialised. The Rabones then discovered that the profit margins on such exports were higher than those on the import of wines, to the point where the Rabone business became exclusively that of exporting.

A knowledge of the Spanish and Portuguese languages was of course critical to the success of the business and, in the immediate aftermath of the Napoleonic Wars, with very many countries in Central and South America gaining their independence from Spain and Portugal, Rabone Bros. had a head start over many of its rivals. The Caribbean, including English-speaking parts in that area, and Central and South America were to remain at the core of Rabone's business success.

George's elder brother Abraham's employment with Rabone Bros. was itself an interesting tale. Dixon's youngest daughter Dora recounted that

> 'A certain Mr. Rabone of Birmingham fell in love with their mother [i.e. father Abraham's wife, Laetitia] but she preferred Mr. Dixon and married him and Mr. Rabone consoled himself with another lady, who was, however, unable to give him children, so when Mr. Rabone was in advancing years he wrote to Mr. Dixon and asked if Abraham, his second son, could come to Birmingham and learn the art of merchandise in his firm of Rabone Bros'.[24]

Dora's sister Katie commented that Rabone 'took the boy in for love of her [i.e. his mother]'.[25] Why Abraham's elder brother, Joshua, was not selected was not clear, but Dixon's grand-daughter, Maidie Rathbone, observed that Joshua 'never married, made a fortune out of some speculation, [and was] generally referred to in a slightly shocked voice'.[26] These are family reports which cannot be externally checked; and the motive for inviting Abraham might have been

23 Ibid., p. 182.
24 K. Rathbone, *The Dales: Growing Up in a Victorian Family* (Ledbury, 1989), p. 118.
25 Ibid., p. 2.
26 Ibid., p. 134.

more utilitarian than romantic. However, this was the way the transaction was explained within the family.

In the middle of George Dixon's schooling, around the age of 12, his education was temporarily interrupted by problems with his eyesight and, during this educational 'pause', his elder sister Mary taught him Spanish. Possibly the importance of understanding Spanish in a future business career, with connections in South America, was a factor behind this choice of subject: it was comparatively rare in England at that time but not necessarily in Leeds. For more than a year George Dixon had to wear a bandage or sit in a darkened room, which made him a captive pupil. How his sister had learned the language is not known.

George Dixon's command of foreign languages was further enhanced when he went to live in France for a year at the age of 17.

Abraham and George Dixon were close throughout their lives and, even though there was another brother between them in years – William, who was to become an Anglican cleric – Abraham made enquiries within Rabone's to see whether George might come as office boy.[27] Employment started in 1838, when George was 18.

It was seemingly a convivial place in which to start his working life. Austen Chamberlain, Joseph Chamberlain's elder son and himself a leading politician, commented in 1913 on the occasion of the centenary of the Birmingham Chamber of Commerce: 'Birmingham has always welcomed visitors and still more residents within its bounds, and much of our Birmingham history has been made by men who were not Birmingham born'.[28] Katie painted the social picture:

> 'Old Mr. Rabone must have been a testy though kind-hearted old man. The two young men used to dine with him on Sundays at his house at Smethwick, and there are tales of rides with talking and smart young ladies. In those days Birmingham being so very much smaller than it is now [this was probably written in the 1940s] it was possible to know and exchange visits with people living all round it by riding through the country lanes, and very pleasant it doubtless was'.[29]

Dixon shared accommodation with his elder brother, initially in a 'pleasant red brick house in Easy Row, a short walk from Bridge Street where another good red brick house facing Broad Street housed the firm' [Rabone Bros].[30]

27 Ibid., p. 118.
28 G.H. Wright, *Chronicles of the Birmingham Chamber of Commerce, A.D. 1813-1913* (Birmingham, 1913), p. 656.
29 Rathbone, *The Dales*, p. 2.
30 Ibid., p. 118. The office premises were at the intersection of the two streets.

In the 1840s, accommodation was being rented in Chad Road. Later, they were affluent enough to be renting the more distant Hay Hall, at Yardley,[31] a fourteenth-century manor-house enlarged in Tudor times. For a time, sister Mary Dixon kept house there.[32]

Birmingham was essentially a town of 'small men', as Austen Chamberlain put it,[33] by which he did not refer to their stature but to the structure of their industry, in which each individual enterprise was notable for its small size, unlike the large factories of the North. Although things were changing substantially in Birmingham as the century progressed, the business environment there was known for its relatively easy relationships between employers and employees.[34] Indeed with Dixon living much of his later life in Edgbaston, and able to walk to work in Bridge Street, he had the opportunity to pass close to some of the poorest and most deprived areas.

1838 was also the year in which Birmingham got its Charter of Incorporation as a Borough. Its 48 Councillors were all Liberals of the Radical persuasion,[35] and one of them was Abraham Dixon, then aged just 23. The Dixon family had entered Birmingham politics at a time of rapid urban growth locally and just as Chartist protests were spreading across the country in their campaign to widen the franchise to include working men.

Around 1840 the Dixon parents had moved to a rented house, 11 Rue de la Régence in Brussels, where Abraham Senior's business contacts included the Belgian government. On occasions it was not all a bed of roses. In 1843 he wrote: 'It would appear (although I am not yet quite certain) that the Belgian government have declined to use Kyam's process [details of which are now obscure]; this is very mortifying after all the trouble and expense I have had with it. I have yet to learn the reason for this apparent determination'.[36]

Nonetheless, it was from all accounts a very happy and hospitable household, although Dixon's mother Laetitia had died by this time. His cousin Mary Taylor later wrote: 'They are the most united, affectionate family I ever met. They have taken me as one of themselves, and made me such a comfortable happy home that I should like to live here all my life'.[37] Dixon remained extremely hospitable throughout his life, and many were the occasions when an invitation to come to his house was the starting-point for the formation of a new movement of one sort or another.

31 [Souvenir brochure] Anon., *Leatherhead Institute: Hall Restoration Project* [n.d.].
32 G. Hayward, 'The Dixon Family of Cherkley Court, Leatherhead', *Proceedings of the Leatherhead and District Local History Society* (1976), Part 2, p. 351.
33 Wright, *Chronicles*, p. 656.
34 Hopkins, *The First Manufacturing Town*, p. 180. This view is not shared by all commentators: see, for example, C. Behagg, *Politics and Production in the Early Nineteenth-Century* (1990).
35 Bird, *Portrait*, p. 139.
36 Brontë Parsonage Museum, Dixon Papers, Letter no. 13, 24 July 1843.
37 Wise and Symington (eds), *The Brontës*, p. 274: letter to Ellen Nussey, 30 Oct. 1842.

Charlotte Brontë was drawn into this circle. She knew Mary Taylor because they had attended the same school, and between 1831 and 1840 Charlotte had spent many weekends with the Taylors at the Red House in Gomersal.[38] It was only about five or six miles from the school at Mirfield, which was located to the south of Gomersal and was thus much closer than her own home at Haworth Parsonage, some 15 miles away.[39] Mary's father Joshua Taylor got on well with the young Charlotte Brontë, encouraging her interest in foreign languages, and even sending a crate of French books to her at Haworth.[40]

After Joshua Taylor died in 1840, the Taylor family fragmented, as his widow Anne was a difficult woman to live with. Instead the Dixon household in Brussels provided an alternative gravitational pull, both for some of the younger Taylors, and also for Charlotte Brontë. Thus it was that on 29 September 1841 she wrote to her aunt, Elizabeth Branwell:

> 'I could go to Brussels, … the facilities there for education [are] equal or superior to any other place in Europe. … Martha Taylor [Mary's sister] is now staying in Brussels at a first-rate establishment there … and, with the assistance of her cousins, I should probably in time be introduced to connections far more improving, polished, and cultivated, than any I have yet known'.[41]

Some time the following year, Mary Taylor was writing to Charlotte's other great friend, Ellen Nussey. Mary was uncertain of her future destiny, and New Zealand was beginning to stir in her imagination:

> 'When in the name of the *grand dieu de la fondue* [i.e. Jupiter] did you find or steal the description of New Zealand? I never knew anything about the country – which however does not prevent my having described it in some overflow of poetic frenzy – if this be the case pray refer me to the volume of my works in which it is to be found or at least mention the date of the night on which I dreamed it'.[42]

The Treaty of Waitangi, giving, from the British point of view, sovereignty over New Zealand, had been signed just two years previously, and no doubt news of this development had considerable attractions, yet Mary Taylor continued cheerfully: 'What do you think of Germany instead of New Zealand? I have heard they are nice and savage there too'.

---

38 See above, Chapter 1, p. 17
39 Hayward, 'The Dixon Family', Part 1, p. 316.
40 Anon., *Red House Museum*.
41 Wise and Symington (eds), *The Brontës*, p. 243.
42 Ibid., p. 268.

Charlotte's close friendship with Mary Taylor and Ellen Nussey is well chronicled, but it is evident that she also found a close rapport with Dixon's elder sister, Mary.[43] In late 1843 Charlotte Brontë wrote to Ellen: 'Miss Dixon is certainly an elegant and accomplished person. When she leaves Bruxelles [sic] I shall have nowhere to go'.[44] That letter was taken to England by Dixon's youngest brother Tom, who was receiving German lessons from King Leopold's librarian in the royal palace itself.[45]

Of Dixon himself, Charlotte had rather different feelings. A little later, against the backdrop of a cold autumn day in Brussels, and feeling intensely lonely, she confided to Ellen: 'Brussels is indeed desolate to me now – since Mary Dixon left I have had no friend… We have as yet no fires here and I suffer much from cold otherwise I am well in health – Mr George Dixon [on a short visit to his father] will take this letter to England – he is a pretty-looking and pretty behaved young man – apparently constructed without a back-bone – by which I don't allude to his corporal spine – which is all right enough – but to his character'.[46]

Despite the editors of the collected letters of the Brontë family observing that 'the censorious reader may discover in Charlotte Brontë an occasional aptitude for a too severe judgement on men and women',[47] there is definitely a point to be answered here. Particularly towards the end of his career, all too often it was said of Dixon that he had never made any enemies. That was not simply due deference, an act of politeness. It was an indication that if he had wished to rise to a higher office than being simply a Member of Parliament, he would have had to develop even further robustness. That was not to say he was not robust. There would be foes all around most especially in the rural areas, for whom he was to develop considerable contempt. On the other hand, Dixon would have a problem in dealing with a rival much closer at hand, right in the centre of Birmingham, an abler politician than he, but a very difficult person to accommodate. He was Joseph Chamberlain, and his powerful character was to feature for virtually all of Dixon's political career. Yet put Dixon's back against the wall, in two distinct eras, it was not to be Chamberlain who would be the victor in their civic confrontations. That, however, is very much for the future.

Throughout his life, George Dixon appeared and indeed was mild-mannered; he did have a political backbone, but not a ruthless ambition.

Meantime Dixon's career as an office boy seemed to prosper and, despite a *faux pas* when he asked who 'that old buffer was?' when Mr. Rabone passed

---

43 W. Gérin, *Charlotte Brontë: The Evolution of Genius* (Oxford, 1967), p. 219.

44 Wise and Symington (eds), *The Brontës,* p. 294.

45 Gérin, *Charlotte Brontë,* p. 219. The Dixon household in Brussels was truly multilingual: Tom was learning German, George and Mary were competent in Spanish, there was fluency in French, besides their own mother tongue of English.

46 Wise and Symington (eds), *The Brontës,* p. 306: letter dated 13 Oct. 1843.

47 Ibid., p. 286.

by, he was admitted into partnership at the age of 24. This development had not been without some initial reluctance on the part of Mr. Rabone when Abraham, already a partner, asked if his younger brother could be taken in too – 'You want George to come into the business. Shan't!'[48] But he remained a full partner until his death, although the amount of time he devoted to the affairs of Rabone Bros. declined substantially in his later years. It was his children's impression that it had been uncle Abraham – rather than their own father – who developed the Rabone business whilst Abraham was still active within the firm (he moved to Leatherhead in 1871, for health reasons), for Katie wrote of him 'I believe it was he who worked the business up'.

Not for nothing was the firm named Rabone <u>Brothers</u>, frequently abbreviated to <u>Bros.</u>. Indeed, in the course of more than 200 years of trading, three pairs of brothers were involved in the running of the business: the original brothers Rabone, involved in the establishment of the business in 1765; Abraham and George Dixon for much of the reign of Queen Victoria; and George's sons Arthur and James Dixon subsequently.

Research has shown that 'rarely was the founder's entrepreneurial drive and commitment matched by his heir, though what was generally required of the second generation was less an entrepreneur's flair than the ability to manage a developing business. The Victorians often solved this by having large enough families for at least one son in each generation to be a successful driver of the business and for others to provide family management in depth, on the old royal principle of "heirs and spares"'.[49]

Such an observation was equally applicable to Abraham Dixon and his younger brother, whose working relationship was very close. Having shared accommodation as bachelors, Katie recorded that, even after Abraham got married, 'they managed to remain inseparable in heart and mind if not in person, and when they were away from each other, interchanged letters every day'.[50] Indeed, 'the same thought often occurred to them at the same moment. When one spoke, the other would say "I was just thinking of that" '.[51]

Such a harmonious business relationship could only have been achieved if there had been a very broad measure of agreement between them on other matters outside the commercial sphere – or, if there had been disagreements, they would have needed the strength of character to accommodate them. Substantial disagreements between the three Lloyd relatives were a powerful factor behind the incorporation and re-organisation of their own banking

---

48 Rathbone, *The Dales,* p. 2.
49 C. Kennedy: *Business Pioneers – Family, Fortune and Philanthropy: Cadbury, Sainsbury and John Lewis* (2000), p. 4.
50 Rathbone, *The Dales,* p. 2.
51 Ibid., p. 82.

business in 1865,[52] but there is no trace of any divergence of opinion between Abraham and his younger brother. On important issues outside the business sphere, such as religion and education – in Dixon's later years, his all-consuming passion – they appeared to be united, and as his elder brother, it would have been natural for Abraham to have had a significant influence on his younger brother's views.

Birmingham's industrial production was extremely diverse. This had two notable consequences for the business. In the first place, it meant that there was a much wider range of products available close at hand for it to sell. Secondly, it meant that if there was a downturn in one particular sector of the economy at any one time, there was always the likelihood that the slack could be taken up, to some extent, by another. With few exceptions, Birmingham prospered strongly throughout the nineteenth century, a factor which helped to give its leading citizens their extraordinary self-confidence as time progressed.[53]

Dixon was able to deploy his strengths within the business: accounting was one. In the process of describing the house in which the family lived, Katie wrote: 'By the window there was a tall burry [bureau], where my father sat, and did his accounts, which he loved'.[54] Interestingly, Joseph Chamberlain, who was to be Dixon's close political friend – and occasional enemy – in later years, was also effectively his own firm's accountant, and this expertise would, as Chamberlain's biographer pointed out, 'help him because of its pertinence to the traditional concerns of British politicians with finance'.[55] Dixon was also self-disciplined; he went to the office 'every morning with the regularity of the clock, walking, in his top hat, umbrella in hand'.[56]

Dixon's business activities led to much travel, and he sought to keep Abraham in touch with all that he was doing. Typically he wrote whilst travelling in Scotland in the summer of 1844, demonstrating as ever his close attention to detail:

> Good land is let at about 50/- per acre – the mountain pasture land £15 to £20 for 100 sheep per annum – the sheep are worth about 23/- each – sometimes they fall as low as 18/- each – the mountain cattle £6 to £10 – they are sent to the Lowlands when fattened by the purchasers – except when speculators buy up for re-sale at the principal markets; many of the farmers here have much money invested….[57]

---

52 See below, Chapter 2, p. 53
53 For a much fuller exposition of this theme, see, for example, C. Gill, *History of Birmingham, Vol. 1* (Oxford, 1952), and A. Briggs, *History of Birmingham, Vol. 2* (Oxford, 1952).
54 Rathbone, *The Dales*, p. 32.
55 Marsh, *Chamberlain*, p. 21.
56 Rathbone, *The Dales*, p. 98.
57 West Yorkshire Archives, Dixon/Stansfeld papers, File WYL 962/2/2, dated 5 June 1844.

In the meantime, the Taylor cousins were beginning to go their own separate ways. The perceived attractions eventually proved too strong, and Mary Taylor left for New Zealand in March 1845. Her brother Waring had arrived in Wellington in 1842,[58] and for many years he conducted a successful merchanting business, became a bastion of the Wellington Chamber of Commerce, acquired substantial property holdings, and for more than a decade represented the City of Wellington in the House of Representatives. Mary was thus not venturing into totally unknown territory, and she did not lose contact with her old friends. Dixon was to make two visits to the far end of the world in the next half-century, even contemplating one more not long before he died in 1898. Indeed, he found the country so attractive, that he suggested to his own family at some stages in his life that they too might emigrate.[59] Thus were sown in his mind the seeds of a belief that New Zealand, in particular, was a place where could be found a better lifestyle than remaining amidst all the deprivations of mid-Victorian England, if only people had the independence and drive to leave.

1846 saw him in Spain, whither his sons also went at later dates, 'to study Spanish and Spanish ways'.[60] Dixon wrote in detail from there as well but, in addition to commercial detail, there were other excitements. His youngest daughter, Dora, recounted some of the detail: 'thrilling letters about his escape from brigands and a beautiful costume he had bought, black boots, white stockings and yellow breeches. There was a [business] crisis going on at the time at home and Mr. Rabone shouted out "And there's George dancing about in his damned yellow breeches"'.[61]

The list of towns and cities he visited in the Spanish Peninsula was impressive, and included Cadiz, Lisbon, Jerez, Seville, Cardova, Gibraltar, Granada, Algeciras, Alicante, Madrid, Valencia, and many others.[62]

In 1847, Abraham Dixon married Margaret Rathbone, from a noted Liverpool merchant family. Although the Rathbones were Quakers, the wedding was at the Parish Church of Childwall, West Derby, and was conducted under licence by William Dixon, then the curate of St Cuthbert's, Carlisle. Through this marital connection, George Dixon moved for many years into the world of William Rathbone, Liverpool MP. Rathbone was to be a useful political ally on occasion, but the connection was never to be as strong as with George's own future brother-in-law, James Stansfeld, a Unitarian.[63] There

---

58 B.R. Patterson, 'Whatever Happened to Poor Waring Taylor? An Address to the Friends of the Turnbull Library', *Turnbull Library Record*, 24 (1991), p. 113.
59 Rathbone, *The Dales*, p. 100.
60 Ibid., p. 99.
61 Ibid., p. 121.
62 West Yorkshire Archive Services, File WYL 962/2/2.
63 The range of connections was considerable. Thus William Rathbone and James Stansfeld went to school together: see R.V. Holt, *The Unitarian Contribution to Social Progress in England* (1938), p. 331.

were no clear party divides in mid-Victorian politics, as Stansfeld was a brewer, a trade mostly associated with the Tories, and had also become an Anglican by the date of his death.

William Dixon was Abraham's younger, and George's elder brother, having been born in 1818, but the relationship was never as close as that between the two Birmingham-based brothers. Nonetheless, William Dixon was to christen all of George's six children, having become the Vicar of Chilthorne Domer in Somerset by the time of his death in 1884. William's own son, the Rev. Frederick Dixon, led the choir at George's funeral in Birmingham in 1898. Some accounts of Dixon's life have mistakenly assumed him to be a Nonconformist.[64] He did live amongst and work with many Nonconformists, to the point where he might have been labelled a 'quasi-Unitarian'.[65] But he remained a member of the established Church of England. There was no doubt of his religious devotion, manifest in his financial support for the construction of Anglican churches, but as is so often the way, home truths often emerge from the mouths of the children, and it was his daughter Katie who opined about church attendance: 'The service was musical, large choir and all that, the way rich people make up for want of ritual; they must have something I suppose'.[66] There was also little doubt that there was to be music in his future life.

As for his business world, the land owned by Rabone Bros. in Bridge Street was always excessive relative to the demands of even a large firm of merchants. So the balance was put to not only good but historic use – first, as premises for the nascent firm of Cadbury Bros., chocolate manufacturers; then when their business prospered to such an extent that they re-located at Bournville, the site was adapted to house a pioneering Technical School.

There are no clear records of the overall site at 297 Broad Street prior to 1846, but photographs contained in Rabone, Petersen and Co. Ltd.'s postwar promotional material show a building described by Katie as 'a large solid red brick building – plain, with a certain dignity, built I suppose by "old Mr. Rabone" '.[67]

The old-established business of Cadbury Bros. occupied that part of the premises not used by Rabone Bros. for 32 years, from 1847 to 1879, during a critical stage in its development, having been forced to move out of its previous premises in Crooked Lane because of the construction of the Birmingham and Junction Railway Company's new line into Snow Hill Station. The period when the two businesses were neighbours was not without its dramas, the sole

---

64 See, for example, D. Cannadine, *Lords and Landlords: the Aristocracy and the Towns* (Leicester, 1980), p. 195.

65 D. Smith, *Conflict and Compromise – Class Formation in English Society, 1830-1914: A Comparative Study of Birmingham and Sheffield* (1982), p. 173.

66 Rathbone, *The Dales*, p. 5.

67 Ibid., p. 98.

surviving communication between the two firms being a letter of considerable appreciation when the Cadbury fire-engine helped to extinguish a fire which threatened the Rabone business in 1874.[68]

A few years earlier the Cadbury business itself had been in financial distress, with staff numbers reduced to a mere twenty at one stage, until a Dutch machine was purchased in 1866 which pressed the butter out of the cocoa, whereupon fortunes were reversed and more than 200 employees were engaged by 1879.[69]

As his tenant and near-neighbour, the younger of the two Cadbury brothers, George Cadbury, made an interesting contrast with Dixon. George Cadbury was a Quaker – and thus a pacifist – whilst the Anglican George Dixon was in the business of supplying arms, albeit in the case of supplies to the Unionist North, there was a moral argument that ultimate victory would lead to the end of slavery, with which cause Quakers would have had sympathy. However, such differences were more than outweighed by their similarities, most especially on the educational front, where Cadbury spent a lifetime involved in the strictly non-sectarian Adult School movement.

After Cadbury Bros. departure in 1879, the site seems to have been unused until 1884, when Dixon decided that it should be used as what turned out to be a pioneering Technical School. The local School Board rented the premises at a nominal figure to serve as a central seventh standard school, accommodating 400 boys.

In 1849, the Dixons tried to re-establish contact with Charlotte Brontë again, extending an invitation to come and stay at Hay Hall for Christmas. But the invitation was declined,[70] although Charlotte corresponded with Mary Dixon for the rest of her life. Abraham Senior died in Brighton in 1850, although he might have re-married after the death of Laetitia.[71]

Around this time, an insight is provided as to how Abraham Dixon might have been an inspiration to his younger brother in the field of educational reform. A Free Industrial School was founded in Gem Street. The first stone of this institution was laid on 12 April 1849, and one of the documents contained in the inevitable bottle, deposited in a cavity in the stone, contained the following account:

LAUS DEO. BIRMINGHAM FREE INDUSTRIAL SCHOOL. This School was erected in the year of Our Lord 1849, the following persons being the promoters thereof:- …. Abraham Dixon, Esq., … This School was instituted

68 I.A. Williams, *The Firm of Cadbury, 1831-1931* (1931), p. 48.
69 Ibid., p. 17.
70 Gérin, *Charlotte Brontë*, p. 417.
71 Hayward, 'The Dixon Family', Part 1, p. 318. After both Abraham Junior and George had married, (sister) Mary Dixon attempted to regain her health after a period of illness by travelling to the sun of the West Indies and Australia. The Commonwealth of Australia was not formed until 1901, and references to 'Australia' before then could have included New Zealand.

for the training and education of 100 boys and 100 girls, children of destitute parents, of all denominations, free of charge, in general accordance with the system of the Elementary Schools belonging to King Edward the Sixth's foundation in this town, the Governors of which charity have granted the land on which the building stands. The system of education provides that the children be taught trades and industrial occupations, besides reading, writing, arithmetic, and Christian knowledge. The said religious instruction being under the direction and superintendence of the Rector of St. Martin's, St. Philip's, St. George's, St. Thomas's, and All Saints', the Head Master of King Edward's School, and the Incumbent of Bishop Ryder's district, for the time being; and that the children of dissenting parents shall not of necessity be compelled to learn the church catechism........[72]*

This was a significant document, for it embraced education <u>and</u> training. It built on the much older tradition of the King Edward VI tradition, and gave a notable clue as to one of the drivers behind Dixon's later campaign for compulsory and free elementary education, leading to Forster's Education Act of 1870. It provided for children of poor parents. It provided for Christian education without denominational bias. And it made specific allowance for Dissenters, members of non-established churches, an issue which was to cause so much controversy in 1870 and the years thereafter.

Thus it was Abraham Dixon, not his younger brother, whose name first appeared in the public domain in support of the reform of elementary education. By contrast, the latter's own first recorded words in the public domain were in an entirely different direction.

The leader of the Birmingham Political Union in 1832 had been the Anglican Thomas Attwood[73] and, although his standing fell subsequently, his views on currency had gained widespread credibility amongst entrepreneurs – he could be said to be the founder of a tradition of economic unorthodoxy, 'the Birmingham School of Political Economy'.[74] It is therefore not entirely unsurprising to find that Dixon's first recorded utterances were on the subject of money-management: 'He [Dixon] counted that this financial matter was a grand battle as to whether the nation should be governed on genteel principles, or the vulgar principles of shopkeeping and commerce. It was a stale thing to tell them that Bonaparte had said that they were a nation of shopkeepers. All he would say was that at any rate they kept their books in a very disgraceful manner [laughter] ... Now, the truth was, that they must become vulgar shopkeeping

---

72 R.K. Dent, *The Making of Birmingham, Being a History of the Rise and Growth of the Midland Metropolis* (Birmingham, 1894), p. 439.

73 Thomas Attwood (1783-1859), campaigner for political reform, banker and economist.

74 R. Ward, *City-State and Nation: Birmingham's Political History, c.1830-1940* (Chichester, 2005), p. 23.

men after all'.[75] The style was distinctive: always wordy, with a tendency to lecture: although not said here, in later years speeches were characterised by a preamble to what he was about to say, and then the phrase '… is this'. Clear, yes, but not always easy to listen to.

George Dixon would not continue to live in the same house as his now-married elder brother for ever and, when the opportunity presented itself, he bought from Lord Calthorpe a 99-year lease on a large house called The Dales, 42 Augustus Road, where he lived for the rest of his life.[76] It was, in the words of his daughter Katie, 'a very large one in a very delightful garden, two fields and a paddock', together with a pond. Dixon had seen it being built in earlier days when he had lodged in Chad Road, and had hankered after it. His elder sister Mary moved in too.[77]

There then followed a substantial gap of about four years in which nothing whatsoever is known of Dixon's movements or activities. It is possible that it was in this period that he lived in Canada for a while, since he referred to such a sojourn very briefly in a speech in 1886.[78] The fact that he scarcely made any other reference whatsoever to the country would seem to indicate that he was not enamoured with it.

The next time when any reference can be found to Dixon was on 20 January 1853, when his name was included in a list to join the Committee of the Birmingham and Midland Institute.[79] This was organised into a general department, providing culture for the upper ranks of Birmingham society, and an industrial department, offering useful knowledge to artisans and clerks.[80] In the next dozen or so months, he made himself very useful to the Institute, attending committee meetings frequently. On 21 March he became Secretary of the newly-formed Sub-Committee to superintend the Canvass for Donations; by 20 June he was signing off a financial statement as Chairman of the Sub-Committee; on 19 September he joined the Land and Buildings Committee; in early May the following year, he was a member of a new Sub-Committee to organise the running of the new Training School; and eventually he became the Institute's first joint auditor.[81]

He was not to be auditor for long, however, and after working hard to raise finance for the Institute, it was recorded that he was tendering his resignation as a member of the Institute's Council. The Minutes continued: 'Resolved. That the Chairman be requested to solicit Mr Dixon to re-consider his

75 *Norwich Mercury,* 10 Feb. 1849; quoted in G.R. Searle, *Entrepreneurial Politics in Mid-Victorian Britain* (Oxford 1993), p. 57.
76 Pictured, in gallery section, The Dales.
77 Rathbone, *The Dales,* p. 1.
78 *The Times,* 3 July 1886.
79 Birmingham and Midland Institute, Minute Book, 20 Jan. 1853.
80 Smith, *Conflict and Compromise,* p. 99.
81 Section 33, of the Act to Incorporate the Birmingham and Midland Institute, 1854.

determination and to express the wish that he would continue to act upon the Council'.[82]

Dixon was also looking for a bride. Nearby in Birmingham's Perry Barr lived a branch of the Kenrick family, and through this connection he met Mary Stansfeld, who was a school-friend of Caroline Kenrick. By the date they were married on 11 September 1855, George was 35, Mary 22.[83] They shared an enthusiasm for riding, but the courtship presented an opportunity for George Dixon to visit and inspect a Mechanics Institute 'with some determination, and possibly greater zeal than was strictly necessary'.[84] His new wife had considerable personal charm, and was a gifted musician; 'her singing especially was recalled with delight', wrote her daughter.[85]

The Stansfeld family lived in Halifax, where Mary's father was a judge. He had been interested in the formation of a Mutual Improvement Society ("Mute Imps"), out of which grew the Mechanics Institute. Rev Millsom, Mary's own brother-in-law, described the judge thus: 'He believed in the value of education, and he gave his help to the cause of popular education all through his long life'.[86] The family was Unitarian, but Dixon was an Anglican. Judge Stansfeld had had good cause to be sensitive of the distinction, describing how in his childhood his own father could not afford 'to give any of us a university education, nor would it practically have availed much, for we were Dissenters select, and I remember being told when I was a boy that there was "no chance of my being made Lord Chancellor", for the Test and Corporation Acts were in operation and the smallest appointment under the Crown could not be held by any one who refused to take the Sacrament according to the forms of the Church of England'.[87]

In an age of considerable sensitivities between different Christian sects, the Dixons' marital union could only be a success if compromises were made. Successful the marriage was, and the spirit of compromise thus rehearsed was to be one factor behind Dixon's achievement in advancing the cause of educational reform, in a field where so many others were failing.

Not only was it the principle of compromise which he practised, but its application which he extended to his own children's education. Katie spoke of it in the following terms: 'At church I liked the singing and so on, but the Creed for instance I thought was a string of words with no particular meaning, made up by some adult or other who thought himself clever. We were not taught any doctrine or church history or anything ... I suppose they [her parents]

---

82 Birmingham and Midland Institute, Minute Book, Minute 190.
83 Rathbone, *The Dales*, p. 2. Mary Dixon (née Stansfeld) was born on 8 Dec. 1832, and died on 25 March 1885.
84 Ibid..
85 Birmingham Archives and Heritage, File MS 2239, Bundle 36, p. 6.
86 Ibid., Bundle 48, p. 5.
87 Ibid., p. 3.

must have agreed that we were not to have any definite religious teaching'.[88] There were consequences. Talking of school exams, she wrote: 'Not taking Divinity was frightfully against us'.[89] Yet there was little doubt as to religious devotion: 'My father read prayers every morning, and every Sunday evening. The coachman and stable boy came in on Sunday evenings, as well as the other servants'.[90] 'My father was a churchman, of the broad kind, I suppose … I don't think he ever went to early Communion, but he stayed to the mid-day one, two or three times a year, perhaps oftener'.[91]

It was Dixon's experience of rearing his own children that no doubt strongly influenced his views on the wisdom of not trying to provide too much doctrinal teaching to the younger generation. This avoidance of doctrinal rigidity was to differentiate Dixon from many of his future colleagues in the field of educational reform. He was always consistent on this point: 'He did not think it necessary to bring before a child under 14 years of age, the doctrines contested by the various denominational bodies. Children of so tender an age were quite incapable of comprehending these doctrines'.[92] 'It was useless to teach children under thirteen years of age abstruse doctrines and creeds – they could not understand them'.[93] On the subject of dogmas, he pronounced about children of the same age: 'though they might be put into the mouth by means of catechisms and formularies, he did not believe they entered into the mind, and certainly not into the heart'.[94] Katie Dixon was a testament to the veracity of that statement: 'I believed in the Bible all right, the stories in it and so forth, but God seemed to be a nebulous something thrown in more for the sake of the story than anything'.[95]

More important than the detail of any religious belief was the moral code which underlay it. In an observation of great significance to what happened more than a decade later, by 1869 Dixon was proclaiming that a child should be learning 'habits of order, punctuality, cleanliness, obedience, refined manners; all these moral qualities in addition to the knowledge that had been placed in his mind – the knowledge of all the wonderful things around him, the knowledge of the elements of science, the knowledge of the works of his God, and through that knowledge he would be able to rise up to his Creator'.[96]

Not long after the wedding, the newly married couple sailed for Australia. Where precisely they went is in considerable doubt, as no record survives of

---

88 Ibid., Bundle 2, p. 13.
89 Ibid., Bundle 26, p. 4.
90 Ibid., Bundle 2, p. 16.
91 Ibid., p. 13.
92 *Birmingham Daily Post* (hereafter *BDP*), 4 June 1868.
93 Ibid., 7 Dec. 1869.
94 Ibid., 4 Sept. 1869.
95 Birmingham Archives and Heritage, File MS 2239, Bundle 2, p. 13.
96 *Bradford Observer*, 1 Dec. 1869.

the two or more years that followed, although they were nearly shipwrecked in a storm in St George's Channel on the voyage out.[97] In his letters home, written later in 1888, George Dixon made comparison with the Hobart, Tasmania[98] that he saw then and on his previous trip thirty years previously, but that is about it. From the enthusiasm with which he spoke about New Zealand, in the 1870s, it can be deduced that he almost certainly went there too, and the fact that his cousins, the Taylors, lived there would have been a substantial draw. He would have experienced an Anglican church without all the associated complications of being an Established Church.[99] This encounter was later invoked by him on the issue of the disestablishment of the Church of England. 'The Church had flourished without state aid in Australia and other colonies of the country, and he was inclined to think that the time was coming when the Church in England would be able to do without such aid'. He would have seen an educational system created without any backdrop of a past.[100] And he would have seen others enjoying a standard of living very different from that enjoyed, if indeed that is the right word, by so many back in England.

It is more than possible that George Dixon visited Sydney, for the obituary of Thomas Lloyd, a fellow partner in Rabone Bros. in this period and later a director of Lloyds Banking Company Limited,[101] showed that he was resident there around this time.[102] Certainly Dixon was resident in the Melbourne area in 1858, for his second child, Helen Margaret, was born in nearby St Kilda in that year.[103]

This period abroad was a valuable experience upon which to found his future career in politics. Dixon had left a minor mark on his adopted town before leaving for the other side of the world: for, on 22 February 1855, he addressed a meeting held in Birmingham Town Hall 'for the purposes of memorialising the Legislature on the necessity of prosecuting enquiry into the causes of the disasters in the Crimea, and on the system of appointments

---

97 Rathbone, *The Dales*, p. 3.
98 Letter dated 20 Sept. 1888 from Dixon to the family in England, written on board the *Doric*, whilst travelling to New Zealand. The reference is to Fern Tree Gully, on Mount Wellington. The manuscript version of this letter is held at University of Birmingham, Special Collections, Joseph Chamberlain Papers. Typescript versions of collected letters (of which this is p.16) are also held there, at Nelson Provincial Museum, NZ, and at Alexander Turnbull Library, Wellington, NZ.
99 *BDP*, 21 Oct. 1868.
100 Dixon's antipodean experience was well remembered by his contemporaries even fifty years later. 'It is possible that he found there conditions regarding education among English people – for at that time they were more English than they are now – suggesting to him what might be acceptable in time even in England itself': see G.H. Kenrick, 'George Dixon: A Lecture', in J.H. Muirhead (ed.), *'Nine Famous Birmingham Men'* (Birmingham, 1909), p. 59.
101 Following a number of changes over the decades, the name of the current organisation, Lloyds Banking Group PLC, is a reversion to its original title.
102 *The Times*, 25 Jan. 1890.
103 Rathbone, *The Dales*, p. 130.

in the army and navy'.[104] It was a pointer to the fact that he had an interest in politics.

A command of foreign languages was no doubt a considerable asset in Dixon's travels around the world. In an era when steamships were in their infancy – although some of the earlier voyages were made under sail[105] – the list of countries visited was impressive. Within Europe, there was frequent travelling, sometimes on business, sometimes on holiday. Trips to Belgium were a mixture of business and pleasure, but there were holiday trips in later years to the Dolomites,[106] the Tyrol, the Alps, and Cap d'Antibes, amongst other places. When his wife Mary's health began to fail in later years, there were trips to Boulogne as 'going abroad was supposed to be good for the health'.[107] Such journeys were done in some style, a substantial horse-drawn coach nicknamed The Ark (of which there is no photographic record) going too.

The enlarged family (both Arthur and Helen Margaret had been born during the absence abroad) returned to England in 1858. Dixon himself was fast approaching the mid-point of his lifespan of $77\frac{1}{2}$ years, and there was as yet no firm indication that the second half of his life was going to be very substantially more newsworthy than the first half.

---

104 *School Board Chronicle,* 29 Jan. 1898.
105 The first trip to the Antipodes was definitely on board a sailing ship: see Rathbone, *The Dales,* p. 130.
106 University of Birmingham, Dixon papers, GD5, letter from Dixon to John Bright, 10 Sept. 1882.
107 Rathbone, *The Dales,* p. 130.

CHAPTER TWO

The Making of the Entrepreneur 1858-67

W HEN DIXON RETURNED from the other side of the world in 1858, he found two important things had changed, one very obvious, the other much less so.

On the political stage, Birmingham had acquired a new MP in the form of John Bright, as a direct consequence of the government's inept handling of the Crimean War. Bright spoke passionately in favour of peace in 1855 but faced criticisms for his views, including among his own constituents. Scorned by those whom he had represented in Lancashire, Bright had now in 1858 been chosen, unopposed, to represent Manchester's rival in the Midlands, Birmingham.

His move south was symbolic of a shift of influence in the provinces. As Richard Cobden,[1] Bright's close colleague in the earlier campaign for the repeal of the Corn Laws, put it:

> He will find Birmingham a more suitable political home than the one he
> has lost. There is more social equality, and a greater faith in democratic
> principles in Birmingham than Manchester ... In Birmingham where a

---

1 For Richard Cobden (1804-65), see *ODNB-online.*

manufacturer employs his three or four hands only, and sometimes but an apprentice or two, there is much more cordial and united feeling among the two [i.e. middle and working] classes.[2]

Another significant change in the mid-1850s was the abolition of the tax on newspapers. Subsequently there was born a whole new generation of provincial newspapers, including in 1857 the *Birmingham Daily Post* (*BDP*). Like the vast majority of merchants at this time,[3] Dixon had Liberal inclinations, and the *BDP* likewise. This was the beginning of a heroic age, lasting for perhaps half a century, when political speeches, both important and less important, were reported verbatim. A great deal can be learned of Dixon's views from the local press, through advertisements, as well as campaigns, and charitable giving.[4]

Little did Dixon realise then, in the late 1850s, what a vexatious instrument the *BDP* could be when the editorship was in the hands of somebody who was to support the ambitions of a rival.[5]

It is from the pages of the *BDP* that Dixon's activities can be traced. He supported the movement to address the inadequacies in the military so apparent at the time of the Crimean War. There had been an unsuccessful attempt to organise a Volunteer Rifle Corps in 1852,[6] and seven years later both the Dixon brothers attended a meeting 'of persons interested in the Rifle Corps movement' convened by Thomas Lloyd as Mayor.[7] Both offered to equip a number of men at their own expense.[8]

Dixon was also keen to make himself known to Birmingham's new MP.[9] Continuing the family's tradition for hospitality, he arranged a large dinner-party, to which a young Joseph Chamberlain was also invited.[10] Chamberlain's first major biographer then took up the tale, the discussion revolving around whether Gibraltar should be handed back to Spain: 'The elders at the table listened in reverence whether they agreed or not. Not so the stripling. Across the table two-and-twenty intervened, controverted the great man [Bright],

2 D. Read, *The English Provinces, c.1760–1960* (1964), p. 156.
3 H.L. Malchow, *Gentlemen Capitalists: The Social and Political World of the Victorian Businessman* (1991), p. 135.
4 In very recent times, the *BDP* was one of the first provincial newspapers to be scanned digitally, which has been of great assistance in redressing the balance resulting from the severe shortage of other primary sources of information. "Dixon" is a comparatively common surname in England, and the task of searching the digitised newspaper has been made much easier by the fact that he was invariably known as "George Dixon", no doubt originally to distinguish him from his elder brother.
5 See below, Chapter 5, p. 170.
6 R.K. Dent, *Old and New Birmingham,* (Birmingham, 1878; repr. 1973), Vol. 3, p. 561.
7 J. A. Langford, *Modern Birmingham and Its Institutions: A Chronicle of Local Events, from 1841 to 1871* (Birmingham, 1877), Vol. 2, p. 82.
8 Obituary, *The Times,* 25 Jan. 1898.
9 Birmingham was represented by two MPs at this time, the second being William Scholefield.
10 The date is uncertain, but would have been in 1858 or 1859, given the reference to Chamberlain's age, and the fact that he was born in 1836.

stood up to him stoutly. So far from resenting it as an impertinence, Bright was magnanimous'.[11] The author of a more recent major biography also added, pointedly: 'With less august opponents Chamberlain's style of argument had a nasty edge, sarcastic and sneering'.[12]

Dixon family dinner-parties were held in some style. No evidence survives to show details of this particular late 1850s function, but it is unlikely that it differed much from what his daughter Katie witnessed a number of years later, as a young child. Creeping into a back passage she peered through a doorway:

> A long long table, with many leaves in it from the stand in the back passage. Huge epergnes of flowers and fruit all down the middle. A pompous parson saying grace – then to it with a vengeance. "Sherry or 'ock Sir?". Clear soup, choice of fish, turbot or red mullet? Two entrees, joint, game, sweets, ice pudding, cheese, savouries, and dessert. There may have been more courses and choices even than that, I don't know, but I do know that dinner began with soup, not grapefruit, and cocktails were not served before dinner till my eldest brother Artie came down from Oxford in the seventies, and solemnly mixed and handed them round in the drawing-room. Every-one refused, my brother's face grew longer and longer, he was absolutely silent and sepulchral. Then my mother dashed in to the rescue, rallied them all with gay words, in the end, they all drank, ...[13]

Some of the parties had a musical flavour, with Mary organising a gathering of 'kindred spirits, and they sang and sang, and someone banged away on the piano'.

The contrast with living conditions experienced by very large numbers of people resident not far away was vast, yet there is no enduring evidence of any manifest expression of envy. Dixon's reputation for philanthropy and fighting for the causes of the working man were to help him in this respect.

This lifestyle could be enjoyed because, as his youngest daughter Dora observed, '[when Abraham and George were partners]… the money came rolling in'.[14] The firm's catalogue in the 1850s shows that it was offering oil lamps, cutlery, garden forks, and many other commodities that helped Britain earn the title of 'workshop of the world'.[15]

In mid-Victorian times, the mainstay of Birmingham's output, taking the town as a whole, comprised items such as guns, nails, locks, wood screws, railway bolts and spikes, buttons, pins, needles, saddlery, electroplate, pens and

---

11 J.L. Garvin, *The Life of Joseph Chamberlain* (1932), Vol. 1, p. 61.
12 Marsh, *Chamberlain*, p. 16.
13 Rathbone, *The Dales*, p. 20.
14 Ibid., p. 121.
15 G. Hayward, 'The Dixon Family', Part 2, p. 351.

papier mâché, ammunition, percussion caps and cartridges, and anchors and chain cables.[16] It is probable that Rabone Bros. had a share in the trade of all these commodities, now markedly less high-value and low-volume than in the previous century, since the construction of railway lines within the country, and the use of steamships overseas, had revolutionised the economics of the business.[17]

One especially large contract was for the supply of rolling stock, bridges and railway track for the construction of a railway line in Cuba, probably in the late 1850s, which necessitated the charter of no less than 47 ships.[18]

As a firm of export merchants, Rabone Bros. was at the heart of the boom which saw exports nationally almost quadruple between 1840 and 1870. This development was in marked contrast with an increase of less than one-half in the succeeding period of 30 years.[19]

There was to be a temporary hiccough in the feeling of national self-confidence at the time of the Paris Exhibition in 1867, but still a leader in *The Times* on 26 September 1871 could say:

> We can ... look on the present with undisturbed satisfaction. Our commerce is extending and multiplying its world-wide ramifications without much regard for the croaking of any political or scientific Cassandras ... Turn where we may, we find in our commerce no traces of decadence.

There are no contemporary records extant of precisely how the firm organised its business, but there is no reason to believe that it differed in any material way from other Birmingham merchants. Most fortuitously there exists a detailed description of the functions of Birmingham merchants in 1860, and subsequently. First published in 1929, it is worth quoting in detail:

> [Merchants] were far from being mere wholesale dealers in the modern sense. Upon them the workshop proprietor or the garret-master depended, not only for the marketing of his goods and for financial help during the period of manufacture, but for the actual organization of production.[20]

In more detail, the writer added:

---

16 W.C. Aitken and G. Lindsey, *British Manufacturing Industries* (1878): chapter headings.
17 W.B. Stephens (ed.), *Victoria History of the County of Warwick, Vol. 7* (1964), p. 125.
18 *Birmingham Post,* 23 April 1965.
19 W. Cunningham, *The Rise and Decline of the Free Trade Movement* (1904), p. 103.
20 G.C. Allen, *The Industrial Development of Birmingham and the Black Country, 1860-1927* (1966 edition), p. 152.

> [A merchant was also] responsible for initiating production, for distributing orders, and sometimes materials, among a multitude of outworkers or small masters, for coordinating their activities when the product was a complicated one, and for financing manufacture, in so far as they relied on him for weekly cash payments when they delivered the products at his warehouse.[21]

With regard to marketing, the small size of the average manufacturing concern was such that it simply could not afford the resources to study market requirements, and to impress its name on the public.[22] Nor was that all, for in the more complex industries, such as gun-making, the factor (and the merchant for export markets) was obliged to possess a wide variety of skill-sets:

> the master gun-maker was required to have an intimate technical knowledge of his trade, and also, since he had to co-ordinate the activities of a multitude of "material-makers" and "setters-up", he had to come into close contact with the manufacturing operations.[23]

Rabone Bros. prided themselves on their skills in this field. No doubt with strong input from members of the staff of the successor company on the occasion of celebrating 200 years of trading, the *Birmingham Post* wrote about its thorough approach in Central and South America: 'for example, a century before the term "market research" was coined, Rabone's representatives were carrying out arduous surveys of the needs of different countries'.[24] Indeed, the same issue recorded that four of Rabone's men died on trips to South America, and others returned home to succumb, eventually, to illnesses contracted abroad.

In essence, the business was not only complex, but also diverse, demanding a multi-skilled workforce, adaptable in its outlook as both production methods and markets changed. It was against this backdrop that Dixon expended much energy in seeking to improve education and training. As a partnership, profits tended to be ploughed back into the business, which on the one hand created some nervousness on account of the risks of unlimited liability, but on the other eventually led to diversification, in the form of money-lending on the other side of the world.

The year 1860 saw a significant new development, for in the autumn there appeared an advertisement in *The Times*:

---

21 Ibid., p. 344.
22 Ibid., p. 153. A more recent study of Birmingham industry suggests that the transition from workshop to small manufacturer was earlier than often portrayed: see Behagg, *Politics and Production,* p. 223.
23 Allen, *The Industrial Development*, p.153.
24 *Birmingham Post,* 23 April 1965.

> Wilson's breech loading rifle. Mr. Thomas Wilson begs to call the
> attention of Volunteers and the public to his new BREECH LOADING
> RIFLE, and to state that he has committed the management of the patent
> to Messrs. Rabone, Brothers, and Co., of 47, Broad Street, Birmingham,
> to whom all inquiries or other communications may be addressed... . The
> guns can be obtained through any gunmaker in the kingdom, and patterns
> may be seen and every information obtained at... [a variety of addresses,
> including that of Rabone's].[25]

The gun trade had been producing at a high level since the Crimean War, but it did especially well during the American Civil War from 1861 to 1865.[26]

The firm's own history gives an indication of the impact on Birmingham, stating that after the Civil War had started 'a visit was received from two representatives of the Washington government, who requested the firm to purchase every available gun in Birmingham and district'.[27] Whatever their share of that substantial market, and all the other items required to fight a war, orders from America resulted without a shadow of a doubt in very big profits for the partners.

This local prosperity had a major impact on Dixon personally, for whilst Birmingham was profiting, Manchester was suffering dreadfully, cut off as it was from supplies of cotton, the raw material for all the mills in the surrounding area. Filled with compassion, it was he who led a mission to establish how one town could help the other. This action thrust him into the public arena for the first time, working with the assistance of a fellow Liberal, John Skirrow Wright.[28] It also meant that he came into contact with many leading figures of the Manchester political world.

As one of the leading merchants in Birmingham, George Dixon played a significant but seldom recorded role in the local Chamber of Commerce. The 1860s were perhaps the most important decade of its existence: the decade which began with the vast majority of the urban population in many parts of the country still lacking the vote, yet participating in significant changes in the industrial infrastructure. And even less has been recorded about Dixon's important role in the very early days of the nationwide umbrella body, the Association of Chambers of Commerce.

In these environs, George Dixon was able to make his name known, to improve his negotiating skills, and to press for changes in the legislation in

---

25 *The Times,* 8 Sept. 1860, and on numerous subsequent occasions.
26 Stephens (ed.), *Victoria County History of Warwick,* Vol. 7, p. 136.
27 Birmingham Archives and Heritage, File MS 2536.
28 For John Skirrow Wright (1822-80), see *ODNB-online.* Dixon and Wright were to become close colleagues as fellow Liberals on the Birmingham School Board in the 1870s.

so many areas that impacted upon not only his commercial organisation, but also those around him. He was working amongst many others of a similar background, and many were, or were to be, members of the Liberal Party. It was not therefore an environment in which he could practise his oratorical skills – a field in which he had significant deficiencies – especially in his early life. This was not an arena for ringing sound-bites. On the other hand, journalists found it very easy to report his slow, clear delivery. Years later, the editor of *The Dart and Midland Figaro* recalled: 'Mr George Dixon was our easiest man to take. He did his thinking as he spoke and a pressman who was fond of snuff had ample time to take a pinch between the sentences'.[29]

The Minute Books for Birmingham's Chamber of Commerce for the years prior to 1861 are missing, but the very first pages of the 1861 Book find Dixon already in post as Vice-President, a position he enjoyed for the year commencing 1862 as well.

At all relevant times, the post of President was occupied by a Birmingham MP, which of course meant that during the Parliamentary session, Westminster duties had priority over Chamber of Commerce duties, and it was the Vice-President ('Chairman' from 1868) who presided over the overwhelming majority of weekly and other meetings[30]. Only the annual and half-annual meetings were invariably chaired by the President.

In early 1861, through his work with the Chamber of Commerce, Dixon had established himself sufficiently as to be one of those on stage at the annual presentation by the town's two MPs,[31] and a couple of months later he was elected a Poor Law Guardian.[32]

The emphasis of the work of the Chambers was very much upon specific problem-solving. The Birmingham Chamber's 1813 terms of reference[33] were clear, the relevant resolution stating: 'That it is expedient to establish a commercial society in the town of Birmingham for the purpose of collecting and representing the opinions of its merchants and manufacturers, of acting as a medium of communication between the community and the Legislature on the subject of trade, and co-operating as occasion may require with other parts of the United Kingdom'.[34]

Throughout its history, there was seemingly a strict adherence to these guidelines, and George Dixon was to play his part in ensuring that. Thus he wrote to *The Times* on 30 November 1861:

---

29 *The Dart and Midland Figaro,* 11 June 1886.
30 In 1867, the Council even met on Boxing Day.
31 *BDP,* 30 Jan. 1861.
32 Ibid., 28 March 1861.
33 Whilst the Chamber was originally founded in 1813, its organisation lapsed before being revived in the middle of the century.
34 Wright, *Chronicles,* p. 600.

A paragraph appeared in your issue of the 28th inst. under the heading "Birmingham Chamber of Commerce" stating that the real meaning of the proposed anniversary dinner of the Chamber is to afford Mr. Bright a convenient occasion for reappearing before his constituents.

As chairman of the meeting of the Council at which it was proposed to have the anniversary dinner in question, I beg to state that this interpretation of the real meaning of the proposal is entirely erroneous, the promotion of the object for which the Chamber was founded being the sole motive for the intended meeting.

A perusal of the minutes in isolation creates the strong impression that there simply were no differences of opinion at all under the heading of religion, when in the world outside the Chamber, this was very far from being the case. To hone his skills in mediating through debates on that subject, George Dixon needed to gain wider experience.

An area in which Dixon established considerable success was in the field of partnership legislation, a somewhat arcane topic today, but certainly a matter for substantial debate in the 1860s. He had a number of axes to grind.

Not for the vast majority of Birmingham businesses were the joys of Joint Stock Company incorporation suitable. In 1861 the Birmingham Chamber of Commerce resolved that '… the Vice President be requested to report to a Special Meeting of this Council upon the desirability of extending the principles of limited liability to private partnerships'.[35] With the local MP, Spooner,[36] in the Chair, this was followed two months later by a call to the Government to introduce a Bill restricting the respective liabilities of some or all of the partners to the amount of capital subscribed.[37] This particular call fell on deaf ears, and indeed it was not until the first decade of the twentieth century that legislation was passed permitting a form of limited liability for some of the partners[38] – by which time, the pressure for change had largely disappeared, since incorporation had by then become an acceptable alternative. In the meantime, however, Abraham Dixon had remained a partner in Rabone Bros. for many years, his capital exposed to risk, even though he was no longer working, due to ill-health.[39]

Other business-related matters also attracted George Dixon's reforming interests. A year later he proposed, and Joseph Chamberlain seconded, a motion in favour of a change 'enabling clerks, managers, etc., to receive a share

35 Birmingham Archives and Heritage, Birmingham Chamber of Commerce Minute Book, 1861-5, 27 Nov. 1861.
36 Richard Spooner (1783-1864), Conservative MP for North Warwickshire.
37 Birmingham Chamber Minute Book, 30 Jan. 1862.
38 Wright, *Chronicles,* p. 181.
39 Abraham finally withdrew from the partnership completely on 31 Dec. 1885. See below, Chapter 7, p. 205.

of profits without thereby acquiring any of the rights and responsibilities of partners'.[40] This proposal reflected Dixon's concern to gain the allegiance of his working managers and to create greater long-term security for the family firm. At the same time, Dixon proposed at Association level a change whereby partnerships would be permitted to borrow money at a rate of interest varying with the profits earned.

Eventually there was success on both fronts, and Birmingham's other MP, Scholefield, ensured that the Partnership Law Amendment Act 1865 passed on to the Statute Book.[41] It would have been that much more difficult for Rabone's to retain the services of several capable senior managers for so many years before being admitted into the partnership, without an attractive remuneration package. Furthermore, without a capable team working for him, George Dixon would not have had the time to pursue his political career as he did.

When Dixon came to be re-elected as Vice-President in 1862, his good friend and sometime partner Thomas Lloyd was elected Treasurer.[42]

Dixon was in office as Vice-President for about three years in all, but his proposer was unknown. Then, as MP, he occupied the post of President for the years commencing 1867 through to 1877 inclusive,[43] and finally for the solitary year commencing 1886.

Dixon never commanded such a leading position in the national Association of Chambers of Commerce as in the Birmingham Chamber. The first recorded attendance by Dixon at an Association meeting was when he was accompanied by Sampson Lloyd [a brother of Thomas Lloyd] in early 1862.[44] Sampson Lloyd was soon to become the Association's Chairman, a post he held for almost twenty years, thereby establishing Birmingham as the pre-eminent member of the Association. He had an interesting relationship with Dixon, for he stood against him on a couple of occasions[45] as a Liberal-Conservative candidate for the Birmingham constituency in Parliamentary elections; and lost on both occasions.

Dixon was appointed one of the Honorary Secretaries in 1864,[46] and re-appointment followed in both 1865 and 1866,[47] but pressures of time caused by his election to Parliament meant that by late 1867 he had to stand down, and the status of Honorary Member was conferred on him.[48]

---

40 Wright, *Chronicles,* p. 184.
41 Ibid..
42 *BDP,* 13 Aug. 1862.
43 This role in this final year is surprising, as Dixon had applied for the Chiltern Hundreds in 1876.
44 Birmingham Chamber Minute Book, 26 Feb. 1862. Also Guildhall Library: Minutes of the Association of Chambers of Commerce of the United Kingdom, MS 14476-1.
45 1867 by-election, and 1868 general election.
46 Wright, *Chronicles,* p. 189.
47 Association Minute Book 21/22/23 Feb. 1865 and 20/21/22 Feb. 1866.
48 Ibid., 26/27 Nov. 1867.

In the strictly commercial environment of the Chambers, both the civic body and the nationwide Association, Dixon was to make the acquaintance of many men with whom he later worked on the wider stage of national politics: amongst them William [invariably 'W.E.'] Forster,[49] after whom one of the most significant pieces of social legislation in the nineteenth century was named; and Anthony Mundella,[50] whose name was much later to be enshrined in legislation introducing compulsory education.

Although Dixon has sometimes been described as a 'single issue politician' in the very few brief references to his life that have been published over the years (and this description is fairly accurate insofar as the vast majority of his speeches in Parliament were to refer to education), the range of topics with which he dealt both in the Birmingham Chamber and, to a lesser extent, in the Association reveal a much broader perspective. As early as 1862 he was to be found negotiating a compromise on a constitutional issue concerning the Association.

The difficulty surrounded the problem of whether the Association could act in its own name, even though not all members might agree with that viewpoint. Dixon suggested that the rules should be amended so that 'no action shall be taken by the Association in its collective capacity except on resolutions carried by a majority of two-thirds of the votes taken'.[51]

Here was one of the first suggestions of compromise that were to become a significant feature of his future life.

Another example reveals the same concern to remedy commercial difficulties. Shipping disputes often led to enormous expenses in relatively unimportant cases, where there was also dissatisfaction with the slowness of the judicial process. Accordingly Dixon became involved in looking into the practicality of Tribunals of Commerce, as an alternative approach, in 1865. As part of this exercise, consideration had to be given to the approach taken by various countries on the Continent, faced with similar difficulties[52] – an example of Dixon looking (as he did with the help of Matthew Arnold[53] and others in educational matters) across the Channel for solutions to problems in Britain. This quest even extended to appeals to the British Government for a better flow of commercial information in the form of consular reports.

With competition from overseas very much in mind, the Chamber spent much time throughout the 1860s debating changes to the legislation on the subject of both Trade Marks[54] and Patents.[55] Dixon played a part in many

---

49 For W.E. Forster (1818-86), see *ODNB-online.*
50 For Anthony Mundella (1825-97), see *ODNB-online.*
51 A.R. Ilersic and P.F.B. Liddle, *Parliament of Commerce: The Story of the Association of British Chambers of Commerce, 1860-1960* (1960), p. 19.
52 Wright, *Chronicles,* p. 202.
53 For Matthew Arnold (1822-88), see *ODNB-online.* Inspector of schools and poet.
54 For example, Birmingham Minute Book, 1861-5: 5 March 1862.
55 For example, ibid., 12 Nov. 1862.

of these discussions which led to involvement with other towns affected by similar issues.

Dixon's many contributions to discussions in the Chamber of Commerce demonstrated his ability to deal with complex issues, such as consideration of foreign tariff negotiations, an area well-suited to his temperament, and fondness for detail. In 1860 an Anglo-French Treaty had been concluded, sometimes referred to as the Cobden-Chevalier Treaty, embracing Most Favoured Nation clauses. Throughout the decade that followed, efforts were made to extend these principles to commercial dealings with other continental countries. Whilst continental Europe was never a major market for Rabone Bros., Dixon became actively involved in proceedings, sitting on the Foreign Tariffs Committee in 1865.[56]

At the other end of the success scale was Dixon's contribution to discussions on banking. He spent much time serving as a member of the Bank Charter Act Committee in 1866, formed in response to the collapse of the Birmingham Banking Company – 'the greatest commercial calamity that has ever happened to this town.'[57] The Committee met at weekly intervals at the height of the crisis. One proposition from Dixon was debated at length, and eventually accepted: 'It is expedient that the issue of Bank Notes should always be based on an undertaking to convert them into gold or silver on demand'.[58]

The Times later gave this short shrift in an editorial that did not mince its words:

> The errors of the Birmingham Committee are legion, but their first and cardinal mistake appears to be that they look upon a time of panic as a time when some mysterious commodity, called "Currency", is in demand, and that it is the peculiar function of the Government to keep a supply of this commodity always on hand.... There is something infinitely childish in this clamour to the Government to help embarrassed speculators, which ought of itself to lead to the Birmingham Committee to suspect the truth of their conclusions.[59]

Dixon made no further comment on the subject, though no doubt he did not agree.

He was at the same time establishing for himself a reputation as a philanthropist. The press was full of announcements of the causes which he was supporting, often in conjunction with his brother Abraham. It is difficult

---

56 Birmingham Minute Book, 1865-8: 31 Oct. 1865.
57 Birmingham Minute Book, 1865-8: 1866 half-yearly report.
58 Ibid., 27 July 1866, and 1 Aug. 1866.
59 1 Feb. 1867.

if not impossible to establish the scale of George Dixon's generosity, nor to measure it relative to the efforts of others in the town, given that in the very nature of things, much work might have been done anonymously. The range of good works with which he allowed his name to be associated, without there necessarily being a financial connection in every instance, was nonetheless impressive and wide-ranging. The following table gives examples, along with the date on which reference is made in the *BDP*:

Date	*Cause*
14/06/1862	General Hospital
27/11/1862	Proposed new church in parish of St Luke's
12/1/1864	Friends of the Birmingham and Midland Free Hospital for Sick Children
17/9/1864	Restoration of Worcester Cathedral
22/9/1864	Birmingham-funded lifeboat at Flamborough Head
24/4/1865 et seq	New church of St Asaph in parish of St Thomas
15/11/1867	Ryland Response Fund, for churches
30/11/1867	Birmingham Music Festival
12/12/1867	Midland Counties Idiot Asylum
21/12/1867	Ancient Order of Foresters
22/7/1868	Loyal Widows' Friend Lodge of Odd Fellows (Manchester Unity)
22/1/1869	Society for the Relief of Destitute Girls
30/7/1869	Baptist Mission School Room, Warwick Street
12/7/1870	Museum of Industrial Art
1/11/1870	War Victims Fund [Relief of Peasantry and other non-combatants in France and Germany]

The scale of his generosity to the Anglican church was significant, his involvement with the church of St Asaph amounting to £1,000, part of the Established Church's achievement in doubling the number of its places of worship between 1850 and 1900.[60] The very much smaller donation to the Baptist Mission School simultaneously demonstrated his ecumenicalism.

Dixon was also one of the many who contributed to the restoration of the Free Library after its disastrous fire in 1879, a fact well remembered at the time of his death nearly twenty years later.[61]

Dixon's philanthropic activities were to translate into an enhanced reputation within Birmingham itself. It has already been noted that through his visit to Manchester with J.S. Wright to establish the scale of the suffering

---

60 A.F. Taylor, 'Birmingham and the Movement for National Education, 1869-77' (Unpublished Ph.D. thesis, University of Leicester, 1960), p. 11.

61 *BDP*, cutting late Jan. 1898: precise date not shown.

arising from the cut-off in the supply of cotton, he came to know much more about politics there. Upon their return in September 1862, he produced a lengthy report as to their findings, ending:

> who can doubt but that this awful famine, as it [foists] itself upon an innocent and patient people, stifling them of all their hardly – [earned] possessions, and shutting out from them all hope of providing for themselves even the commoner necessaries of life, will also open the hearts of their wealthy neighbours, as that the wants of the poor shall be the only limit to the contributions of the rich?[62]

This exhortation for donations did not fall on deaf ears, for Dixon was promptly appointed honorary secretary of a relief fund, and a few days later addressed a public meeting: 'although Birmingham men, as a rule, were not gifted with eloquent speech, they now had an opportunity of speaking directly to the hearts of the Lancashire men by a good subscription list'.[63] There were two interesting aspects to this observation, other than the obvious philanthropic one: Dixon's propensity for self-deprecation, which was to endure throughout his life (and may be one factor why history has for so long overlooked him); and the undoubted fact that alongside so many other masters of oratory, he was not the ultimate champion.

Of his very considerable fund-raising skills there was not a shadow of a doubt. Years later, at the conclusion of the American Civil War, there was still a small amount of the Lancashire relief fund remaining,[64] and it was then planned to use this to construct a sanatorium. In spring 1866 a public meeting was held in the Town Hall at which one speaker praised Dixon, saying 'there should be no misunderstanding as to the gentleman to whom Birmingham and its working men and its poor were indebted for the Sanatorium'.[65]

Within a few weeks of his 1862 report, Dixon was acquiring new responsibilities. The Mayor had been presiding over another public meeting in the Town Hall when he had to leave for another appointment, and suggested that Dixon should take the chair:

> He thought, if he was not very much mistaken, they would have a great deal of work out of Mr Dixon yet. He believed that Mr Dixon was cut out for public work, and that he would be a great blessing to the town.[66]

---

62 Ibid., 4 Sept. 1862.
63 Ibid., 10 Sept. 1862.
64 Ibid., 8 Feb. 1866.
65 Ibid., 16 March 1866.
66 Ibid., 10 Oct. 1862.

Other duties followed. The next spring Dixon was a member of a sub-committee to promote the establishment of working men's clubs in the town;[67] by the summer he was a member of the provisional committee of the Birmingham Dining Halls Company (Ltd.), whose objectives encompassed 'the comfort and well-being of the working classes'. Quite probably he had subscribed for shares, but 'it was not to be seen as an investment for the sake of profit', the dividend was not to exceed 5%, and it should be 'free from all appearance of patronage or charity'.[68] In the autumn Dixon was chairing a meeting of the Birmingham Central Working Men's Clubs, fixing their rules and constitutions.[69] The following spring he was a new borough magistrate,[70] and by that autumn he had been elected unopposed to the Town Council, a vacancy having arisen in the Edgbaston Ward.[71]

If that were not enough, a year later he was appointed visiting justice of Birmingham Gaol. Undoubtedly, there were diary clashes, and a feature of the next few years of his busy life was the occasional complaint of failure to attend meetings. This problem was especially the case in connection with his election for Mayor a few years later. He stood down as a Town Councillor in February 1868, with six councillors voting against the resolution thanking him for his services, on the basis that he had attended so few meetings.[72] It is scarcely surprising to find a report on 11 February 1870 that he had by then become an inactive member of the Board of Guardians.

The circumstances of his not seeking re-election in 1863 as Vice-President of the Chamber of Commerce were revealing, for they show what Dixon had come to achieve in a short space of time.

The half-yearly meeting took place seemingly without drama on 30 July 1863, R. Spooner, MP, in the chair.[73] Within days, *The Times* published an intriguing editorial,[74] which started off with an account of Birmingham's turbulent past, of the days of the First Reform Act:

> We are beginning to fear that a glory has departed, and that Birmingham has passed through its heroic stage. … Birmingham has had its stirring times, its demigods, its TITANS, and its crusades. It is only a generation since a hundred thousand Birmingham men were on the very point of marching upon the metropolis to compel the Lords to accept the Reform Bill, and were only stopped, as some maliciously say, by the want of shoes,

---

67 Ibid., 26 March 1863.
68 Ibid., 11 June 1863.
69 Ibid., 20 Oct. 1863.
70 Ibid., 27 April 1864.
71 Ibid., 23 Nov. 1864.
72 Ibid., 18 Feb. 1868.
73 Birmingham Archives and Heritage, Birmingham Chamber of Commerce Minute Book, 1861-5.
74 3 Aug. 1863.

but, as is far more probable, by finding their services were not wanted and they would simply have to march back again.

It moved on to Dixon's era:

> Since then Birmingham has proved its strong nature and its good fighting spirit by refusing to accept Mr. Bright's peace doctrines, and on that point he does not represent the town. In other respects, as far as can be judged, from the opinions of the representatives, the town is disposed to go ahead in every department of reform, and may be safely counted upon to support any moderate revolution likely to create a demand for small arms. But there is nothing great just now for Birmingham to do.
>
> ... Its Chamber of Commerce is driven by mere force of events into the utilities of life, and, under the judicious presidency of Mr. Spooner, talks prose. Its proposals, if they do not excite astonishment, strike terror, or provoke opposition, claim our assent upon more reasonable grounds....
>
> ... If you set about altering the whole world, and turning society upside down, you will probably find yourselves like the naughty child who has covered the drawing-room floor with litter, and finds himself under peremptory orders to pick it up and make all straight again. Birmingham, after indulging in various eccentricities, or at least allowing her name to be associated with them, is now quite as reasonable as the rest of the world, clothed, and in her right mind. The change is remarkable, and it is impossible not to remark it without drawing a useful lesson and pointing a moral.

Birmingham was earning a reputation for increasing moderation, and it was proper that Mr. Spooner as President should get some credit, but the reality was that Dixon had for the past few years been doing much of the hard work. Who, however, outside of Birmingham had heard of 'George Dixon'?

Things then moved quickly. At the Council meeting on 11 August, with Spooner in the Chair, Minute 1258 records: 'Resolved that George Dixon, Esq., be re-elected Vice President for the following year'. Dixon had other plans, however, and the following Minute records that he declined office, giving reasons, which unfortunately were not specified. This was the second time in his life when he had tendered his resignation and was asked to re-consider his position.[75] He was showing his capability as a team player.

Meanwhile, Dixon played another role as public benefactor in the aftermath of the notorious 'Female Blondin' incident.

---

75 The previous occasion was eight years previously, when he had tendered his resignation from the Birmingham & Midland Institute.

Blondin was a tightrope artiste who unfortunately fell to her death in 1863 whilst performing at Birmingham's Aston Park, which had been opened to the public some years previously by Queen Victoria and her Consort, Prince Albert. Victoria learned of the episode and was distinctly not amused. Then George Dixon and his elder brother Abraham headed a public subscription list with contributions of £1,000 each, which led to the Park being acquired by the Corporation of Birmingham – and gaining better management.[76]

Around this time, Dixon became a member of the Birmingham and Edgbaston Debating Society,[77] a forum in which he gained closer acquaintance with several of those who were to feature significantly in the town's municipal life. This group saw itself as a

> training school in which the intellectual athlete has prepared himself for the more vigorous, if not the more difficult, conflicts of public life.[78]

However, a local periodical did not rate Dixon's early performance too highly:

> when he first began public life, [he] was diffuse and somewhat "wordy". In these respects he has greatly improved. His speeches are now concise, lucid, and distinct. They are carefully prepared, and are models of arrangement and perspicuity. They give one the idea that he is completely at home in his subject, and thoroughly in earnest. He makes no attempt at oratorical display, and aims rather at convincing his audience….[79]

The same periodical was equally severe about Joseph Chamberlain's early days there too, describing him as 'a very impetuous and rapid speaker'.[80]

It was in 1864 that Dixon began to get involved in local politics, albeit very much on the margins, supporting Birmingham's two MPs, John Bright and William Scholefield, at a meeting calling for electoral reform.[81] He was also a member of a committee to organise Garibaldi's visit to Birmingham, which, as it happened, never took place.[82]

---

76 *The Times,* 25 Jan. 1898: obituary of George Dixon.

77 He had previously been the last President of the Birmingham Debating Society – see C. Wade, *The Lucid Expression of Thought: A History of the Birmingham & Edgbaston Debating Society, 1846-2006* (Studley, 2006), p. XV. He had been a member of the earlier organisation since at least 1849.

78 Langford*, Modern Birmingham,* Vol. 1, p. 247; quoted in S. Gunn, *The Public Culture of the Victorian Middle Class: Ritual and Authority and the English Industrial City* (Manchester, 2000), p. 99.

79 *Edgbastonia,* Jan. 1886, p. 2.

80 Ibid..

81 Langford, *Modern Birmingham,* Vol. 2, p. 343.

82 Ibid., Vol. 2, p. 264.

Throughout his life, Dixon had very little to say about foreign affairs, despite travelling abroad extensively, and frequently making comparisons with the state of foreign competitors' economies, and their provision of education. Whilst his mother's side of the family had had strong connections with Italy, and his brother-in-law James Stansfeld spoke of Joseph Mazzini, the Italian revolutionary, in the most reverential of terms,[83] it was that connection which nearly brought Stansfeld's political career to a premature end.

After an unsuccessful attempt to assassinate Louis Napoleon, the spotlight fell on Mazzini as one of the perpetrators. In the process, Stansfeld became implicated, with accusations being made that he had allowed his house to be used as a poste-restante. This Stansfeld vigorously denied, and in 1864 he only just survived a vote of no confidence in the House of Commons. Upon returning home, his wife confessed that all along she had been forwarding letters to Mazzini behind his back, and Stansfeld felt obliged to tender his resignation to Palmerston.

Stansfeld's own obituary told a slightly different tale: 'Letters had been with his assent addressed to Mazzini as M. Fiori [nom-de-plume] at his house, but he repudiated the notion of Mazzini's complicity with the conspirators'.[84]

Whatever the truth of his involvement, the debacle may have been sufficient to persuade Dixon, with a very full agenda of other issues to deal with throughout his life, that foreign affairs were not for him.

Meanwhile, a new local issue had emerged. As a former grammar school pupil himself, in Leeds, Dixon was appalled to find that the Birmingham School, intended for the education of the children of the poor, had in effect been hijacked by the middle classes – and some of the children of his colleagues in commerce were indeed being educated free of charge.

A Free Grammar School Association (FGSA) had been founded in 1864, with J.S. Wright one of the two honorary secretaries. Its aims were to extend educational provision and to displace the old establishment from its privileged position.[85] The hub of the problem was ably described by Jesse Collings,[86] who delivered a paper at the Social Science Meeting in Birmingham in October 1868, entitled *On the State of Education in Birmingham*: 'one feels drawn to the conclusion that the state of education in Birmingham would have been as good at the present time if the Grammar School never existed'.[87] Disturbingly, the

---

83 'I speak of Joseph Mazzini, long my revered friend, whom I, in intimate daily life, know perhaps better than any other living man, English or Italian, knows him…': James Stansfeld, *The Italian Movement and Italian Parties* (1862), p. 39.

84 *The Times,* 18 Feb. 1898.

85 Dennis Smith, *Conflict and Compromise – Class Formation in English Society 1830-1914 – A Comparative Society of Birmingham and Sheffield,* (1982), p. 176.

86 Jesse Collings (1831-1920) was an advocate of both educational and land reform, in which context he is often remembered for the phrase 'three acres and a cow'. He was also a close friend of Joseph Chamberlain.

87 Jesse Collings, *On the State of Education in Birmingham* (Birmingham, 1868), p. 6.

very effect of its existence was to destroy all the private schools in the area. Furthermore, those attending were the children of parents who could well afford to pay for education elsewhere, thus depriving children of poorer parents a place. Entrance to the school had been by nomination, although a very recent policy change had resulted in admission being by competitive examination.[88]

The administration of the charity was by a self-elected Board of Governors, very few indeed of whom were either Nonconformists or Liberals. 'These facts give ample ground for the strong feeling that exists in the town, that the elections were made in the interests "of a particular political and ecclesiastical party"'.

Sargant[89] was the first President of the FGSA and, like Dixon who quickly succeeded him, was an Anglican.[90] Dixon was faced by a deplorable situation: large numbers of middle class children received an excellent education free of charge, whilst children of such poorer parents who could afford to pay anything received an education that was practically worthless.[91] On two significant occasions he made his views known very publicly.

Before the Schools Inquiry Commission,[92] he outlined his concept of the way forward, after setting out the facts, 'Whereby the poorest boy in Birmingham should have the opportunity, if he were qualified by his industry and talents of availing himself of that opportunity, that he should have the opportunity of rising from those lowest schools up to the highest'.[93] Dixon was also wary that local connections were being lost, suggesting that the share of resources devoted to boarders should be diminished.[94] He further objected to the requirements that the headmaster and second master should be selected from among the Anglican clergy, and urged that the magistrates and town council should share in the appointment of governors.[95]

Dixon reverted to the subject once again before the Royal Commission on Endowed Schools two years later, complaining that it was manifestly unfair that the rich and well-to-do classes should absorb some three-fourths of the income of the charity, to the exclusion of those for whom the school was founded.[96]

The headmaster was Rev. Charles Evans, who wanted to take more boarders, make fee-paying general, extend the teaching of Latin into the elementary

---

88 Ibid., p. 7.
89 William Lucas Sargant (1809-89).
90 Smith, *Conflict and Compromise*, p. 177.
91 Taylor, 'Birmingham Movement', p. 44.
92 Smith, *Conflict and Compromise*, p. 177.
93 Question asked before the Schools Inquiry Commission: Q. 18,037.
94 Ibid., Q. 18,049.
95 Ibid., Q. 18,039-45. This issue was a foretaste of the battle that was to rage again some 12 years later: see below, Chapter 6, p. 182.
96 *BDP*, 9 March 1868.

schools, and generally free himself from 'local pressure which may often be unwisely exerted'.[97] Just as the Leeds case culminating in the Eldon judgment had rumbled on for many a long year at the turn of the century,[98] so would the issues surrounding the management of the King Edward's Foundation more than half a century later.

Dixon was becoming increasingly concerned with the welfare of the working classes. But the path of reform was not straightforward. Just two years after becoming involved with a working men's club, he had to admit defeat. The aim of the promoters had been to 'help working men to help themselves, rather than to establish or manage institutions for them, this being as essential for the moral usefulness as for the permanent success of our endeavours'.[99] However, two years later 'The Working Men's Club, which was commenced with so much promise and hope, had to be abandoned. Every attempt was tried, but after considerable loss, principally borne by Mr George Dixon, the friend of every movement for the education and elevation of the working classes, the promoters had to close its doors'.[100] No explanation was forthcoming.

Dixon was able to support reform causes because he was by the mid 1860s a man of some considerable financial standing, as was evident from his involvement in the reorganisation of the Lloyds banking business in 1865.

It is known that Rabone Bros. had banked with the firm of Messrs. Taylor and Lloyd as far back as 1841,[101] and it is not impossible that the relationship went back many years before then.

The general trend towards joint-stock banking, and a failure in a local banking business, Attwoods,[102] resulted in the Lloyd family (between whom 'perfect uniformity of view was not always possible') deciding to review their position, and they made this the occasion to inject fresh blood from powerful business circles in Birmingham.

Dixon was an obvious choice, not only because he was by then a man of considerable stature in the local business community, but also because of close ties with the Lloyd family. Thomas Lloyd had been a partner in Rabone Bros., and 'a very great friend', in Katie Rathbone's words.[103] Sampson Lloyd of course had had many contacts with Dixon at the Association of Chambers of Commerce. The third member of the Lloyd family who made up the partnership prior to incorporation was Sampson's younger brother, George Braithwaite. That there was scope for disagreement was obvious: Thomas was

---

97 Smith, *Conflict and Compromise,* p. 179.
98 See above, Chapter 1, p. 18.
99 Langford, *Modern Birmingham,* Vol. 2, p. 251.
100 Ibid., Vol. 2, p. 284.
101 *The Times,* 16 Aug. 1841.
102 Marsh, *Chamberlain,* p. 20.
103 Rathbone, *The Dales,* p. 27.

a Liberal, and Sampson a Conservative. But the introduction of new faces spelt the way forward.

Dixon was not alone, for there was a long list of local notables who attended the first meeting of the Provisional Committee which met on 29 March 1865. Joseph Chamberlain was amongst them,[104] and he, Dixon and Edward Gem, another merchant, were the largest shareholders when the time came to allot shares, with £2,500 invested apiece.[105] Individual members of the Lloyd family subscribed rather less at that time.

Dixon played a prominent part in the initial proceedings, his name being associated with all of the first three Resolutions passed at that first meeting. The size of Dixon's shareholding also showed that he had considerable funds at his disposal, and these were to be a feature of his life more and more often, as he put his money where his mouth was, demonstrating his own personal support for the causes he espoused.

The pressures on George's time were, however, considerable, and by the early months of 1867 not only was he Mayor, but he had set the ball rolling on the formation of the Birmingham Education Society [BES]. It is therefore not surprising to find the Bank's Board passing a Minute on 18 March 1867 calling on the Secretary to inform him that his resignation as a director was accepted 'with regret'.[106]

One of the reasons for his being so busy was that he had taken his first tentative step into the field of politics, pure and simple. A pattern was about to emerge, and a circular did the rounds of Birmingham.[107] His name was the first on the list.

> Dear Sir,
>
> It has for some time been a matter of regret that the Liberal party in Birmingham has no recognized organisation by which its opinions can be expressed and its interests promoted. We desire to see some course taken which should unite all the Liberals of the town, and provide them with a regular and efficient method of exercising a legitimate influence in favour of their political principles. In furtherance of this object we request your attendance at a meeting.
>
> 11 February 1865

Other names on the list comprised many who were to feature prominently in the history of the town over the next few years: Thomas Phillips, Arthur

---

104 Lloyds Banking Group Archives, Board Minutes: File Ho/D/Boa/Min/1.
105 Lloyds Banking Group Archives, Share allotment book: File HO/S/Sha/1.
106 Lloyds Banking Group Archives, Board Minutes: File Ho/D/Boa/Min/2.
107 The story is told by Frank Schnadhorst, later to be a significant figure in the National Liberal Federation. See *BDP,* 24 March 1885.

Ryland, J.S. Wright, William Holliday, William Harris, John Jaffray, Thomas Lloyd and William Middlemore.

The meeting duly took place six days later in a committee room of the Town Hall, and after much discussion as to a name ('Radical Reformers Association' was one suggestion), the Birmingham Liberal Association (BLA) emerged in its first incarnation. A member of the long-established Birmingham Muntz family, P.H. Muntz was its President, and Dixon its Honorary Secretary.[108]

Established shortly before the General Election of that year, its objects were stated to be 'To maintain the Liberal representation of the Borough. To assist in obtaining the return of Liberal members for the county. To promote the adoption of Liberal principles in the Government of the country'.[109] As such it was an election committee put on a permanent basis. In its way, it was a ground-breaking development in British politics, for hitherto all election activities had been conducted on an ad hoc basis, with organisations, such as they were, created and then subsequently dismembered before and after each election.[110]

Dixon's nomination of Bright as a candidate in that election was made with considerable reservation: 'he was not prepared to endorse all that Mr Bright had said – and he was sure that everyone would agree with him – that England had never produced a more outspoken or a more honest politician'.[111] What Bright thought of this was not recorded but Scholefield took the opportunity to compliment Dixon on his work in connection with partnership legislation.

The BLA from the outset was a body of some substance: Dixon's name had appeared on an advertisement calling for support in the form of petition signatures for the Six Pounds Franchise Reform Bill,[112] and there appeared two weeks later an advertisement for a paid secretary.[113] No doubt the response to the call for signatures had been significant.

The general election in 1865 was not an unqualified success, for G.F. Muntz had not been returned for the nearby constituency of North Warwickshire. However, Dixon's close friend, Thomas Lloyd, had by now replaced P.H. Muntz as chairman. It was Dixon's task to read the report on what had happened in the general election, and called for a post-mortem, which could not be carried out successfully 'unless the organisation hastily formed for the contest just over be rendered permanent and effective' ... 'The Liberal organisation, defective as it may hitherto have been, has led to the discovery that sufficient material for

---

108 Dent, *Old and New*, Vol. 3, p. 542.
109 *Birmingham Journal*, 18 Feb. 1865, as quoted in E.P. Hennock, *Fit and Proper Persons. Ideal and Reality in Nineteenth-Century Urban Government* (1973), p. 131.
110 Ward, *City-State*, p. 63.
111 *BDP*, 13 July 1865.
112 Ibid., 14 March 1865.
113 Ibid., 30 March 1865.

complete and immediate success lies around it'.[114] Thus was the genesis of a permanent political organisation.

Not content with having an involvement in temporal politics, George Dixon also became involved in ecclesiastical politics.

Anglicanism itself was far from united, and Dixon declared his stance at a meeting convened by the Bishop of the diocese[115] to consider measures for the extension of the church in the borough. He denied that he was either High Church or evangelical. 'If he was of any party in the church at all (which he would rather not consider himself to be) it would be of the Broad Church. Indeed so broad might he think himself that he might fairly hesitate as to whether it was right for him to come there that day…'.[116]

In fact, Dixon became embroiled in a vigorous debate over the manner in which clergymen should be appointed to the new churches which were springing up all over Birmingham. Dixon was opposed to the concept of patronage, and preferred an approach for selecting a new pastor which was variously described as 'congregational' or 'democratic'.[117] In this, he was supported by Rev William Gover, principal of the Worcester Diocesan Training College, who published a pamphlet describing Dixon's stance as 'a novel proposal for vesting the patronage of incumbencies, established under the Birmingham Church Extension Society, in representative trusts, superseding self-elected and ex-officio trusts'. The pamphlet continued: 'I have, at this momentous crisis of the history of the church in Birmingham, spoken out for the principle of representative self-government on behalf of the laity, and for that freedom of thought which was the backbone of the early church, and is the ground work of the Reformed Church of our land'.[118]

Three years later, George Dixon supported the argument for the disestablishment of the Church in Ireland, but not yet in England, on the basis that it was doing good work, especially in agricultural areas. There was good reason for maintaining the status quo in England. As Dixon's thoughts turned to an agenda which would eventually culminate in calls for compulsory and free education, it would be a step too far to disrupt the existing infrastructure of largely Church-funded elementary education, inadequate as it might be in many areas.

The central dilemma for Victorian education was that 'whilst it was very clear that there was a need for broader access to education, so too was the perception that it must include instruction in moral values'. But moral values were perceived as inseparable from religious instruction, and religious

114 Ibid., 2 Aug. 1865.
115 Birmingham at this time lay within the diocese of Worcester.
116 *BDP*, 1 Feb. 1865.
117 Ibid., 15 March 1865.
118 Ibid., 13 Feb. 1865.

instruction would almost certainly be denominational. This basic starting point was further complicated by the fact that there was an established state church, which would almost certainly have a substantial role in any provision by the state.[119] The differences between the views of Anglicans and Dissenters on the question of religious instruction ran very deep, cropping up again and again throughout very many of the debates on educational reform in the coming years.

Superimposed on that conundrum was another conflict of ideologies. On the one hand, the Anglican model envisaged the labouring population being cared for through the charitable endeavours of a patrician establishment, which cultivated its connections with the county and metropolis. Yet an alternative view proposed that care for all members of the community should be a prime function of public institutions rather than of private charity. In between lay a gradation of differing views; and the issue remains a contested one to this day.

Dixon himself was to pursue his overall ambitions for education as President of the Birmingham Town Mission, clause 2 of whose constitution read: 'The object of this institution is to extend the knowledge of the Gospel among the inhabitants of Birmingham and its vicinity (especially the poor), without any reference to denominational distinctions, or the peculiarities of church government'.[120]

1866 was a turning-point for Dixon personally. His elder brother Abraham, who had not been in the best of health for some time, decided to move to the countryside. He chose Cherkley Court in Surrey, located overlooking the Mole Valley between Leatherhead and Dorking. The estate, comprising 90 to 95 acres of yew trees,[121] had previously been owned by the banking firm, Overend, Gurney & Co. The run on this bank in 1866 which triggered the sale was the last in the United Kingdom before the crisis of Northern Rock in 2007. Abraham Dixon commissioned a substantial new building, but it was not until 1871 that he finally moved south. There he was able to enjoy his hobby of cultivating exotic plants, many of which had been imported from South America, and to engage in lengthy correspondence with the Director of Kew Gardens. The fresh air obviously suited him, for he outlived his younger brother by nine years, dying aged 92.

---

119 R.F. Spall, 'Free-Trade Radicals, Education, and Moral Improvement in Early Victorian England', in M. H. Shirley and T.E.A. Larson (eds), *'Splendidly Victorian': Essays in Nineteenth- and Twentieth-Century British History in Honour of W.L. Arnstein* (Aldershot, 2001), p. 70.

120 Langford, *Modern Birmingham*, Vol. 2, p. 196. There were representatives from 24 different organisations at Dixon's funeral on 28 Jan. 1898, at the Church of St. Augustine in Edgbaston. One body represented was the Birmingham Hebrew Congregation: see West Yorkshire Archive Services, WYL/962.

121 J. Lowe, *The Yew-Trees of Great Britain and Ireland* (1897), p. 196. The house was subsequently purchased by Max Aitken, later Lord Beaverbrook, in the ownership of whose family it remained until 2011.

That younger brother, however, remained committed to Birmingham, for a great deal of work lay before him. As one commentator put it: 'There was no storm and stress in his [George Dixon's] private career; he was not one of the under-privileged: his course through life was certain, and eased by parental wealth; his own fortune, by middle life, was considerable, and like many another, he might easily have bought land and joined the squirearchy. Instead, he chose to throw himself into the agitation for a national system of education: indeed, it was he who by his own deliberate action gave the impetus to the whole movement in Birmingham'.[122]

By contrast, 'after 1860 many [Birmingham businessmen] sought rural retreats close enough to the city to be able to continue to play an active part in business but distant as possible from the encroaching lower-middle and middle-class suburbanites'.[123] Dixon decidedly bucked the trend here, and resolutely stayed put at The Dales, in the heart of fashionable Edgbaston, and within walking distance of his offices in the centre of Birmingham.

The Dales was eminently suitable for entertaining, built in sizeable grounds. Located in Augustus Road, Edgbaston, The Dales was used for a while after Dixon's death as student accommodation by Birmingham University, (founded 1900), before demolition some time in the 1970s.

Like his brother, Dixon was a keen gardener, and so was naturally interested in the affairs of the Birmingham Botanical and Horticultural Society, which was in some financial difficulty. At the annual meeting in 1866, he suggested ways of improving profitability, such as rearing young plants on spare ground, and selling them.[124] Almost a year later, he was thanked for his advice, which had led the Society to pay off its mortgage debt.[125]

Other significant annual meetings were being held around this time. The first annual meeting of the BLA was held on 10 May 1866, but was not especially well-attended. Dixon summarised its achievements, most notably that the Liberal party of Birmingham now had a recognized organisation. Its purpose was to unite all the Liberals in the town, and provide them with a regular and efficient method of exercising a legitimate influence in favour of their political principles.

A mere 28 people attended the annual meeting in the following year, the year of the Second Reform Act. The existing BLA constitution was out of line with the new circumstances – there was a recognition that the extension of the right of voting to the working men of the town carried with it the right to a voice in the selection of the men for whom they should be asked to vote.[126]

---

122 Taylor, 'Birmingham Movement', p. 21.
123 Malchow, *Gentlemen Capitalists,* p. 370.
124 *BDP,* 13 Dec. 1866.
125 Ibid., 1 Nov. 1867.
126 Ibid., 24 March 1885.

Thus was born the 'Birmingham caucus' as it came to be popularly known, with the 400 becoming 600 in 1876, 800 in 1880, and 2000 proposed in 1885. William Harris was initially its organising genius, but Francis Schnadhorst became secretary in 1873. With three Liberals returned unopposed for Birmingham in 1874, despite a national swing in favour of the Conservatives, other parts of the country looked to it for inspiration. Thus in 1885 Schnadhorst could proclaim that then 'began the missionary era', and 'Birmingham had revolutionised political organisation in the United Kingdom'. It had indeed, and Dixon had played a small part in its beginnings.

Against this backdrop of vigorous activity in Birmingham on a large number of fronts, it was not surprising that Dixon should become a candidate for the mayoralty in the autumn of 1866. He was then aged 46, and by comparison with the relative obscurity of just five years previously, his rise had been rapid – indeed, too rapid for some who, perhaps reliant on the concept of seniority, considered that others might have had a stronger claim than he.

One view came from Alderman Goodrich, who disclaimed his own nomination. 'Dixon has served the town for many years, and has been foremost in supporting every great movement with his purse, his influence and his labour. He is not seeking this office, but has been urged into it'.[127] There were other views. Alderman Brisley hinted that 'he was sure Mr Dixon would not be elected for any ward in the borough other than Edgbaston'.[128] But such reservations came to nothing. Dixon was elected Mayor on 9 November 1866, with 43 votes in support, 1 opposed, and 16 abstaining.[129]

In the years before Dixon became Mayor, there had been a period of strict economy and civic stagnation, most especially during the period when Joseph Allday had been leader 'whose course of proceeding had excited a strong feeling of hostility, personal, political and municipal', according to the traditional view of this period.[130] However, more recent scholarship argues that Allday was made into a scapegoat for perceived municipal backwardness.[131] Whatever the truth of the matter, the atmosphere had soured. Indeed, it was commented that 'so many efficient members of the Council had been sickened of public life that the status and the value of the governing body had been lowered'.[132]

Nonetheless, by the 1860s things had changed. The years 1866 to 1873 have been described by Asa Briggs as veritably 'the seed-time of a "civic renaissance"' in Birmingham.[133] This flowering encompassed the years when

127 *Aris's Birmingham Guide*, quoted in Taylor, 'Birmingham Movement', p. 22.
128 *Aris's Birmingham Gazette*, 10 Nov. 1866.
129 J.T. Bunce, *History of the Corporation of Birmingham* (Birmingham, 1885), Vol. 2, p. 564.
130 Bunce, *History*, Vol. 2, p. xxxii.
131 R. Ward, 'Joseph Allday: Scapegoat for Municipal Backwardness', *Birmingham Historian*, 32 (2008), p. 18.
132 Bunce, *History*, Vol. 2, p. xxxiii.
133 A. Briggs, *Victorian Cities* (1963), p. 202.

Joseph Chamberlain was Mayor, and launched the policies often described as 'gas-and-water socialism'. Dixon had his part to play also, focusing especially upon educational improvements.

To all accounts, Dixon and his wife did the town proud during his mayoralty. Katie recorded: 'They gave some big parties in the Town Hall. I have heard they were better parties than any that had been given there before, my mother had a genius for entertaining'.[134]

Within weeks of coming to office, a very severe winter coupled with a trade depression afflicted the country, and the main problem for many of the population of Birmingham was to stay alive.[135] As Mayor, Dixon started a fund for the relief of poor families, and he himself contributed £100 per week.[136] Except for one very important matter, Dixon's period in office was not significantly different from those who immediately preceded him, nor immediately followed him. That matter was education.

Only a couple of months after taking office, Dixon penned a long letter to interested parties.[137] It merits reproduction in full as characteristic of the campaign style of the era, and of the man:

The Dales, Augustus Road, Edgbaston,

January 21st, 1867.

Dear Sir,

By this post you will receive copies of the paper contributed by the Manchester Education Aid Society to the Social Science Congress in October 1866, and heads of a Bill prepared by the same Society, and adopted by a meeting of the inhabitants of Manchester presided over by the Mayor.

I have to ask the favour of a careful perusal of these important documents as information has reached me that it is probable that Birmingham and other large towns will be called upon to aid Manchester, in an endeavour to get the Bill passed through Parliament during the coming session.

In preparation for a formal request to this effect, I beg also to invite you to a private meeting of some of the leading friends of education in Birmingham, which I propose to hold at the Dales on the evening of February 13 at which meeting it is my intention to submit for consideration, whether it is desirable that some action should be taken with reference to this Bill:- whether for instance it would be advisable at once to call a Town's Meeting to discuss the Bill, or whether the example

---

134 Rathbone, *The Dales*, p. 26.
135 Taylor, 'Birmingham Movement', p. 22.
136 *BDP,* 12 July 1867.
137 Birmingham Archives and Heritage, File MS 725/8.

of Manchester should be more closely followed, and a Birmingham Education Aid[138] Society be first established, deferring to a later period the consideration of the principles and details of the proposed measure.

If the latter course were to be adopted it might be thought desirable that the Society should embrace in its operations a wider range of objects than that of the Manchester Education Aid Society. It might be formed for the purpose of:-

(1) Collecting and disseminating information respecting the state of Education in Birmingham.

(2) Stimulating and assisting existing educational agencies.

(3) Discussing the merits of such new agencies as the Factory Act, and the Manchester Scheme, and to take action with reference thereto if it should seem desirable.

The hour of assembling will be 6.30 and the proceedings will commence at 7 precisely.

In addition to a large number of those Gentlemen in the town who have taken a leading part in all educational questions, the following have been invited, and I hope will be able to attend.

The Right Hon. the Lord Leigh

Dr. Temple, Head Master of Rugby, late H.M. Inspector of Training Colleges

H.M. Inspectors of Schools connected with the Privy Council Office in this Town

I.A.P. Bremmer Esq., Hon. Sec. Manchester Education Aid Society

Dr. Wilkinson

The Honble. and Rev. G. Yorke

Rev. Charles Evans

Rev. W. Gover

I shall be glad if you will inform me at your early convenience whether it will be agreeable to you to attend.

I have the honor

To Remain

Yours faithfully

George Dixon

Mayor

---

138 Subsequently, 'Birmingham Education Society' (henceforth 'BES') became the body's name, 'Aid' being omitted.

What had triggered this initiative? The Chambers of Commerce at this particular juncture were not yet expressing any significant concerns about educational issues, and so it is necessary to look back to the early 1860s, if not even earlier, to understand the pressures for change that were developing nationally, in order to understand how these impacted upon Birmingham in particular.

In 1973, E.P. Hennock observed: 'The history of the making of the 1870 Education Act and its implementation, complex as it is, has never been written though much has been written about it'.[139] The same remains true even today. This account of Dixon's life cannot possibly touch upon all the factors that bore upon possibly the most important piece of social legislation in the nineteenth century, symbolising as it does a turning-point between two eras, between the individualist earlier period, and the more collectivist later period. Of necessity, the focus here must be on Dixon's own contribution to these events.

The issue of educational reform had been before Parliament very many times in previous decades, to the point where Parliament had earned the reputation in the 1850s of being 'the great cemetery for the interment of defunct Education Bills'.[140] Throughout this period, state provision of finance for education was regarded primarily as an adjunct to the provision of relief of poverty.[141] Nonetheless, there were straws in the wind that the state needed to go further. Thus J.S. Mill was arguing: 'Is it not almost a self-evident maxim that the state should require and compel the education up to a certain standard of every human being who is born its citizen?'[142]

That there was general unease with regard to the provision of education generally was reflected in the proliferation of Royal Commissions appointed to look into various aspects. The crucial Newcastle Commission reported in 1861, calling for 'the extension of sound and cheap education'.[143] This stress upon cost was no doubt one reaction to the fact that the education estimate had risen from £160,000 in 1853 to £836,920 in 1859, and there was a 'strong and just presumption that the efficiency and utility of the system were not advancing in proportion with the cost'.[144] The mainstays of that system were

---

139 Hennock, *Fit and Proper Persons*, p. 80.

140 F. Smith, *The Life of Sir James Kay-Shuttleworth* (1923), p. 257.

141 J.W. Adamson, *A Short History of Education* (Cambridge, 1919), p. 307. The contrast between England and Prussia was extreme: not long after Victoria's accession, the latter was spending £600,000 annually on education, whilst the former a mere £30,000 (and £70,000 for royal stables), as Brougham bitterly said: see Garvin, *Chamberlain*, Vol. 1, p. 89. For the career of the Whig lawyer and politician, Henry Brougham, 1st Baron Brougham and Vaux (1778-1868), see also *ODNB-online*.

142 J.S. Mill, *On Liberty* (1859), p. 157, quoted in H.C. Barnard, *A Short History of English Education from 1760 to 1944* (1947), p. 133.

143 Barnard, *Short History*, p. 127.

144 F. Adams, *History of the Elementary School Contest in England* (1882; in new edn. Brighton, 1973), p. 177.

the National Society, and the smaller British and Foreign School Society. The former was exclusively Anglican, the latter less so.

The upshot was the introduction of Robert Lowe's Revised Code, based on the principle of payment by results, with a variable scale of grants depending on the number of children enrolled, and a sliding scale of payments for the total number of days in the year each child attended. In addition, pupils were assessed by inspectors' tests of attainment in the three core subjects of reading, writing and arithmetic.[145]

Whilst the Revised Code undoubtedly succeeded in securing economies,[146] it was vulnerable to the criticism that it encouraged the neglect of the intelligent and the reduction of all pupils to the level of the lowest capacity in a given school.[147] In today's parlance, it would be called 'dumbing down'. Lowe himself was however unrepentant, declaring in the Commons in 1863: 'I cannot promise the House that this system will be an economic one and I cannot promise that it will be an efficient one, but I can promise that it shall be one or the other. If it is not cheap it shall be efficient; if it is not efficient it shall be cheap'.[148]

However, within a decade there was to be a further fundamental change – Forster's Education Act. 'It seems extraordinary that a decade which had begun so unpromisingly should have closed with a commitment to a national system of elementary schools' observed Gillian Sutherland.[149] Historians have spent much time debating the nature of the predominant driving force behind the Act: was it England's growing awareness that it was beginning to lag behind in terms of international industrial competitiveness? was it a realisation that Parliamentary reform was incompatible with the country's perceived level of literacy? or was it something else? In truth, there were so many currents that they combined into an incoming tide – and it so happened that Dixon was one key activist who rode the wave that finally broke the dam.

Sutherland also noted that there were prosaic and very domestic reasons for supporting reform[150], and in Birmingham there was scarcely anything less prosaic than the Factory Extension Act and the Hours of Labour Regulation Act (Workshops Act).[151]

These pieces of legislation were ultimately to have the effect of changing the workshops,[152] of which Birmingham had proportionately far more than any other major industrial town, given its industrial structure, by emptying them of

---

145 J. Bowen, *A History of Western Education*, (1981), Vol. 3, p. 310.

146 The grant declined to £636,806 in 1865: see Barnard, *Short History*, p. 130.

147 Adamson, *Short History*, p. 308.

148 Bowen, *History*, p. 311.

149 G. Sutherland, *Elementary Education in the Nineteenth Century* (1971), p. 27.

150 Ibid..

151 A.J. Marcham, 'The Birmingham Education Society and the 1870 Education Act', *Journal of Educational Administration and History*, 8 (1976), p. 11.

152 G. Best, *Mid-Victorian Britain* (1971), p. 136.

their children. Dixon wrote his circular letter just ten days before the Chamber of Commerce minuted the extension of the new factory legislation.

In the Chamber's half-yearly report twelve months later there was considerable concern: 'It would appear that the new laws are even now leading to the discontinuance of the employment of children in many of the factories.'[153] The youngsters were left to roam the streets, being all too visible as Dixon walked to and from his office. As a debate in Parliament within a couple of years was to reveal, a miniature crime wave had broken out, and references to 'street arabs' abounded.

The immediate trigger[154] for the meeting mentioned in the letter of 21 January 1867, was an appeal for help by the Manchester Education Aid Society, which had been founded in 1864.[155] Such co-operation was very much in the same idiom as the manner in which the Birmingham Chamber of Commerce had co-operated with the Sheffield Chamber of Commerce, for example, over the issue of Trade Marks and Patents. However, it was foreseen at the outset that Birmingham might wish to do more than Manchester, although much could be learned from the latter. A formidable body of experience had accumulated there some years earlier when Manchester was at the heart of the campaign for the repeal of the Corn Laws, and when Bright himself had then been its MP.

Nonetheless, Manchester and Birmingham were very different: 'In many ways the change from Early to Late-Victorian England is symbolized in the names of two great cities: Manchester, solid, uniform, pacific, the native home of the great economic creed on which aristocratic England has always looked, and educated England was beginning to look, with some aversion and some contempt: Birmingham, experimental, adventurous, diverse, where old Radicalism might in one decade flower into lavish Socialism, in another into a pugnacious Imperialism'.[156]

The aims of the BES at the outset were loosely defined, and embraced paying school fees for poor children, raising and distributing funds for the enlargement, building and maintenance of schools, taking steps for obtaining local rating on behalf of education, and collecting and disseminating information on the subject.[157] Whilst a number of those involved in the BES also played a major part in the National Education League (NEL) which chronologically followed it, the two were distinctly different in character.

---

153 Birmingham Chamber of Commerce Minute Book, 1865-8: 30 Jan. 1868.
154 The genesis of the Society has been said to have originated in a conversation between Jesse Collings, shortly to become Honorary Secretary of the Society, and Dixon, in which the former said: 'If we could have an Education Society on the right lines, the very stones in the street would rise and join us': see A.Briggs, 'Introduction', Adams, *History of Elementary School Contest*, p. xvi.
155 Briggs, 'Introduction', p. xiii.
156 G.M. Young, quoted in Briggs, *Victorian Cities*, p. 185.
157 Langford, *Modern Birmingham*, Vol. 2, p. 399.

The BES was a local educational agency, not a national pressure group. It did not engage in any agitation. It pursued a philanthropic tradition of doling out education, or the means to obtain education. It could not appeal to working-class participation, requiring as it did a subscription of one guinea. And it did not contemplate legislation, other than that necessary to obtain local rating powers. Nonetheless both the BES and the NEL engaged in extensive collection and dissemination of information.[158]

What was significantly absent from any of these early discussions was what might loosely be termed 'the religious difficulty',[159] which had thwarted so many previous initiatives, and was to bedevil the affairs of the NEL, which was to follow. However, it is important not to overstate the strength of religious devotion in Birmingham. One measure which can is the combined attendance at church on Census Sunday in 1851, the only occasion on which an attempt was made to take stock of congregations in the nineteenth century. Birmingham was amongst the towns with the lowest index of attendance.[160] From the volume of the arguments, it would have been easy to conclude that the numbers were far higher.

Dixon duly had the formation of the BES discussed in the Town Council, on 5 March 1867, as mooted in his letter of invitation, and the meeting concluded with a vote of thanks, praising 'the ability, courtesy, liberality, and impartiality which have marked his conduct in the chair'.[161] That impartiality, involving as it did a need to compromise at critical moments, was crucial to the future campaign. The timing was such that in the following month he was able to provide local support for a Bill which had originated in Manchester, but which like so many that gone before, failed to reach the Statute Book.

A later meeting in June established a committee of which Dixon, an ecumenical Anglican, became president. As if to acknowledge the potential for religious discord, there were two vice-presidents, the Hon. and Rev. G.M. Yorke (Anglican) and the Dr. R.W. Dale, (Congregational),[162] who was to become one of Dixon's good friends. The committee as a whole was drawn from all sects, including a Roman Catholic, several more Anglicans, the renowned Nonconformist orator, George Dawson, and the Unitarian Joseph Chamberlain.[163] Thus through the conduit of the Society a number of able

---

158 Marcham, 'Birmingham Education Society', p. 14. See also H. Roper, 'Towards an Elementary Education Act for England and Wales, 1865-8', *British Journal of Educational Studies,* 23 (1975), p. 194.

159 For what constituted the difficulty, see below, Chapter 3, p. 93.

160 Gunn, *The Public Culture of the Victorian Middle Class,* p. 106.

161 Langford, *Modern Birmingham,* Vol. 2, p. 398.

162 The Rev. R.W. Dale (1829-95) did not use the title 'Reverend', and is here referred to as Dr. Dale. A leading exponent of the Civic Gospel, he was Chairman of the Congregational Union of England and Wales in 1868.

163 Marcham, 'Birmingham Education Society', p. 13.

recruits were to find their way into municipal politics, brought there by their interest in the extension of popular education.[164]

One of Chamberlain's biographers has perceived a community of interest between Dixon and Chamberlain at this stage. Both were concerned about the widening chasm between the middle and working classes in the town, and keen to see free education provided.[165] The constitution was 'wholly independent of party politics or sectarian bias' as the secretary of the NEL was later to describe it.[166] Indeed, the Conservative *Aris's Birmingham Gazette* said of Dixon: 'The Mayor, who is ever willing to spend and be spent for the public good, is taking active steps to bring this vital question before the public of Birmingham … There is ample room for such a society, and ample work for it to do; and the thanks of every friend of education are due to the Mayor'.[167] But the ecumenical approach was not to endure for long, as some of the members were shortly to find themselves agitating on behalf of the National Education Union (NEU), the League's Manchester-based rival.

The BES duly produced statistics as Dixon had intended, and these in absolute terms made depressing reading. They were, however, statistically unsound, for what was needed was some idea of the proportion of children among the total living in Birmingham for whom better provision was needed: Birmingham was a substantial town, and the government would need a better idea of the scale of the problem nationwide. Lord Robert Montagu, Vice-President of the Council of Education, was not slow to highlight the point, once the figures had been drawn to his attention: the canvas had deliberately excluded streets occupied by members of the middle classes.[168]

Dixon had to tread warily, for one of those whom he had invited to his home for the meeting on 13 February 1867, Rev. William Gover, had written a letter drawing attention to the very considerable variation in educational facilities, comparing one district with another. Whilst there was only enough room in local schools to accommodate 8% of the school-age population, attendance was irregular, so that such places as were available, were not always filled. Further, despite the Society providing much assistance, no more than half the beneficiaries attended at all regularly.[169] On the other hand, Rev. Gover pointed to the abundance of provision in certain country districts, and observed: 'It were an egregious

164 Hennock, *Fit and Proper Persons*, p. 82.
165 Marsh, *Chamberlain*, p. 30.
166 Adams, *History of Elementary School Contest*, p. 196.
167 *Aris's Daily Gazette*, 26 Jan. 1867.
168 *Hansard*, Vol. 192, Col. 2001, 24 June 1868.
169 Marsh, *Chamberlain*, p. 36. Montagu was an awkward opponent with whom to deal: once, responding to Forster's reliance on BES statistics, he said that 'it was commonly known that the paid secretaries of such institutions "wrote up" their reports to induce silly women to part with subscriptions'. Eventually it transpired that Montagu simply had not read the report in question: Taylor, 'Birmingham Movement', p. 64.

folly to attempt to apply the same plans universally; to small parishes as well as to great towns'.[170]

Comments such as this would not have fallen on deaf ears, for Dixon had robustly made a pitch for variety in the Town Council meeting – although he had yet to learn to be less 'wordy':

> It was most important that they should seek in all educational work that they took in hand, to make the ultimate end of that work a gradation of schools – schools that is, not uniform, not of the same character, but so diverse that they should be adapted to the wants of every class of the community, from the richest down to the very lowest, and that they should be so easy of access from the lower schools to the higher that they should feel that there was not one boy in Birmingham, however low in the school, or however indifferent his parents might be to his education, if he had really those natural powers which would enable him to profit in an extraordinary degree by the advantages offered, who would have anything in the shape of a barrier put in the way of his progress upwards, even to the highest honours of the University.[171]

This bore all the hallmarks of the meritocrat. Kenrick described these words as 'remarkable', adding:

> These words – more or less varied – have been used by so many speakers since then that they have become almost the watchwords of education in England, and I make no apology for quoting them again.[172]

One such variation was reportedly[173] used by Thomas Huxley a few years later and has become much better known, not least because of the use of the word 'ladder' in place of Dixon's unwieldy 'gradation':

> He believed that no educational system in this country would be worthy the name of a national system, or fulfil the great objects of education, unless it was one which established a great educational ladder, the bottom of which should be in the gutter and the top in the University, and by which

---

170 Rev. William Gover, *Day School Education in the Borough of Birmingham: Our Progress, Position and Needs: A Letter to George Dixon, Esq., Mayor* (1867), p. 15. As it transpired, Dixon was just as concerned about the inadequacy of school provision in the countryside as in the towns: see below, Chapter 5, p. 153.

171 Kenrick, 'George Dixon', p. 55.

172 Ibid., p. 54.

173 See P. White, *Thomas Huxley, Making the 'Man of Science'* (Cambridge, 2003), p. 129, where it is suggested that *The Times* reporter present at the London School Board meeting concerned paraphrased Huxley's conclusions.

> every child who had the strength to climb might, by using that strength, reach the place for which nature intended him.[174]

Progress was being made in drawing local people's attentions to shortcomings in educational provision, but Dixon needed a wider audience if he were going to secure action, and achieve his ambitions. Then suddenly, out of the blue, two things happened which thrust him on to the national stage: as Mayor, he bravely took a leading part in the suppression of Birmingham's Murphy Riots in June 1867; and almost immediately after that, William Scholefield, Bright's colleague as MP for Birmingham died, and Dixon won the ensuing by-election. To a minor extent, the two events were inter-connected.

So far as Dixon's obituarist in *The Times* was concerned: 'His year of office was rendered memorable by the occurrence of the Murphy "No Popery" riots, which were the outcome of a series of lectures on the Confessional by an itinerant demagogue who succeeded in rousing the fanaticism of the mob against their Roman Catholic fellow-subjects, and keeping the town for several days in an uproar. That the consequences were not much more serious was largely due to Mr. Dixon's firmness and energy.'[175]

It was the last of a 'long series of riots which have rendered the town of Birmingham infamous in that respect'.[176] Murphy was a fanatical Protestant Electoral Association rabble-rouser who exhorted the crowd to attack ritualism of any kind.[177] The chief magistrate had declined the use of the Town Hall for the purpose of these lectures, and this tacitly gave the rough element in the town to understand that he was not to be afforded any protection. 'A number of the lowest roughs, delighted at the opportunity of a "row" and probably not caring two straws for either cause, took possession of Park Street, stripped many of the houses of their contents, tore off the tiles from the roofs of most of the buildings in the street, and there ensued such a scene of destruction as had not been equalled since the Chartist riots of 1839'.[178] With a squadron of Hussars lurking in the background, and a stone being thrown in his direction, Dixon bravely rode into the midst of an angry crowd in Birmingham's Bull Ring, and there read the Riot Act.[179] These were the days when the text of the Act had to be read aloud – literally – and within hearing of the crowd.

---

174 H.B. Philpott, *London at School* (1904), p. 153.
175 *The Times,* 25 Jan. 1898.
176 Dent, *Old and New,* p. 569. In fact, it was not the last: the Aston Park riot of 1884 was still to take place.
177 Bird, *Portrait,* p. 102.
178 Dent, *Old and New,* p. 569.
179 *BDP,* cutting late Jan. 1898: precise date not shown. A graphic account of the riots is to be found in *Reynolds's News,* 23 June 1867.

Aris's Birmingham Gazette had some reservations about Dixon's conduct, commenting initially that 'the result, so far, has certainly not been altogether unsatisfactory',[180] whilst three weeks later criticising him for not having the police in the right place at the right time.[181]

But Dixon's handling of the situation overall did his reputation no harm. Around this time, 'he was probably the most popular man in Birmingham'.[182] Two very distinct points emerged from this episode, however, which many historians have overlooked. Firstly, there was scarcely a person in the whole country who knew better than Dixon the consequences of religious discord. This experience would have strengthened his natural resolve, wherever possible, to seek a compromise when difficulties abounded. And secondly, despite the 'religious difficulty' surrounding the 1870 Education Act being invariably portrayed as a conflict between the Established Anglican Church and the Nonconformists, in this instance the conflict lay between the Nonconformists and the Catholics – religious problems, through Dixon's eyes, were multi-dimensional.

After William Scholefield's death on 9 July 1867,[183] there was immediate support for Dixon's candidature from the BLA and the Reform League. So immediate was the response that it has been suggested that the Liberal nomination 'was snatched almost before most people knew what was happening'.[184] And the by-election process was remarkably rapid. Dixon resigned the mayoralty on 15 July,[185] and a Town Hall meeting of his supporters was held on 18 July.

With the by-election following on so soon after Dixon's election to the mayoralty, it is not surprising to find that the arguments advanced in his support were very similar.

Once again, Dixon attracted some criticism for his shortcomings in not attending meetings. His opponents in the Liberal-Conservative Association however had a problem in opposing his candidature: they did not know too much about him. Bizarrely, it was reported that 'Mr Dixon was not transcendently qualified as a commercial man', although little further was said on that subject.[186] The fact that his Conservative opponent, Sampson Lloyd, was standing for a party that included 'Liberal' in its name (as Liberal-Conservative) reflected that already the town was well deserving of its

---

180 *Aris's Birmingham Gazette,* 22 June 1867.
181 Ibid., 13 July 1867.
182 Kenrick, 'George Dixon', p. 53.
183 Langford, *Modern Birmingham,* Vol. 2, p. 359.
184 Hennock, *Fit and Proper Persons,* p. 132.
185 Bunce, *History,* Vol. 2, p. 564.
186 *BDP,* 11 July 1867. With the destruction of records in 1941, the historian is similarly unable to comment in detail on the conduct of the business of Rabone Bros..

contemporaneous description 'as Liberal as the sea is salt'.[187] No candidate who did not possess some Liberal inclinations was likely to be successful.

Nonetheless, the Conservative press had a number of criticisms to make, portraying Dixon as a 'rider of dead horses'. One was particularly intriguing: 'Mr Dixon is a sound Protestant, and hates the Romish system as a system. We don't doubt it. But what is he prepared to do?... the Protestant horse that Mr Dixon rides is as dead as the rest of the stud. No web nor spur will ever get him to show his paces'. For Dixon, this cautious trait was something of a useful weapon. By frequently appearing to compromise, and often refraining from sticking his neck out on contentious issues other than education, he did not leave too many hostages to fortune. This quality is one explanation for his long-term ability to stand apart from the turmoil that periodically beset Birmingham Liberals.

The parliamentary contest put Thomas Lloyd, brother of one of the candidates and former partner of the other, in an awkward position, which he resolved by writing to Dixon that he could not support either side. He did not wish to jeopardise his relationship with 'either of my two best friends'.[188] There was a widespread desire to keep personalities out of the contest, for connections were intimate: Thomas Lloyd's sister-in-law married George Dixon's younger brother, another Thomas.[189] It was all rather bewildering for the younger generation, though, for Katie recalled as a child that she was confused between Murphy and Sampson Lloyd. 'I suppose Murphy was an Irish stump orator – not a very elevated character. I always thought he and Sampson Lloyd were in league together, and both bad characters'.[190] Only later when she grew up did she realise that the respectable Sampson Lloyds were friends of the family, and that her father George Dixon had been one of many involved in the re-organisation of the Lloyds banking business.

Dixon addressed his election committee just four days after Scholefield died. This was the first major occasion when he had had an opportunity to air his views on the issues of the day. Not surprisingly, matters connected with Parliamentary reform headed his agenda but, with regard to the recent riots, religious matters were also to the forefront of his mind. He said that he had nothing against Catholics as individuals, but 'there is not a man in this country more willing to lift up his voice against the theology and the practice of the Roman Catholic Church than I am myself'.[191]

---

187 *Birmingham Mail,* 24 Jan. 1898: obituary of George Dixon, in which the phrase was used to describe the outcome of the general election which followed the next year.
188 *BDP,* 13 July 1867.
189 Rathbone, *The Dales,* p. 27.
190 Ibid..
191 *BDP,* 13 July 1867.

Significantly, there was virtually no mention of education at all, other than an oblique reference to the welfare of the town. An explanation is not hard to find. His colleague J.S. Wright observed that on education: 'they might not all go quite so far with him in that matter, but his motive must command the respect of everybody'[192] This comment was particularly significant as it came from one of his two friends who had nominated him.[193] George Dawson and Dr. Dale were also prominent in supporting Dixon, whilst one contemporary described Chamberlain's speech in support as his 'first political performance'.[194]

Dixon's election address, published a few days later, revealed the range of issues in which he was interested, in one of the last elections where the electorate was defined by the provisions of the Reform Act 1832. He welcomed the current Reform Bill, whilst opposing its rate-paying clauses, and the inadequacy of the Redistribution Clauses; he sought a further extension of the franchise, and the secret ballot; he demanded economy of administration; he urged an alteration of the land laws which tended 'to the excessive accumulation of landed property in individual owners', whilst seeking an amendment of the Game Laws; he wanted enactment of just and equal legislation on the relations of employers and workmen; but, above all, (without shouting it from the rooftops) he wanted a national system of education.[195]

He drew support from many quarters, including Sandford,[196] with whom he was closely associated in the BES. By contrast, Bright's support for the candidate-in-waiting can scarcely be described as overwhelming. His speech in support of Dixon was lengthy, but made virtually no reference to him until its concluding moments, when he said that there were at least a dozen men in Birmingham of his ability. By contrast, Dixon was much more respectful, saying that 'of all the placards that have been put forward in Birmingham, the one that I least object to, was that which alluded to my "big brother"'.[197]

It was the first contested election in Birmingham since 1859. The contest was intense, with suggestions of intimidation and skulduggery, although Sampson Lloyd exonerated Dixon personally for any of this.[198] Katie Dixon, then aged six, later recounted that a little cart was made covered with posters, 'Vote for Dixon' and 'Sampson Lloyd is a beast', or 'something opprobrious and childish of that kind', which was then taken up the road to an aunt's house, 'keeping the rude part next the hedge'.[199] The poll on 23 July showed Dixon substantially ahead, with 5,819 votes against Lloyd's 4,214. In just a few days,

192 Ibid..
193 Anon., *Birmingham Faces and Places: An Illustrated Local Magazine* (Birmingham, 1893), Vol. 5, p. 36.
194 J. M. Davidson, *Eminent Radicals In and Out of Parliament* (1880), p. 86.
195 *BDP*, 16 July 1867.
196 John Sandford was Archdeacon of Coventry from 1851 to 1873.
197 *BDP*, 19 July 1867.
198 Ward, *City-State,* p. 64.
199 Rathbone, *The Dales,* p. 27.

however, Lloyd had managed to spend £5,009.6s.2d., whilst Dixon an almost equally staggering £3,658.11s.10d.[200]

Dixon was embarrassed by the situation, but turned it to his advantage. Speaking in the House of Commons a year later, and with more than a little irony, he said:

> Personally he should hail any increase in the election charges [consequent upon a substantial increase in the size of the electorate] with satisfaction, because it would lessen the chances of any opposition to his return on the part of gentlemen who were not able to expend as much as he could afford to; but he trusted that the House would not consent to any course which would make wealth the passport to that assembly. The squires of this country must not expect that they were to continue to be the only class who could get into the House; for he would warn them that the traders and manufacturers were rapidly passing them in wealth, and were prepared to spend more money to get into the House than the landed aristocracy ….[201]

The biggest opportunity in his life now lay before him, and he was going to make the most of it.

200 Langford, *Modern Birmingham*, Vol. 2, p. 361.
201 *Hansard*, Vol. 193, Col. 1716, 24 July 1868.

CHAPTER THREE

Getting Organised for Reform 1867-70

S O FAR AS his family was concerned, George Dixon had now 'gone
into politics'. The period of thirty months which followed his successful
by-election victory were the most hectic of his life, and were almost all
devoted to educational reform.

Within weeks of Dixon becoming an MP, Royal Assent was given to the
Second Reform Bill,[1] although its provisions were not to be 'put to the test'
until the 1868 General Election, more than a year later.

In light of what was to follow, not only in the aftermath of the Act, but for
years to follow, Dixon's personal views on the representation of the people
were highly revealing. On 6 August 1867, no more than two weeks after being
elected to Parliament, he wrote to his distant relative William Rathbone:

> What I think would be the best plan of all for Gt. Britain & Ireland would
> be equal electoral districts each returning one member. By this plan I think
> that wealth, intelligence, education, experience, & high moral character
> would rise to the highest places – & there would be sufficient diversity

---

1 The Second Reform Act of 1867 was passed by the Conservative Government led by Benjamin Disraeli,
and enfranchised a proportion of the urban working class.

of constituencies & of representatives – also the elections would be conducted with the greatest simplicity & the least trouble & cost.[2]

But the electoral system introduced by the Conservatives under Disraeli was far removed from this dream. Above all, it never embraced simplicity, amongst other things retaining two- and three- member seats plus special representation for the ancient universities; and it certainly provoked trouble.

Although John Bright led the calls in Birmingham and elsewhere for Parliamentary reform during the 1860s, Dixon himself had not played a totally insignificant part. Even before he became Mayor, it was he who moved the adoption of addresses to Scholefield and Bright at a Town Meeting after an enormous pro-reform demonstration in Birmingham's Brook Fields. He was seconded by Lampard of the Reform League, which powerful association could call upon 200,000 people at a week's notice for a meeting such as this.[3]

One of the devices which Disraeli as Prime Minister sought to introduce into the Reform Bill was specific to large towns such as Birmingham. Originally, Birmingham was to have only two members, but Dixon as Mayor, together with a local Conservative representative, led a deputation to Disraeli to seek parity with other towns, such as Manchester, Liverpool and Glasgow, and award Birmingham three MPs.[4] Ostensibly to protect the rights of minorities – which would be Conservative minorities in this instance – each elector would be restricted to two votes only.

With a substantially enlarged electorate nationwide, a feeling was abroad that this change made educational reform much more urgent. This view was voiced most eloquently by Robert Lowe: 'I believe it will be absolutely necessary to compel our future masters to learn their letters'.[5] Whilst debate has continued ever since as to the impact the new legislation had on the campaign for better education, the point was not lost on Dixon. Indeed, Kay-Shuttleworth,[6] a major figure in the national educational debate, had earlier taken the view that improving the conditions of the working-classes was a means of averting social revolution.[7]

The new electoral roll created by the 1867 Act showed 830,000 new urban voters nationwide.[8] Their children were all consumers, or potential consumers,

---

2 Liverpool University, file RPXXI.2.8(3): Rathbone Family Autograph Collection. This William Rathbone was the uncle of Margaret Dixon, Abraham Dixon's wife.
3 *BDP,* 28 Aug. 1866.
4 Ibid., 26 June 1885.
5 A.P. Martin, *Life and Letters of the Rt. Hon. Robert Lowe* (1893), Vol. 2, p. 323. For Robert Lowe (1811-92) see *ODNB-online.*
6 For Sir James Kay-Shuttleworth (1804-77), see *ODNB-online.*
7 B. Simon, *Studies in the History of Education, 1780-1870* (1960), p. 338.
8 T.J. Elkington, 'Elementary Education in the 1860s in Birmingham, Leeds, Liverpool and Manchester' (Unpublished M.Phil. thesis, University of Leeds, 1998), p. 1.

of the educational system. Whilst some members of society fretted about the dangers of educating the working classes, 1868 saw the formation of the Trades Union Congress (TUC) and many union leaders saw education and trade unionism as allied questions. Applegarth of the Associated Society of Carpenters and Joiners (ASC&J) proclaimed: 'Opposition of masters and men does not arise from a desire of either to oppress each other, but rather from ignorance. I look to education to teach all parties better'.[9] Indeed, the ASC&J went further: it initiated classes in technical instruction – the first example in the industrial history of the country of a trade union planning education for its members. Applegarth added the hope that this measure will 'do something towards securing what the working class have so long desired, namely a national, compulsory and unsectarian system of education'.[10]

The passage of the Reform Act also had other effects. In October the Congregational Union decided, using the Act as a pretext, that it was no longer in a financial position to play a part in the voluntary sector[11] (of which it formed a component), without the acceptance of Treasury Grants in future.[12] This development marked a significant change, for some other Nonconformist bodies refused to share in the Grant on the principle that no state interference of any kind could be accepted.[13] Moreover, acceptance necessarily implied inspection. Yet those very people had a fundamental problem to address, as Matthew Arnold – a Schools Inspector as well as a man of letters – pointed out:

> What is the capital difficulty in the way of getting them [the working classes] public schools? It is this: that the public school for the people must rest upon the municipal organisation of the country. In France, Germany, Italy, Switzerland, the public elementary school has, and exists by having the commune and the municipal government of the commune, as its foundations, and it could not exist without them. But we in England have our municipal organisation still to get; the country districts, with us, have at present only the feudal and ecclesiastical organisation of the Middle Ages, or of France before the Revolution. This is what the people who talk so glibly about obligatory instruction, and the Conscience Clause, and our present abundant supply of schools, never think of. The real preliminary to an effective system of popular education is, in fact, to provide the country with an effective municipal organisation: and here, then, is at the outset

---

9 B. Simon, *The Two Nations and the Educational Structure, 1780-1870* (1974), p. 360.

10 Ibid., p. 361.

11 The 'voluntary sector' was the phrase used, more especially after the passage of the Elementary Education Act 1870, to describe schools not financed in part by local rates. The largest organisations in the sector were the National Society for Promoting Religious Education and the British and Foreign School Society.

12 Hennock, *Fit and Proper Persons*, p. 84.

13 Simon, *Studies,* p. 338.

an illustration of what I have said, that modern societies need a civic organisation which is modern.[14]

The issue was eventually to be resolved through the creation of School Boards, but much had to be done before this proposal came before Parliament.

Other debates in Parliament in 1867 also served to arouse public discussion of education generally: an Agricultural Children's Bill was introduced, as was Bruce's[15] Education Bill,[16] but neither reached the Statute Book, whilst in the House of Lords, Earl Russell[17] intervened, advocating the right of education for every child.[18]

The pressure for educational reform was also building up in the commercial world. After just four months as MP, Dixon was chosen as one of eight delegates from the Birmingham Chamber to attend a Special General Meeting of the Association of Chambers of Commerce. At this gathering Mundella (with Forster in attendance) proposed a resolution, which was carried unanimously. It stated that:

> the rapid progress and high excellence of Continental Manufactures are, in the opinion of this Association, mainly attributable to the Schools for Technical Education which have for many years been established in Germany and other parts of the Continent, and by means of which the art of design and other valuable scientific knowledge have been very generally acquired, to the great advantage of industrial pursuits; and that, in order to enable our manufacturers to maintain the position they have so long enjoyed, the necessity of establishing in this country Institutions of a similar character be urged upon the Government and that for this purpose a Committee be appointed by the Associated Chambers to assist in the promotion of Art and Industrial Education.[19]

When this resolution was reported back to the Birmingham Chamber, it was supplemented by the observation that

> a system of primary instruction was first essential as a basis for any efficient carrying out of the Technical Education sought and that this

---

14 Hennock, *Fit and Proper Persons,* p. 91.
15 For H.A. Bruce (1815-95), see *ODNB-online.*
16 R.C. Raffell, 'The Radical and Nonconformist Influences on the Creation of the Dual System of Universal Elementary Education in England and Wales, 1866-70' (Unpublished Ph.D. thesis, University of Hull, 1993), p. 168.
17 For John Russell, 1ˢᵗ Earl Russell (1792-1878), see *ODNB-online.*
18 Raffell, 'Radical and Nonconformist Influences', p. 471.
19 Guildhall Library, Minutes of the Association of Chambers of Commerce of the United Kingdom, MS 14476-1, 26/27 Nov. 1867.

primary education should be compulsory was largely advocated and your delegates believe nowhere opposed.[20]

On Boxing Day, a further meeting of the Birmingham Chamber asked Dixon, by then President, to invite Mundella to meet the members of the Chamber and to address them on the question of Technical Education. They collectively sought to answer four key questions which Lord Robert Montagu, on behalf of the Government had posed, via the Association:

1. What trades are now being injured by the want of a technical education?
2. How and in what particulars are they being injured?
3. How do other countries from their greater attention to technical instruction abort our trade? (Give instances and if possible statistics)
4. What plan of technical education would remedy the evil?

Measures were taken to ensure that as many businesses within Birmingham as possible were consulted on these matters, and Mundella attended a special meeting of the Chamber on 6 January, 1868. Things were moving fast. Dixon was in the Chair:

> The great importance of the subject was beyond a doubt in Birmingham; ... They had Art Schools. The question now was about having Science Schools; and they must show to the Government that they could no longer afford to wait; the time had come when the Government must take the matter in hand completely.[21]

Mundella spoke at length, comparing the English position with that prevailing in France, and more especially in Germany. He suggested that Saxony had the best educational system in Europe. With regard to manufacturing industry, he noted that:

> unfortunately other countries were progressing much faster than we are; they are applying art and science in a way which we do not at present understand .... The defective education among our people was truly lamentable; .... many years must elapse before much could be done, but we must set about it at once.

He concluded with an open statement:

---

20 Birmingham Archives and Heritage, Birmingham Chamber of Commerce Minute Book, 1865-8: 5 Dec. 1867.
21 *The Times*, 7 Jan. 1868.

> What the country wanted was as thorough a man in the education movement as Mr. Cobden was in free trade.

He did not mention George Dixon by name but, in the circumstances, he was the obvious candidate. Certainly, through his career as a very successful merchant, and through his extensive commitment to the Chamber of Commerce movement, Dixon had developed many skills and contacts. There was a growing awareness in the heart of England's industrial landscape that its competitive position was in jeopardy and, whilst this situation was not capable of immediate resolution, other factors nationwide were combining to make the case for change – radical change – in the provision of education, overwhelming.

One such factor was the cost of crime. This issue Dixon broached whilst laying the foundation stone of a new church school at St Mary's, in Aston. He made the point robustly: 'unless they could provide schools of that kind it was ridiculous to talk about technical education, for technical education must have a foundation of elementary education on which to rest'. He took the opportunity to praise the Church of England in the educational sphere, and called for local taxation to support local education, whilst making comparisons with Boston in America. 'In spending money in that way they would only be laying out what would amply be returned to them in the saving in poor rates and in the cost of criminals, gaols and asylums'.[22]

Much interest was being expressed in educational provision abroad at this time. Not only was Mundella explaining in depth his own first-hand experience of Saxony (through owning a factory there), but Collings was writing a pamphlet on the schools system in the USA. Using the Anti-Corn Law League as a model, he called for the creation of a society that would publish propaganda, send out lecturers, encourage the formation of local branches, and thus mount a national campaign.[23] In October 1868, Collings was to read a paper at the Social Science Meeting in Birmingham, entitled *On the State of Education in Birmingham.*[24]

So were being sown the seeds of what was to become, in the following year, the NEL.

The early months of the Birmingham Education Society witnessed more co-operation on the educational issue than at any time either before or after, for it temporarily drew together individuals who had been on both sides of the recent dispute on the grammar school issue,[25] whilst subsequently, from 1869 especially, there was some divergence with the formation of the NEL.

---

22 *BDP*, 17 Dec. 1867.
23 Marsh, *Chamberlain*, p. 36.
24 See above, Chapter 2, p. 51.
25 Smith, *Conflict and Compromise*, p. 183.

Dr. Dale later reflected that 1868 was the first year in which 'there was a sweeping movement of spring in the air' and 'the city struggled, revelled more truly, in a maelstrom of controversy in which national and local issues in religion, politics, education, public health and the whole range of social life were fiercely and bitterly debated'.[26] Whilst Asa Briggs may have dated this epoch as beginning in 1866,[27] the year Dixon became Mayor, Dr. Dale preferred the year when the Liberals swept back into power, under Gladstone. At the heart of this civic renaissance were the three Nonconformist Ministers, Dr. Dale, Dawson and Crosskey, and it was Dr. Dale's son who traced its progress:

> It began, as all such movements do, in the dream of solitary and silent hours. Then it made its way into the minds of a few men of kindred spirit. And the dream became an ideal; and the ideal grew into a conviction; and conviction flamed into enthusiasm; and enthusiasm took shape in policy, and passed from the study and the club to the platform and the pulpit, and swept through the wards of the city, and fired men's minds and kindled their hearts, until the ideal that had once been a dream had become a reality. Those years in which the new gospel began to spread and to prevail – those glorious hours of crowded strife – can we ever forget them?
>
> 'Bliss was it in that dawn to be alive;
> But to be young was very heaven'.[28]

And all around them were new buildings. In the final years of the century, Birmingham was to see itself as latter-day Renaissance Venice, and some of them, as latter-day oligarchs. J.T. Bunce, editor of the *Birmingham Daily Post*, wrote that 'Art must … permeate and suffuse the daily life, if it is to become a real and enduring influence'. There must be 'public buildings, ample and stately and rich enough in their ornament to dignify the corporate life', which would promote 'a municipal life nobler, fuller, richer than any the world has ever seen'.[29]

Dixon himself was never at the heart of what came to be called the 'Civic Gospel'. Its main exponents were all Nonconformists. Chamberlain's son Austen many years later summarised Dixon's role: he was 'one of that band of

---

26 C. Gill and C.G. Robertson, *A Short History of Birmingham* (Birmingham, 1938), p. 57.

27 See above, Chapter 2, p. 59.

28 A.W.W. Dale, 'George Dawson', in Muirhead (ed.), *Nine Famous Birmingham Men*, p. 105.

29 D. Cannadine, 'The Bourgeois Experience as Political Culture: The Chamberlains of Birmingham', in M.S. Micale and R.L. Dietle (eds), *Enlightenment, Passion, Modernity: Historical Essays in European Thought and Culture* (Stanford, 2000), p. 151.

workers who presented here to the city, and in Parliament to the country, the new ideas of government, … , which were started in this active hive of industry, and no less active hive of thought'.[30]

Disseminating these ideas around the country of necessity involved much travel, and it was a feature of these years that much use was made of the national railway network, still expanding rapidly in the middle of the century.

In January 1868 Dixon attended a conference in Manchester (with his brother-in-law, James Stansfeld, amongst others), whose agenda included the provision of education in rural areas.[31]

The full significance of Dixon's interest in the countryside would only emerge after 1870,[32] but amongst those who were for a while involved in the affairs of the National Education League was the Radical, Henry Fawcett,[33] who believed that the provision of education was even more urgent in the countryside than in the towns. Besides later becoming Postmaster-General, he was also a friend of the family, joining them when they took a holiday in the Lake District in 1873. Although blind, Fawcett went out in a boat with Arthur, Dixon's eldest son, for a bathe. Standing up, he would ask 'Am I facing right?', and then dive in.[34]

Dixon was beginning to get restive for, whilst the Conference generally wanted merely to re-introduce Bruce's Bill of the previous year: '… the great mass might, and he hoped would, rise up and say "We won't wait" '.[35]

The interesting point to note about public opinion generally on education was that there was no dispute as to the need for reform. There was however widespread disagreement as to its speed. The slowest merely wanted increased state aid given to the denominational system; in the middle lay the moderates, such as Bruce, Forster and the Manchester Education Aid Society; then in the vanguard lay the advanced Radicals, who wanted to inject a greater degree of urgency into the situation.[36] Dixon would shortly emerge as being a leader of the advanced Radicals.

That Conference was followed shortly after by another, this time on technical education. Despite this topic being the main thrust, the first subject for discussion was 'the necessity for improving national education for the working classes', with subheadings of '[a] improved primary education and measures for securing it; [b] additional facilities in the primary schools for

---

30 *Birmingham Post,* 5 March, 1934. Of the other Birmingham MPs during Dixon's first term in office, Bright remained Rochdale-resident, and engaged himself on a much wider range of national and international issues; and Muntz made much less impact.

31 Roper, 'Towards an Elementary Education Act', p. 199.

32 See below, Chapter 5, p. 153 et seq.

33 Briggs, 'Introduction', p. xv.

34 Rathbone, *The Dales,* p. 64.

35 Raffell, 'Radical and Nonconformist Influences', p. 235.

36 Ibid., p. 474.

affording the elder children the means of learning the elements of scientific knowledge'.[37]

Securing a seat in Parliament meant for Dixon personally much more travel to and from London, to the point where he took a furnished house in Cromwell Place, Kensington, for the Session of 1869.[38]

Whilst he remained at the head of the Birmingham movement which he had launched, in the wider context Jesse Collings now set the tone, beginning to abandon the effort to secure a broad consensus within the BES, and instead pressing for uncompromising action.[39] Meantime Dixon had been introduced to the House of Commons by Bright as his fellow Birmingham representative, and by his brother-in-law, James Stansfeld. In his former position as Mayor of Birmingham, Dixon's name was certainly not unknown to his new Parliamentary colleagues, for there had been no less than five questions asked about the Murphy Riots in the weeks immediately preceding his by-election.[40] At this point, Dixon moved more into Bright's orbit than he had done hitherto. In educational matters, this change was not to Dixon's advantage, as he and Bright did not exactly see eye-to-eye.

Typically Bright was reported as saying, on 5 February 1868 that 'he knew nothing about it except that it [education] was in a deplorable condition, but that he could see no reason for the Government to intervene either by grants or by giving rating powers: existing endowments would be sufficient if properly utilised; he was opposed also to State establishment of Technical Colleges: technical education was not necessary – boys should use their own initiative; furthermore, he deprecated the feverish activity about the education question which he saw around him'.[41]

This declaration did not go down at all well. George Dawson commented in characteristic style: 'John Bright came here recently in the character of a fire engine … it was a novelty to see him come with his pitiful wet blanket and endeavour to chill the holy zeal of the people for the education of the nation'.[42]

Amidst all this growing clamour, Dixon was continuing to press for educational changes far wider than mere elementary education. In his second speech in Parliament,[43] he pressed for a Select Committee on the subject of Scientific Education. He specifically alluded to the recent Paris Exhibition in 1867, and 'letters written by jurors … [which] showed that we had not kept

---

37 Roper, 'Towards an Elementary Education Act', p. 201.

38 Rathbone, *The Dales*, p. 52: the parliamentary session at that time typically lasted for six months each year, from February through to August.

39 Marsh, *Chamberlain*, p. 36.

40 *Hansard,* Vol. 188, Col. 17, 18 June 1867; Col. 88, 19 June 1867; Col. 925, 3 July 1867; Col. 1262, 9 July 1867; and Col. 1764, 19 July 1867.

41 Taylor, 'Birmingham Movement', p. 39.

42 Ibid..

43 His first speech had been on the subject of Compounding for Rates.

pace with Continental nations'.[44] A subsequent speaker was dismissive about the call for Government support in this field, when exports had doubled in the previous twelve years, despite heavy duties at very nearly every Continental seaport. But the next sentence must have been music to the ears of the BES and Dixon: 'All that we required and all that our manufacturers had a right to ask for was that our working classes should receive a sound and solid primary education'.[45]

For his pains, Dixon was one of eighteen Members appointed to the 1868 Select Committee appointed to inquire into the provisions for giving instruction in theoretical and applied Science to the Industrial Classes.

As one of Birmingham's two representatives in Parliament, he did not neglect other issues, including most especially the thorny issue of drink. On this point, Dixon's views were equivocal. Shortly after being elected to Parliament, he wrote a letter to the UK Alliance, the temperance pressure group, excusing himself for being unable to attend a meeting: 'I have not yet arrived at conclusions which will admit of my appearing on your platform. Yet my desire to diminish drunkenness is scarcely less than that of the advocates of the Permissive Bill'.[46] He significantly failed to attach his colours to any mast, a pattern of behaviour which was to be repeated several times over in his political career. But it was a strategy which helped him survive in the turbulent waters around him.

A few months on, Dixon took an ecumenical approach. This time, presiding at the annual dinner of the Birmingham Retail Brewers Association, he acknowledged that some people had apparently expressed surprise that he should associate with such a body, but he had made it plain at the time of his election that he represented all the town, not just part of it.[47]

What he did not express so brazenly was the fact that his own brother-in-law, James Stansfeld, owned a brewery in Fulham;[48] and he did not have too many other close friends and colleagues in London.

Dixon was certainly not teetotal himself, although one particular 'misadventure' might have led to incorrect assumptions being made about his liking for sherry. As his daughter Dora recorded, 'in a blithe spirit he ordered a dozen small casks of sherry to be sent to The Dales, for he was by then married. Weeks after, looking out of his study window he saw the sherry arrive, not twelve small casks but twelve enormous barrels and £400 to pay. A man was in the cellar for days bottling the sherry'.[49]

---

44 *Hansard*, Vol. 191, Col. 165, 24 March 1868.
45 Ibid., Col. 169.
46 *BDP*, 11 March 1868.
47 Ibid., 23 July 1868.
48 Stansfeld owned the Swan Brewery in Fulham.
49 Rathbone, *The Dales*, p. 121.

By this date, nearing the age of 50, Dixon was taking on more and more commitments. Whilst he had the good sense to stand down from the Town Council on 14 February 1868,[50] (to be replaced by Jesse Collings, a couple of months later), on 25 April Dixon found himself elected the President of the first annual meeting of the Birmingham Society of Artizans. This body's main aims comprised the delivery of papers on trade subjects, by the members themselves; the presentation of lectures by qualified persons upon subjects connected with the application of science and art to trade; and the formation of science classes for adults.[51] Nobody could argue that Dixon was failing to keep closely in touch with the educational world at grass-roots level.

Once more he engaged in the problems of the Free Grammar School Association. In the same month he chaired a meeting at which a resolution was passed: *'That this meeting is of opinion that it is not necessary to extend the advantages of the endowment to those who are not inhabitants of Birmingham or the adjoining parishes; and that some considerable portion of the funds should be used to promote the elementary education of the poorest classes'.*[52]

He was very irritated by certain fellow citizens, and appealed to them for assistance. Looking in the first instance to those who sent their sons to the nearby public school of Rugby, he urged them to make donations to the BES, which by this time had been in existence for a year. 'Had these men nothing to spare for these destitute children who were perhaps destined to live alongside these Rugby boys, and perhaps to work for them?' He appealed to the middle classes who used the Grammar School: 'surely no one who got free Grammar School education for his own son could refuse to help?'[53]

Some time later, irritation turned to disgust. The Annual Report of the BES for the year ended 31 March 1870 reported tartly that: 'The Committee announce with much disappointment that they have not obtained any assistance, beyond the trifling amount stated in last year's Report, from the parents of children who are receiving free education at the cost of public funds in King Edward's Grammar School'.[54]

Behind this irritation lay grim statistics, which the BES was beginning to amass. Of the 45,051 children between the ages of 3 and 15 in the town, 17,018 were at school, 6,337 were at work, and 21,696 were neither. This latter category, the 'street arabs', represented 48.2% of their age group.[55] Philanthropy was not working as intended. At the end of January 1868, 4,729 free places had

---

50 C.A. Vince, *History of the Corporation of Birmingham,* (Birmingham, 1902), Vol. 3, p. 377. Dixon never became an Alderman.
51 Langford, *Modern Birmingham,* Vol. 2, p. 406.
52 Ibid., p. 306.
53 *BDP,* 18 April 1868, as quoted in Taylor, 'Birmingham Movement', p. 61.
54 *Third Annual Report of the Birmingham Education Society,* p. 10.
55 Elkington, 'Elementary Education', p. 141.

been granted, yet a quarter of them were not being used.[56] At the end of the first year of its existence, the Committee concluded that no voluntary agency could overcome 'the apathy of parents and the wilful disregard of offers of education'. This fact led many, including Dixon, to the conclusion that compulsion must be part of their agenda. But this logic presented a huge quandary. Even though there were unfilled vacancies in the existing schools, in no way were there enough spare places for all those who would start to attend, should compulsion be introduced.

Interestingly, the objectives of the BES extended far beyond the provision of mere elementary education. The First Annual Report of 1868 had commented that: 'when children left the primary school, there would be some chance of success in imparting to them technical instruction. The night school would become a "*Fortbildung*" – continuating school – affording to them what would then be a relaxation after physical labour, and a mental relaxation, in the place of what is now a toilsome struggle to overtake the days gone by'.[57]

From this analysis, it was very clear that Dixon foresaw the need for educational reforms across the board, and that elementary education was but one facet. Indeed, part of the BES's exercise in gathering information included research into the attainments of those in the age group 13 to 21.[58]

Throughout this period, Dixon had as his business tenants the chocolate firm headed by George Cadbury and his brother, and it is a great shame that no records survive – they may never have existed, given the fact that the two businesses were neighbours, and most communications may have been by word of mouth – as to what input George Cadbury may have had on the issue of education, given that Cadbury also devoted much of his life to the Adult School movement, and especially to the Severn Street school where Cadbury taught which was entirely non-sectarian in its organisation.[59]

Dixon had been supportive of Manchester as it twice presented Bills to Parliament, in 1867 and 1868, in the name of Bruce and with the support of Forster. But to no avail, in the dying days of the Conservative government.[60] Dixon thus expected much to be heard in the coming election, 'and he trusted that Parliament would not be satisfied to allow sectarian jealousies and religious bigotries to stand, as they had stood too long, in the way of the education of this country'.[61] Nor was he in much doubt whence much of the pressure for change was coming: 'The great importance of the subject was being more and more

---

56 Marcham, 'Birmingham Education Society', p. 13.

57 *First Annual Report of the Birmingham Education Society* (1868), p. 15.

58 Marcham, 'Birmingham Education Society', p. 13: the figures made depressing reading: over two-fifths failed in reading, over half in writing, over three-quarters in spelling, four-fifths in general knowledge, and nine-tenths in arithmetic.

59 W. Stranz, *George Cadbury: An Illustrated Life of George Cadbury, 1839-1922* (Aylesbury, 1973), p. 6.

60 Hennock, *Fit and Proper Persons*, p. 85.

61 *Hansard*, Vol. 192, Col. 1991, 24 June 1868.

recognized by those in whom the wisdom of Parliament had decided that the greatest portion of political power should be vested. The working classes were beginning to consider in what manner they should use that power in regard to education as the very first question'.[62]

Dixon was thus clear that the state had to take the lead in educational reform. He argued that on the grounds that some people were unable, or unwilling, for whatever reasons, to provide or purchase such facilities for themselves. Yet the opposition to a greater state came from all quarters. Herbert Spencer[63] was one outspoken opponent of state interference, having published *State Education Self Defeating* as long ago as 1851. Robert Lowe was also to be found saying that 'I hold it as our duty not to spend public money to do that which people can do for themselves'.[64] Many were devotees of Samuel Smiles's doctrine of <u>Self Help</u>, which he published at his own expense in 1859. But it was left to Matthew Arnold to write in 1868 that 'Our dislike of authority and our disbelief in science have combined to make us leave our school system … to take care of itself as best it could. Under such auspices, our school system has very naturally fallen all into confusion; …'[65] The intellectual battle continued, but with the evidence all around getting stronger by the day that something was seriously amiss, the individualists were very much on the back foot.

But did Dixon have a sufficiently strong constituency to support him in his campaign?

One of the issues that began to emerge in the run-up to the 1868 General Election, was whether there should be a working man to represent the newly enfranchised working classes, given that the number of seats in Birmingham had risen from two to three. This issue had increased potency as time progressed, but for Dixon personally this was not perceived to be a problem. One letter to the press stated explicitly 'In Mr Dixon, the working men have found a true advocate, who has ever shown a willingness to serve them on every occasion'.[66] In an electioneering speech, Dixon declared that 'He had not been able to retire wholly from business'.[67] Evidently his conduct in business matters was as upright as it was in public affairs, and he was not seen as an oppressive employer.

---

62 Ibid., Col. 1989.
63 For Herbert Spencer (1820-1903), see *ODNB-online.*
64 G.W. Roderick and M.D. Stephens, *Education and Industry in the Nineteenth Century: The English Disease?* (1978), p. 6.
65 Ibid..
66 *BDP,* 13 July 1868.
67 Ibid., 31 July 1868.

Almost two years later, immediately after Forster had presented his Bill to Parliament, the Chairman of the local Labour Representation League[68] was able to say of Dixon: 'he had become a power in the House, and he had attained his position by unflagging industry, inexhaustible energy, backed by the noblest constituency in England'.[69] The tribute, it may be noted, was not only to George Dixon but also to his constituents.

The 1868 General Election was not only the last parliamentary election before the introduction of the secret ballot, but it was also highly controversial in Birmingham.

John Bright had dubbed the minority clause, by which each elector in the three-member constituency got just two votes, as 'the offspring and the spawn of feeble minds'.[70] Nonetheless, with the structure in place, the Liberals could scarcely avoid taking the opportunity to capitalise on the situation. Strict Liberal party discipline was needed to implement the plan drawn up by William Harris,[71] whereby precisely one-third of members would cast their votes for the first and second candidates; one-third for the first and third candidates; and one-third for the second and third candidates. Dixon's electoral address spoke of it in the following terms:

> I accept, without hesitation or reserve, the plan laid down by the Liberal Committee for the conduct of the election; believing that by these means, notwithstanding the insidious and mischievous device of the restricted vote, a great victory may be achieved by the return of three Liberal Members for Birmingham.[72]

Chamberlain joined in the general clamour: 'the operation of the minority clause in elections was inconvenient, expensive, uncertain, unneeded'.[73]

The inconsistency was stark: writing about the life of his late father, A.W.W. Dale, observed that 'Mr Bright in the House of Commons had lavished his scorn upon the scheme, and the Liberal party in the borough, no less indignant, were bent on retaining the representation unbroken'.[74]

It was a reflection of the state of public opinion generally that Dixon could stand accused of making the education issue a 'hobby'. His supporters rallied to his side. 'We don't mind taking it that way. I can recollect that Henry Grattan [eighteenth century campaigner for legislative freedom for the Irish

---

68 The Labour Representation League was founded in 1869, its mission being to register the working class to vote, and to return workers to parliament.
69 *BDP*, 29 March 1870.
70 Ward, *City-State,* p. 62.
71 See above, Chapter 2, p. 55.
72 Langford, *Modern Birmingham,* Vol. 2, p. 370.
73 *BDP,* 21 Sept. 1868.
74 A.W.W. Dale, *Life of R.W. Dale* (1898), p. 264.

Parliament] had a hobby. I know that Mr Wilberforce had a hobby; Richard Cobden was a hobby-rider; Milner Gibson is a free-trader',[75] said one.

Katie Rathbone recollected one Tory poster of Sampson Lloyd putting an extinguisher on little George Dixon in petticoats.[76] In response, one Liberal made the quip that Birmingham 'has its George, whose lance has made more than one gallant thrust at the hydra-headed dragon of ignorance'.[77]

Dixon's electoral address was an interesting document. Educational reform was not high on his agenda. This is surprising, given that he might have been expected to set out his priorities in order of importance. Other than a couple of introductory paragraphs which would normally be expected by way of formality, Dixon made mention of the Irish question, which of course was to dominate Gladstone's early days in power; further electoral reform, spoken of as 'Completion of Reform Act'[78]; and equalisation of rates, including restoration of compounding; before touching on the educational issue, in the following terms:

> The establishment of a national and compulsory system of education, based upon local rating and local management, supplemented by State aid and Government inspection, must also engage the support of earnest Liberals in the next Parliament.

The paragraph that followed also intrigued, in the light of the controversy over the size of the Civil List in the later years of this Parliament:[79]

> Immediate attention must also be directed to the state of the national expenditure, which has largely increased under a Conservative Government, and is likely still further to increase, unless determined means are adopted to enforce rigid economy.

It was paradoxical that Dixon was calling for economy on the one hand, while in the preceding paragraph he had been calling for increased expenditure on education – and compulsory education at that. Had he done his sums? Moreover, it was not inferior education that Dixon had in mind either: whilst he accepted the existence of the Anglican Church schools – he had little choice in this matter, given their considerable number – he argued that in time they

---

75 *BDP,* 17 Nov. 1868.
76 Birmingham Archives and Heritage, File MS 2239, Bundle 2, p. 20.
77 *BDP,* 3 Nov. 1868.
78 Specifically he wanted [a] further reduction of the qualification for the county franchise; [b] repeal of the so-called minority clause; [c] the adoption of the ballot; and [d] a re-distribution of seats, advancing as far as possible in the direction of the only permanent settlement – equalised constituencies, with one representative to each.
79 See below, Chapter 5, p. 148.

would be superseded, not supplemented, by rate-aided schools, simply because the latter would offer better teaching.[80] Indeed, some twenty years later, in his capacity of Chairman of the Birmingham School Board, he was to point with some satisfaction to that trend in the town, although to what extent that was achieved by dipping into his own capacious pocket, will always remain unknown.[81]

A final substantive paragraph embraced a raft of issues, all of which Dixon supported at various stages in his career: *reforms in the administration of the army and navy* – he had been concerned with problems in this arena as long ago as 1855;[82] *the discontinuance of wasteful Government manufacturing establishments, to the increase of expense and the detriment of private trade* – no doubt the question of government manufacture of arms would have been foremost in his mind here; *the amendment of the laws of entail and the game laws* – his concern for the state of affairs in the countryside was to manifest itself in his later links with Joseph Arch;[83] *the opening of the Universities fully and freely to Nonconformists* – he had already been concerned with the Midland Institute,[84] which some saw as 'Birmingham's earliest University for the working classes',[85] and his interest in the tertiary sector of education was to become further manifest much later in his career.[86]

Dixon also had a long-term agenda. It was one 'possibly not [capable of being] realised in his lifetime, but he would be content to spend his life labouring towards it: universal suffrage; equality of suffrage; primary and secondary education for all – free, unsectarian and compulsory; open diplomacy; return of all overseas Conquests; the break-up of large estates; re-distribution of wealth by legislation; nationalisation of communications, railways, gas and water; and all class distinctions swept away'.[87] These long-term aims meant that he could quite rightly call himself an advanced Radical.

It was against this background that Gladstone won his convincing election victory of late 1868. All three Liberal candidates for the multi-member Birmingham constituency were elected. Dixon headed the poll with 15,098 votes, ahead of Muntz (the newcomer) with 14,614 and Bright with 14,601.[88] But no personal significance whatsoever can be attached to these figures, given that Liberal supporters had all been told how to vote, to counter the mischief of the new system, as already explained. One contemporary was torn in differing

---

80 Briggs, 'Introduction', p. xxi.
81 See below, Chapter 6, p. 196.
82 See above, Chapter 1, p. 33.
83 See below, Chapter 5, p. 153.
84 See above, Chapter 1, p. 30.
85 J.E. Jones, *A Short History of Birmingham* (Birmingham, 1911), p. 152.
86 See below, Chapter 6, p. 193.
87 Taylor, 'Birmingham Movement', p. 66.
88 Langford, *Modern Birmingham,* Vol. 2, p. 378.

directions: 'the temptation to disobey orders in wards instructed not to vote for Mr. Bright was very strong'.[89] As Dixon himself put it, 'it is a mere chance which of the Liberal candidates was first', although he kindly regretted that Bright had not headed the poll.[90] Sampson Lloyd once again stood, under the banner of the Liberal-Conservatives, and once again lost.

The first full year of the new Liberal administration dawned in a spirit of commercial optimism in Birmingham, for 1869 witnessed two notable events: the opening of the Suez Canal and the passage of the Telegraph Act. The former promised better trading prospects through much improved communications,[91] and an increasing taxation yield to the government. The latter demonstrated the ability of the state, through the Post Office, to better manage an otherwise inefficient, if not chaotic, sector of the economy.

On 7 January 1869, Dixon convened another meeting – at The Dales, again.[92] William Adams, who was to become the paid secretary of the NEL, recorded that 'The League had its origin in a conversation between Mr. Dixon and Mr. Collings, when it was resolved to call a private meeting to consider the advisability of organising a National Association for the purpose of agitation'.[93] This genesis was very similar to that of the BES some two years earlier.

Those attending were the stalwarts of the BES but, insofar as it is possible to make any generalisations about the pattern of attendance, those staying away were largely those who believed in the extension of the existing voluntaryist structure. They also tended to be based further away from Birmingham. For the essence of the NEL, which emerged from this meeting, was that its core was essentially Birmingham-based; and almost without exception, they were Liberals. However, such loyalty often conflicted with loyalty to the NEL itself, for the two were often to be at odds, especially from 17 February 1870, when Forster was to present his Education Bill on behalf of Gladstone's government. All shades of religious opinion, except Roman Catholicism, were represented.[94] Whilst rank-and-file membership was largely Nonconformist, mainly driven by antagonism to the Established Church, four out of the eight executive officers were Anglican.[95]

Shortly after this inaugural meeting a circular was distributed, which 'invited adhesions to the League on the following basis':

---

89 Dent, *Old and New,* Vol. 3, p. 546.

90 *BDP,* 19 Nov. 1868.

91 Birmingham Archives and Heritage, Birmingham Chamber of Commerce Minute Book, 1868-72: 3 Feb. 1870.

92 Adams, *History of Elementary School Contest,* p. 197; Briggs, 'Introduction', p. xvi; Marsh, *Chamberlain,* p. 37.

93 Adams, *History of Elementary School Contest,* p. 197.

94 Ibid., p. 206.

95 Marsh, *Chamberlain,* p. 39.

OBJECT

The establishment of a system which shall secure the education of every child in the country.

MEANS

[1] Local authorities shall be compelled by law to see that sufficient school accommodation is provided for every child in their district.

[2] The cost of founding and maintaining such schools as may be required, shall be provided out of local rates, supplemented by Government grants.

[3] All schools aided by local rates shall be under the management of local authorities and subject to Government inspection.

[4] All schools aided by local rates shall be unsectarian.

[5] To all schools aided by local rates admission shall be free.

[6] School accommodation being provided, the State or the local authorities shall have power to compel the attendance of children of suitable age not otherwise receiving education.[96]

It is interesting that there are six issues identified here, just as there were six points to the People's Charter a generation previously.

This agenda bore much in common with what Collings had recently proposed, based on his review of the American common school system.[97] What was not addressed, however, was the inter-action between the proposed local authority schools, on the one hand, and the existing, very substantial voluntary school system. In particular, there was the thorny question which was to be at the heart of the turmoil in the coming months and years: what would happen if voluntary schools were to be funded out of local rates, as the third point implied being subject to Government inspection?[98]

2,500 people responded to this circular, and Dixon found himself chairman of a provisional committee, appointed to organise a general conference of members. Chamberlain was Vice-chairman; Collings the honorary secretary; and John Jaffray the treasurer.[99] Dixon was thus notionally in charge at this juncture, but as time progressed, the perception was to grow that Chamberlain ran the organisation.

That general meeting established a structure which has sometimes been mis-described. The historian Tristram Hunt, for example, wrote that

---

96 Adams, *History of Elementary School Contest,* p. 197.
97 Ibid., p. 198. See also above, Chapter 3, p. 78.
98 Marsh, *Chamberlain,* p. 37.
99 Adams, *History of Elementary School Contest,* p. 198. John Jaffray, an Anglican, was co-founder of the *BDP* in 1857.

'Chamberlain manoeuvred himself into the post of Chairman'.[100] But Dixon was chosen chairman of the Council, a consultative body, 'consisting of all members of Parliament who joined the League, donors of £500 and upwards, representatives appointed by the branches, together with nearly 300 ladies and gentlemen chosen from the general body of members'.[101] Dixon was thus the Parliamentary leader and adviser of the League until he applied for the Chiltern Hundreds in 1876.[102]

Local reaction to the formation of the NEL was not entirely sympathetic. One response was that it was the parents' job to pay for education. If the state took on this obligation, then the provision of food and clothing would become a public charge, which in its turn would lead to communism, and 'to the position when private property will not be worth six months' purchase'.[103] An angry letter to the *BDP* added that the NEL apparently offered 'a premium to improvidence and intemperance'.[104]

As the campaigns developed momentum, Dixon changed too – into an agitator. One of his obituaries pointed to the importance of this at this particular juncture: 'he [Dixon] was not, of course, a "great educator" in the same sense as Thomas and Matthew Arnold …; but in his capacity of a "fighting man" he probably did quite as much for education as any of them'.[105]

In its first year, the League 'served as the pace-setter in what was unquestionably one of the nineteenth century's most crucial social reform movements'.[106] Dixon had a difficult job as leader. Not only had he to contend personally with the challenging character of Joseph Chamberlain, but he also faced some fundamental dividing issues: whether the NEL sought unsectarian or secular education; whether free schooling should be confined to the poorest pupils alone; what share of the costs should be borne out of the rates; and just how compulsion should be enforced.[107]

As if that were not enough, Dixon was fully alert to the grounds of opposition that lay ahead of the NEL nationally. Its proposals would be held to be unjust to existing schools; the costs would be too high; the new schools would be seen as irreligious; and direct compulsion was not only objectionable, but impossible to achieve.[108]

There was no doubt whatsoever that Adams, the paid secretary of the NEL, was utterly loyal to Dixon. Writing in 1882, by which time Dixon

---

100 T. Hunt, *Building Jerusalem: The Rise and Fall of the Victorian City* (2004), p. 246.
101 Adams, *History of Elementary School Contest*, p. 200.
102 Ibid., p. 204.
103 Taylor, 'Birmingham Movement', p. 74.
104 *BDP*, 8 Feb. 1869.
105 *Graphic*, cutting late Jan. 1898: precise date not shown.
106 V. Skipp, *The Making of Victorian Birmingham* (Birmingham, 1983), p. 159.
107 Smith, *Conflict and Compromise*, p. 184.
108 *BDP*, 12 Jan. 1870.

had become well established as chairman of the School Board, he recorded that:

> After the Parliamentary struggle began, his [Dixon's] attention was necessarily confined to the proceedings of the House of Commons, but at all times, and wherever and whenever they could be best employed, his services were at the disposal of the Executive. The pains which he has since bestowed upon the local administration of the Education Act, and the development of the resources and powers of School Boards, are well known throughout England. It is perhaps the best refutation of the calumnies which were heaped upon the League, that the leader of those who were branded as sectarians, revolutionists, irreconcilables, sciolists,[109] infidels and communists, has devoted himself unremittingly for fifteen years with many of his colleagues, in the first place to secure an efficient education law, and afterwards to derive the largest possible product which able administration is capable of leading.[110]

There were many changes in the Executive of the NEL during its eight-year existence.[111] As Dixon was physically absent in Westminster for much of the time, local leadership fell effectively to Chamberlain, who was throughout chairman of the Executive Committee.[112] Sixteen years separated the two men in age. Not only was the elder an Anglican and the younger Unitarian, but in addition their temperaments were utterly different. Just how different was shortly going to be made manifest.

For the time being, the fortunes of the NEL were looking bright. At the outset, it was thought that it would take ten years of agitation before its objectives were attained. This appraisal was realistic. The financial arrangements were unusual, with a guarantee fund established, one-tenth of which was due each year – eight instalments were eventually called up. The total amount of the guarantee fund was £60,000 (towards which Dixon and many others subscribed £1,000 each), yielding £6,000 each year. On top of this, special funds were raised for electoral purposes, to which guarantee subscribers also contributed. Special donations also came in, together with subscriptions for purely local purposes, 'which were also large'.[113]

The availability of these resources meant that it was not difficult to set up a country-wide organisational structure, with local committees in a variety

---

109 Those with only superficial knowledge.
110 Adams, *History of Elementary School Contest*, p. 204.
111 Ibid., p. 200.
112 Hennock, *Fit and Proper Persons*, p. 87.
113 Adams, *History of Elementary School Contest*, p. 203.

of towns and cities,[114] with Birmingham at the hub. Membership of the NEL in London was comparatively small, making the movement essentially a provincial one.[115] Nonetheless, Parliamentary work was a prominent feature in the NEL programme.[116]

An element of continuity stretched from the Anti-Corn Law League of the 1840s, whose organisational model inspired the Manchester Education Aid Society, through the BES, with whom it had contacts, in turn to the NEL, and finally to the National Liberal Federation.[117]

Money and organisational experience could not, however, paper over the very real cracks on the 'religious difficulty', even though these were not markedly divisive at the outset of the NEL's campaign. There were many aspects to this issue, which for much of the nineteenth century had every appearance of being completely intractable.

In retrospect, it could be said that difficulties were bound to happen in a society which prized its religion highly, whilst at the same time was politically freer than any other in Europe.[118] Religion can, after all, become a deeply emotional issue for the individuals involved, expressing their views about God's will for his flock – and the pathways to eternal doom or salvation. In the early stages, the battles were not between warring churches, nor between principles of religious and sectarian education, but between two irreconcilable ideas of what really was 'religious education'. At the core was a dispute between the doctrinal idea and the undenominational idea.[119]

Underlying this state of affairs was the complication of the existence of the Established Church in England.[120] Not to be an Anglican meant varying degrees of exclusion from society, although with the passage of time these areas of exclusion were diminishing. However, the development of a concept of generalised Christianity was discernible in the middle of the nineteenth century, devoid of any particular denominationalism. It was espoused by campaigners like Lord John Russell. Critics of this stance condemned it as an attitude, not a creed; and because it meant nothing precise, it was held to be reducing standards of religious commitment. In particular, it was described as being 'ignorant and heedless of dogma, concerned chiefly with conduct, imparting a gloss of Christian imagery and sentiment to a moral code which, as the dogmatically minded did not fail to point out, was

---

114 Ibid., p. 198.
115 Read, *English Provinces*, p. 170.
116 Adams, *History of Elementary School Contest*, p. 201.
117 A. Briggs, *History of Birmingham*, Vol. 2, p. 101. See below, Chapter 6, p. 182.
118 G.F.A. Best, 'The Religious Difficulties of National Education in England, 1800-70', *Cambridge Historical Journal*, 12, No. 2 (1955), p. 173.
119 Ibid., p. 161.
120 Ibid., p. 162. The very recent Compulsory Church Rates Abolition Bill of 1868 indicated that its position was not impregnable.

indistinguishable from the enlightened paganism of Greece, Rome and the State of Massachusetts'.[121]

This ecumenical concept did, however, suit Dixon, whose Broad Church Christianity appealed to many, and provoked less hostility than did the views of many other educational campaigners of his day.

The Protestant Nonconformists were particularly vocal at the time, although the position of the Catholics could not be overlooked. In many parts of the country, especially in rural areas, distances and transport problems meant that parents had no choice but to send their children to the one single school that might be available there. Hence the prospect of a 'conscience clause', whereby parents might elect to keep their offspring out of religious classes that promoted Anglican doctrines, was all very well in theory, but somewhat daunting in practice.

And once the children were in school, what should they be taught? 'Secular' education caused particular problems for those who were shocked at the omission of all religious instruction.[122] Dixon and others foresaw this difficulty, and decided that the NEL's policy should be to compromise and strive for 'unsectarian' education. He later wrote to the *BDP*, saying that 'it was decided' at the first meeting in January 1869 'that the word "secular" did not represent the views we entertained, and "unsectarian" was inserted in the programme without a single dissentient voice'.[123] Yet in October 1869 Dixon had to be more specific as to what this wording meant in practice. It did require the exclusion of 'all dogmatic, theological teaching, creeds and catechisms'. On the other hand, the exclusion of Bible-reading 'without note or comment' was 'not necessarily' intended.[124] This phrasing was very much the language of compromise and the apparent unanimity of the first meeting was not to endure.

George Dawson highlighted the absurdities of the debate, in his typically humorous style: 'I have no more notion of sectarian education than I have of a denominational water-cart or a sectarian vaccination'.[125]

On occasion, Dixon spoke more frankly. 'We are not here to patch the existing system – to patch the garment of semi-charity and semi-ecclesiasticism … Looking over the Church flock we find a sheep that belongs to us, and that is education, the primary education of the nation. It does not belong to the Church in any sense – it belongs to the whole nation.'[126]

There were also fissures within the NEL on other issues. The concept of free education did not appeal to all (despite the view of the BES, on the basis of its

---

121 Ibid., p. 170.
122 Murphy, *Education Act,* p. 31.
123 Briggs, 'Introduction', p. xix: date of letter to *BDP* 29 Nov. 1870.
124 Adamson, *English Education*, p. 350; Briggs, 'Introduction', p. xx.
125 Raffell, 'Radical and Nonconformist Influences', p. 315.
126 J.S. Hurt, *Elementary Schooling and the Working Classes, 1860-1918* (1979), p. 78.

earlier research, that the lack of money was a major stumbling block to many parents). As a doctrinaire political economist, Fawcett took exception to such a proposal,[127] and even Dr. Dale had objections initially, on the grounds that it would bring the new schools directly into competition with the existing ones. He also contended that if free education was to be supplied to the working classes, it could not justly be withheld from the middle classes.[128]

Amidst all the considerable upheaval involved in the establishment of the NEL, Dixon continued to be mindful of his constituents' many other concerns.

As relative newcomers to the Westminster scene, Dixon and his new fellow Birmingham MP, Muntz, kept a close eye on electoral malpractices, and intervened in the case of the nearby borough of Bewdley, where corruption and treating were allegedly endemic. Dixon went so far as to suggest that bribery appeared to be diminishing, whilst 'treating' (giving free food and, especially, drink to supporters) might have been increasing,[129] but subsequent research shows that he had little evidence for this suggestion. Soon electoral malpractices were flourishing on a larger scale than ever before.[130]

Dixon also supported Birmingham's gun-manufacturers on the question of arms for India.[131] As a merchant in the trade himself, this was one of the rare occasions when Dixon could have been accused of being self-serving. The industry was, however, such a staple for Birmingham that his concern was hardly surprising. Nonetheless, these were minor diversions by comparison with Dixon's main agenda, education.

With a strong organisation in the making, and not daunted by the fissures already apparent, Dixon pressed on in Parliament. On 12 March 1869, he seconded a motion proposed by one George Melly[132] for a Select Committee to investigate 'the number of young children in our large towns who are growing up without any education'.[133] Forster had now replaced Montagu as minister and, whilst refusing a Select Committee, promised on behalf of the government to carry out an exercise, seeking to establish once and for all the number of schools and scholars in the four largest towns in the country.[134] He expressed 'great faith in the returns which had been obtained by the Manchester Society and the Birmingham Society … Still, as their correctness had been disputed, it would be an advantage for the Government to endeavour to ascertain how

---

127 Briggs, 'Introduction', p. xix.
128 Dale, *Life of Dale*, p. 273.
129 *Hansard*, Vol. 194, Col. 666, 4 March 1869.
130 H.J. Hanham, *Elections and Party Management: Politics in the Time of Disraeli and Gladstone* (1959), p. 266.
131 *Hansard*, Vol. 194, Col. 1653, 18 March 1869.
132 Melly was a cousin of William Rathbone.
133 Marcham, 'Birmingham Education Society', p. 15.
134 Elkington, 'Elementary Education', p. 1.

far they are correct'.[135] This was the genesis of the Fitch/Fearon Report. With the exercise undertaken in the closing months of 1869, the Report was not published until 2 March 1870, two weeks after the First Reading of Forster's Bill.[136] No doubt the government had had some inkling as to what was likely to be divulged.

For the first significant time, Melly introduced the view that there was a correlation between the increase in crime and decrease in the provision of education.[137] An overall 'decrease', as Dixon was subsequently to explain, occurred because the growth in the population was outstripping the provision of new resources.[138] Melly highlighted the current comparative costs of policing and gaols in major towns, compared with the future cost of provision of free education there, which would be very much smaller. There was an implication of a direct trade-off. He even invoked the Vaccination Act, whose powers of compulsion were for the common good. 'Crime was more contagious than disease'.[139]

Both Melly and Dixon were singing from the same hymn-sheet. Dixon was quite clear as to why the country had a problem: 'We can no longer rest on the system of voluntaryism and its twin sister denominationalism' [to] reach the masses in those large and populous areas.[140]

Meantime, the BES was still active – or as active as it could be, given very limited funds. Its defining moment came with the Second Annual Report, for the year to 31 March 1869, in which it declared: 'The experience of this Society leads to the conclusion that sufficient money for the maintenance of schools for all the children requiring them, cannot be raised by voluntary agency; and your committee trust that the Government of the country will not let another session pass without introducing some efficient national system which shall secure the education of every child'.[141]

The BES was by this time in debt, and Dixon's subscription represented more than one-eighth of its income for the year.[142] It had to scale back its activities. Indeed, a fundamental weakness was all too apparent: whilst men of very different backgrounds had come together with a mission, they could proceed only by creating two different funds and allowing subscribers to allocate their money either to denominational or undenominational schools.[143]

---

135 Marcham, 'Birmingham Education Society', p. 15.
136 Raffell, 'Radical and Nonconformist Influences', p. 295.
137 *Hansard*, Vol. 194, Col. 1196, 12 March 1869.
138 Ibid., Col. 1210.
139 Ibid., Col. 1202.
140 Ibid., Col. 1212.
141 [IoE], National Education League pamphlets Vol. 4, pamphlet 4, *Second Annual Report of the Birmingham Education Society* (1869), p. 16.
142 Ibid., p. 30.
143 Hennock, *Fit and Proper Persons*, p. 86.

Whilst its Secretary, Jesse Collings, was concluding that poverty was the principal cause of the absence of children from school,[144] the Society's reputation was being tarnished by abuse of its benevolence, for some fee-paying pupils were being lured away from local schools by the offer of free places elsewhere.[145]

In absolute terms, the town was slipping backwards educationally. In the 18 years between 1851 and 1869, Birmingham's population grew from 232,841 to 380,846, whilst the number of scholars on the books of schools rose from 22,183 to 27,826. Expressed as percentages, this change represented a drop from 9.5% to 7.7%.[146]

But action followed. On 9 April 1869, Dixon petitioned the House of Commons in favour of the general establishment of Elementary Schools to educate the children of the working population, partially funded by local rates.[147] At the annual meeting itself, a couple of weeks later, he urged:

> Looked at from a financial point of view, it was admitted that a result of the education of children would hereafter be higher wages and greater wealth later in life, a saving in the reduction of taxes, and in the cost, the enormous cost, to the country of drunkenness and crime. Who, again, was there who did not admit that education had become a political necessity – that to withhold education from those to whom they had given the franchise would be little short of madness?.[148]

Then the BES made its last major contribution to the debate when it reported significantly that 'want of accommodation is not the cause of the absence of children, as there are very few schools which cannot receive more'. It continued by observing that there were problems with those attending school for far too short a period in their lives; or not attending school at all. Parental apathy was part of the problem, but poverty was also a major factor.[149] Little wonder then that the NEL wanted both compulsory and free education. And Dixon himself was clear that national action was needed, stating in Parliament that 'the control of the Government would be more wise and efficient than that provided by localities'.[150] He further explained:

---

144 Elkington, 'Elementary Education', p. 157.
145 Ibid., p. 167.
146 Ibid., p. 131.
147 [IoE], National Education League pamphlets Vol. 4, pamphlet 5, *Third Annual Report of the Birmingham Education Society* (1870), p. 9.
148 *BDP*, 29 April 1869.
149 Langford, *Modern Birmingham*, Vol. 2, p. 410.
150 *Hansard*, Vol. 197, Col. 438, 22 June 1869.

He had no fear of the results of giving more power to the central authority; for, although the system of centralisation had always been looked upon in this country with great fear and apprehension, they might be dismissed now that we had a reformed House of Commons. ... And the wisdom and experience which might be collected in a central Board might be of enormous use if it were diffused all over the country, fertilising every distant and ignorant union, where everything in the shape of innovation was shunned.[151]

Overall, Dixon saw the need for a judicious balance in these matters: 'We should avoid the evils of centralisation on the one hand, and of local inefficiency on the other'.[152]

As the 1869 Parliamentary session drew to a close, Forster announced that a Bill on education would be introduced, if public business permitted.[153] Dixon wondered whether the government was holding back on the grounds of cost. He suggested that Forster 'stood somewhat in awe of the Chancellor of the Exchequer and of the Secretary to the Treasury, who occupied something like the position of dragons in reference to the national expenditure'.[154] But Dixon stated boldly in Parliament:

It was the first point in the political creed of the new constituencies that education of the best possible character must be given, and be given quickly, to the people. All other considerations were of secondary importance; and while he by no means desired to advocate a lavish expenditure of the public money, he could assure the right hon. gentlemen that the working classes ... would be greatly disappointed if he were deterred from carrying out an object which they had so greatly at heart simply by consideration of finance.[155]

As if on cue, the fanatical rabble-rouser Murphy[156] once more put in an appearance in Birmingham. Dixon then found himself defending the actions of the current Mayor, who arrested Murphy before he had the opportunity to make a speech.[157] 'Small wonder that enlightened leaders of political reform dreaded giving votes to ignorance'.[158]

---

151 Ibid., Col. 439.
152 [IoE], National Education League pamphlets Vol. 1, pamphlet 5, *Report of the First General Meeting of the National Education League, 12/13 Oct. 1869* (1869), p. 66.
153 *Hansard*, Vol. 198, Col. 170, 18 July 1869.
154 Ibid., Col. 188.
155 Ibid., Col. 189.
156 See above, Chapter 2, p. 68.
157 *Hansard*, Vol. 198, Col. 611, 23 July 1869.
158 Garvin, *Chamberlain*, Vol. 1, p. 90.

Something of the same concern was expressed by Charles Dickens, by then a venerable reformer as well as Britain's paramount literary figure. As president of the Birmingham and Midland Institute, he had delivered a very long speech without a note of any kind. Dixon had the opportunity to express a vote of thanks to Dickens in tribute to his support. Dickens then responded with the famous words: 'My faith in the people governing is, on the whole, infinitesimal; my faith in the people governed is, on the whole, illimitable'.[159]

The NEL organised a two-day meeting on 12/13 October 1869, the main business being a debate 'That a Bill embodying the principles of the League be prepared for introduction into Parliament early next session'.[160] By this time, 2,500 'influential persons' had become members, of whom 40 were Members of Parliament, and somewhere between 300 and 400 were ministers of religion, although the sects were not specified. Dixon himself read a paper entitled 'On a system of national schools based on local rates and Government grants'. This contribution led the 1930s historian John Adamson to observe that Dixon was 'the real originator of the Elementary Education Act of 1870; here he not only outlined the Bill but sketched almost uncannily the early history of the school boards after the Bill became an Act'.[161] This compliment acknowledged Dixon's importance, although it must be noted that not dissimilar claims were made for Bruce, whose earlier attempts to introduce legislation in 1867 and 1868 had failed. Certainly, if Adamson had claimed that Dixon to be 'an' originator of the 1870 Bill rather than 'the real' originator, that would have been nearer the truth.

Dixon ended his paper with a caution that 'The choice before us is expenditure on education, or expenditure on paupers and criminals'[162] – a theme he had developed with Melly in the Commons six months previously. Lightening the atmosphere, the ebullient George Dawson added his own touch of humour. Addressing the assembly, he said of the Anglican Archdeacon Sandford: 'He has told you he has ceased to regard me as a firebrand. Well, I have long since ceased to regard him as a fogey'.[163]

Dixon supported Forster, who was essentially an ally, in the autumn of 1869, but with reservations. On the one hand, there was a need to lead the campaign, and to inspire his followers at the first annual conference; on the other, there was a risk of upsetting the leading Liberals in the Government. Dixon addressed a wider audience in the Town Hall after the Conference was closed, and gave a very clear indication as to the direction in which the campaign would go.

---

159 Dent, *Old and New*, Vol. 3, p. 571: 27 Sept. 1869.
160 J.W. Adamson, *English Education, 1789-1902* (Cambridge, 1930), p. 349.
161 Ibid., p. 350.
162 [IoE], National Education League pamphlets Vol. 1, pamphlet 5, *Report of the First General Meeting of the National Education League, 12/13 Oct. 1869* (1869), p. 69.
163 Ibid., p. 32.

We now have a Minister of Education, in Mr. Forster, who, in my opinion, has the will to do it; but I am not so certain that he has the power. But what we are going to do is this: by means of this League and its branches, we are going to rouse the people – in whom now, happily, is placed political power – in order that we may say to Mr. Forster, 'Be our leader, and give us what we want; we'll support you'. But if Mr. Forster should hesitate, if he will not transfer the education of this country from the voluntary and denominational basis, upon which it now rests, to the basis of taxation and self-governing energy of this country, then, much as we respect Mr. Forster, much as we esteem his character, his excellent will and his great skill, it will be our duty to say, even to Mr. Forster, our hitherto leader, that we can follow him no longer. We shall say, 'We have taken upon ourselves the performance of a duty than which, none can be higher – the duty of seeing to the education of every child in this country; and that duty we shall perform – with you as our leader, if you will, but if not, in spite of you'.[164]

That meeting had one unusual feature: members of the League had been invited by the Mayor to a 'soirée',[165] not perhaps the type of social gathering to which union leaders such as Applegarth were accustomed to attend. It gave a clue as to the essentially middle-class core of the organisation, although the invitation to the trade union leaders showed a desire for ecumenicalism.

In sending a warning of this nature in Forster's direction, Dixon was fully conscious of what he was doing. He confided to his fellow MP, Melly: 'We do not assume that Forster will bring in a "rotten bill" … But what I do assume is this, that exactly in proportion to Forster's estimate of the strength of the League, will be the Liberal colouring of the Bill – he will be afraid of the Churches until we convince him that we are stronger – he is not yet so convinced – he thinks that the Manchester Union [i.e. the National Education Union [NEU]] will grow faster than the Birmingham League'.[166]

The recently-formed NEU to a point concurred with the NEL on the issue of compulsory attendance, but fundamentally disagreed on the manner in which that should be achieved. Its object was 'the primary education of every child by judiciously supplementing the present denominational system of national education'.[167] Support for the NEU was drawn overwhelmingly from Anglican quarters, amongst whose supporters numbered two archbishops, five dukes, one marquess, eighteen earls, twenty-one bishops, and twenty-one barons,[168] and tensions between the two bodies were becoming fraught.

---

164 Ibid., p. 201.
165 Langford, *Modern Birmingham,* Vol. 2, p. 419.
166 Raffell, 'Radical and Nonconformist Influences', p. 299.
167 Adamson, *English Education,* p. 351; Briggs, 'Introduction', p. xxiii.
168 Briggs, 'Introduction', p. xxvi.

At the same time, there were developments in government circles. In October 1869 Forster submitted a memorandum to the Cabinet, his objective being 'to supplement the present voluntary system – that is to fill up its gaps at least cost of public money, with least loss of voluntary cooperation, and with most aid from the parents'.[169] Furthermore, he envisaged a real – although perhaps slightly exaggerated – threat which the NEL's stance represented: the cost of free and compulsory education would be enormous but, even worse, it would drive out most of those who supported and worked in the voluntaryist sector, thereby obliging the Government to provide even more educational resources than were otherwise mooted.[170] Becoming aware of the way the wind was blowing, the NEL changed tack somewhat, and briefly sought a postponement of new legislation,[171] whilst the Government sought to move quickly.

Dixon meantime faced opposition on his own front doorstep. The recently-formed and predominantly Anglican Birmingham Education Union [BEU] took an oppositional stance, bemoaning the fact that Dixon was sounding the death knell of the existing system. The BEU feared that education was no longer to be associated with the clergyman, the parsonage, the annual tea-party, the parish church. Instead, it was to be relegated entirely to the policeman, the magistrates and the prison. Dixon was a man of one idea: 'such men were bores, and he would be well advised to talk of anything rather than education – even his wealth'.[172]

Then there was the question of the local Catholics, who featured seldom in Dixon's life, not least because he made it very clear that he had little time for their faith. Their leader, Bishop Ullathorne, asked of his audience: 'Is it your wish that the tax gatherer should come to your door to demand by law a part of your money, all which money is to go to those godless schools, while your own schools are to have no part of that money?'[173]

An editorial in *The Times* rode quickly to Dixon's defence. Significantly, so far as the press in London was concerned, Dixon was then the leader of the NEL, and nobody else.

> With a dexterity that ought not to be called dexterity – for it is to the unconscious twist of a mind which has become so habitual to colour what it looks upon that it can now never describe things exactly as they are – the Bishop represented Mr Dixon's League to his Fellow Catholics at Birmingham in a way to excite their vehement indignation against proposals which they did not understand.

---

169 Ibid., p. xxii.
170 Ibid..
171 Adams, *History of Elementary School Contest,* p. 208.
172 Taylor, 'Birmingham Movement', p. 88.
173 *The Times,* 17 Nov., 1869.

So it was that during the months of November, December and January 1869/70, the leading figures in the NEL, including Dixon, Chamberlain, Dr. Dale and Collings, toured the country giving a series of speeches to arouse popular enthusiasm. The distances they covered in a relatively short time were considerable, thanks to the development of the railway network in the previous three or four decades. It was even reported that a spare railway carriage was kept in a siding at New Street Station, ready to be coupled to any regular service whose destination was a town which an NEL spokesman wanted to address. 'Out of Birmingham' went the word, and the country was listening.

The arguments varied quite naturally according to the audience to whom Dixon was talking. In Bradford, for example, 'he contended that enjoyment was absolutely essential to life; and how could a man deprived of the power of reading and writing easily, how could he enjoy himself? What was there left to him to enjoy? … in too many cases the temptation to go to the drinking shop was greater than they could overcome'.[174]

He tackled head-on the fears of the existing voluntary sector about the new competition which it would face from the state-funded schools. Dixon argued that if there were two sets of schools side by side, there would be a rivalry between them; and both would benefit from that rivalry.

In late November 1869 the NEL and NEU held a joint conference in Newcastle, but this encounter emphasised to the wider public the very real differences between the two bodies. The NEU distrusted town councils and boards of guardians as education authorities,[175] but the Liberal government, the NEL and even the Manchester Bill Committee had agreed that local school rates necessarily implied management by elected local authorities – in practice, a body selected by the Town Council.[176] Membership of the Town Council was therefore an attraction in its own right, and Chamberlain needed no second bidding when a deputation headed by William Harris asked him to stand.

With Christmas fast approaching, there appeared the following satire upon religious wrangling in the *Greenwich and Woolwich Gazette*:

'Who bids for the little children –
Body, and soul, and brain?
Who bids for the little children –
Young and without a stain?'
'Will no-one bid', said England,
'For their souls so pure and white,
And fit for all good or evil

174 *Bradford Observer*, 1 Dec. 1869.
175 Adamson, *English Education*, p. 351.
176 Hennock, *Fit and Proper Persons*, p. 87.

The world on their page may write?'
'Oh shame!' Says true Religion,
'Oh shame, that this should be!
I'll take the little children,
I'll take them all to me.
I'll raise them up with kindness
From the mire in which they'd trod;
I'll teach them words of blessing,
I'll lead them up to God.'
'You're not the true Religion,'
Said Sect with flashing eyes;
'Nor thou,' said another scowling –
'Thou'rt heresy and lies.'
'Thou shalt not have the children,'
Said a third, with shout and yell;
'You're Antichrist and bigot –
You'd train them up for hell.'
And England, sorely puzzled
To see such battle strong,
Exclaimed with voice of pity –
'Oh friends you do me wrong!
Oh cease your bitter wrangling,
For till you all agree,
I fear the little children
Will plague both you and me.'
But all refused to listen; -
Quoth they – 'we bide our time';
And the bidders seized the children –
Beggary, Filth and Crime;
And the prisons teemed with victims,
And the gallows rocked on high,
And the thick abomination
Spread reaking to the sky.[177]

There were increasing pressures for action – after all the talking. So in the closing weeks of 1869, there was an interesting dialogue between Manchester and Birmingham as to whether a combination of resources would be to mutual advantage. The initiative actually came from the Manchester Bill Committee, with a letter in the *Daily News* stressing that there was very little difference between the opinions of the two bodies. On 1 December, speaking

---

177 *Greenwich and Woolwich Gazette,* 4 Dec. 1869.

in Manchester, Dixon said 'he agreed it was wiser they should not waste their forces but by union increase them'.[178]

This observation from Dixon showed that he was willing to subordinate his own position for the sake of the cause to which he was so passionately committed. There were however sticking points. Manchester was seemingly suggesting that Birmingham should adopt the Bill proposed by Manchester,[179] and intimated that the proposed new Bill from Birmingham would have no chance.[180] Such emollience contrasted with the more spiky personality of the ambitious Joseph Chamberlain.

Dixon would have none of this, as he explained in a letter to the *Manchester Examiner and Times*:

> that not only was the Bill of the League [NEL] a more complete measure than that of the [Manchester] Education Bill Committee, but, also, that the operations of the League extended far beyond the enforcement of certain views upon a Minister ... The work we have set our hands to, is to arouse the whole country to a sense of the extent and dangers of our present educational destitution; to create and guide a strong public opinion: and thus to make possible a bold and comprehensive measure. ... The Education Bill Committee is composed of gentlemen to whom the friends of education owe much, but their numbers are insignificant, and, as a body, they are scarcely known beyond their own locality. It was my desire that they should extend their organisation, so as to become national instead of local, but I was informed this could not be done. Had my suggestions been favourably received by the gentlemen to whom they were made, Birmingham would not have originated the League, but would have followed Manchester, which in my opinion, ought to have headed, and was entitled to lead a national movement.[181]

Herein lay a fundamental difference of temperaments between Dixon and Chamberlain: the former, for ever diplomatic, was inching his way towards a solution which would carry general assent; the latter was self-assertive and domineering. Briggs wrote of this episode, 'It is doubtful if Chamberlain would ever have assented to this proposition'.[182] Dixon was, however, aware of his younger colleague's oratorical skills. Unable to attend a meeting in Wolverhampton, Dixon wrote to apologise: 'but the chairman of our

---

178 S.E. Maltby, *Manchester and the Movement for National Elementary Education, 1800-70* (Manchester, 1918), p. 109.
179 Adams, *History of Elementary School Contest*, p. 194.
180 Maltby, *Manchester*, p. 109.
181 Letter dated 10 Dec. 1869: see Adams, *History of Elementary School Contest*, p. 194.
182 Briggs, 'Introduction', p. xii.

Executive Committee, Mr Joseph Chamberlain, who is a better speaker than I am, will go'.[183]

As the New Year was about to dawn, a hostile little poem appeared in the *Daily Gazette*:

> There rose up a house without mason or tool,
> A dismal house which I know was a school;
> A school in St Pancras Guardian style,
> A brick-and-a-half thing, built by the mile,
> All shabby and gloomy, yet new to boot,
> As of fresh from the wreck of a Chancery Suit.
> The jambs of the door were of stucco, all wet,
> The flaws not puttied and painted yet:
> But over the doorway, and cleft by a crack,
> Was the one word, LEAGUE, grim lettered in black.
> 'Twas the dismallest house the world o'er saw;
> Where to pray to God was to break the law.[184]

This barracking against unsectarian education was scarcely the kind of Christmas present that Dixon might have been wishing.

He stuck to his position, however, with his usual doggedness and belief in civic service. In 1870 Dixon was asked about the composition of the current House of Commons. In typically self-effacing and long-winded form, in one long sentence addressed to his constituents he replied: 'It seemed to me that men who had fought their way up to the House of Commons through a life devoted to private and public business, men who were trained in habits of method, of diligence and of concentration, who were fond of work for its own sake, and full of experience of life, that if such men were to devote themselves to special subjects, although they might not be brilliant, yet still they might have qualities that would be more useful, perhaps, to their constituents and to their country, and who would occasionally originate useful reforms'.[185]

His declaration was not the stuff of outstanding leadership, but it was sincere. And on the following day, Dixon expanded on these thoughts: 'it would be to the interest, not only of the working classes, but of the country at large, that there should be in the House of Commons a certain proportion of representatives who were themselves working men. I say this not because I wish to have any class representatives, for I am very much adverse to it. I wish in every case the constituencies should elect the man who, on the whole, is most suitable for them, irrespective of his class and position in life'.[186]

---

183 *BDP*, 11 Jan. 1870.
184 *Daily Gazette*, 24 Dec. 1869.
185 *BDP*, 12 Jan. 1870.
186 Ibid., 13 Jan. 1870.

There followed one of the most dramatic months of Dixon's entire life. The Queen's Speech on 8 February 1870 announced a Bill for the enlargement, on a comprehensive scale, of the means of national education.[187] The following day, John Bright retired from public life.[188] Dixon became the senior Birmingham MP, and whilst Bright's retirement removed from the stage one of the most revered Radicals of the day, he could hardly have been described as one of Dixon's most enthusiastic supporters. However, Bright's departure was an opportunity for Chamberlain, an opportunity he was shortly to grasp.

Eight days later, Forster presented his landmark Bill to Parliament. The first rung in Dixon's educational ladder was to be put in place. At long last, the state was prepared to accept responsibility for the elementary education of every child in England and Wales, and the path was paved for it to be compulsory and free. There was widespread acclaim on the day, and Dixon's name featured prominently in Forster's speech:

> what is the principle relied upon by the hon. Member for Birmingham [Mr. Dixon] and the hon. Member for Sheffield [Mr. Mundella], to whom so much credit is due for stimulating educational zeal in the country? It is the education of the people's children by the people's officers, chosen in their local assemblies, controlled by the people's representatives in Parliament.[189]

Four days later, Forster's brother-in-law, Matthew Arnold, felt able to write in one of his frequent letters to his mother: 'I think William's Bill will do very well. I am glad it is so little altered since I heard its contents in November. His speech in introducing it seems to have been a great success'.[190] Adams described the initial reaction in welcoming terms: 'The precise effect of the bill was hardly perceived upon its introduction, and it was received with a chorus of satisfaction from the Liberal benches'.[191]

Dixon, however, was placed in a severe quandary. The Bill was manifestly not what the NEL had been campaigning for. He was flattered by the tribute paid to himself and Mundella, and he must have been impressed, as would have been so many others in the Commons that day, by the masterful way in which Forster had tackled head-on so many of the contentious issues.

It would have been churlish to launch a bitter attack immediately given the sentiment in Parliament. It was also extremely difficult to consider every aspect of a topic so complex. The speech was far longer than many Budget

---

187 Taylor, 'Birmingham Movement', p. 109.
188 Ibid..
189 *Hansard*, Vol. 199, Col. 465, 17 Feb. 1870.
190 G.W.E. Russell, (ed.), *Letters of Matthew Arnold, 1848-88* (1904), Vol. 14, p. 219.
191 Adams, *History of Elementary School Contest*, p. 212.

speeches delivered by Chancellors of the Exchequer over the years and, as many opposition leaders have learned to their cost, the devil is often in the detail.

That context explains Dixon's quandary in response, which led to a challenge to his leadership of the educational reform campaign. With his customary politeness, Dixon expressed thanks: 'He felt persuaded that the country generally would support them in their endeavours to carry its provisions out'.[192] 'Generally' gave a clear indication that total support was not to be expected. On the other hand, it expressed support rather than opposition.

He continued with further compliments: 'He believed that the promise given in the Speech from the Throne was now fully redeemed by the introduction of this Bill, and in supplementing it by giving compulsory power of attendance through the school Boards throughout the country. The school Boards formed the backbone of the Bill, and made it a measure which he felt assured would be acceptable to the country'.[193]

Then Dixon began his litany of reservations, which deserve quotation at length:

> There were, however, some provisions of the Bill which, in his opinion, deserved the serious consideration of the House, and which, he thought, should be modified … [Furthermore] He did not look upon it, for instance, as wise that a whole year should be allowed to elapse before the school Boards caused the necessary schools to be erected. He hoped that that point would not be insisted upon by the Government … With regard to the religious difficulty, he entertained little doubt that the view which was gaining ground throughout the country, that no Conscience Clause could be devised which would prove satisfactory to a large portion of the population, was becoming too strong to be successfully resisted even by the most powerful Government … In all probability, therefore, it would be regarded as the great weakness of the Bill that the separation which it was desirable should be made between religious and secular instruction should be left to the decision of an innumerable number of Boards throughout the country, into whose election religious feeling must necessarily enter, instead of being directly effected by Parliament … He could not, under these circumstances, look with approval on the method by which his right hon. Friend proposed the religious difficulty should be met, although, in leaving to the various Boards the means of solving it, the way was paved for its ultimate removal.
>
> He was sorry it was thought necessary to give merely permissive powers to the School Boards to enforce compulsory attendance. That

---

192 *Hansard*, Vol. 199, Col. 475, 17 Feb. 1870.
193 Ibid..

House ought to decide whether it should not only be made compulsory on parents to send their children, but on the School Boards to enforce such attendance.

He was not surprised to find the Government shrinking from the responsibility of abolishing entirely all school fees. But his faith in the principle of the Bill was great, and his confidence in its wisdom was so full that he had no doubt the time would soon arrive when the school Boards would be convinced of the utility of entirely abolishing those fees. As he understood, power would be given to the school Boards to solve this question. Although he did not think the way to this end was the wisest, and certainly would not be the shortest, he was nevertheless convinced that its solution would be ultimately reached.

He would not say he regretted to find no clauses in the Bill providing for the establishment of a purely educational Department of the Government, because he hoped that the omission of such clauses could not find a proper place in the Bill. He, however, hoped that before the Session was over a measure of that character would be introduced. The experience of even the last two months was sufficient to convince them of the absolute necessity of establishing the office of a Minister of Education, whose duty should be to attend exclusively to the working of the system.

Dixon's final remarks were polite, but qualified: 'He felt quite sure that the people at large would be satisfied with the efforts of the Government, and he was still more certain that those efforts would be crowned with success'.

However, he had significantly failed to highlight the features offensive to the mainstream of the NEL.[194] This caution was perhaps not surprising, given Dixon's ecumenical tendencies, as the problems all centred on religious aspects.

Just how substantial was the religious difficulty? Dixon touched on the issue in his response to Forster, and Mundella elaborated on the point: 'He had never regarded the religious difficulty as being of any considerable magnitude, because he believed that the people of this country generally desired that their children should receive religious teaching, and in support of that proposition he might state that a very able man belonging to the working classes had told him that the religious difficulty had been made for and not by the lower classes'.[195]

Forster himself quoted Frederick Temple, one-time Headmaster of Rugby, at that time Anglican Bishop of Exeter, and subsequently Archbishop of Canterbury, as believing that 'the religious difficulty was immensely exaggerated and that once we were inside the school it vanished'. And the point

---

194 Marsh, *Chamberlain,* p. 43.
195 *Hansard,* Vol. 199, Col. 477, 17 Feb. 1870.

was pursued further in Committee: 'I venture to assert with great respect to those who are agitating the religious difficulty that the difficulty is one which has not sprung from the people themselves. It is a grievance which has gone down from London into the country, and which would never have struck the minds of the people, unless they had been told by those having authority over them that they ought to raise the question'.[196]

In the immediate aftermath of Forster's speech, there were only two significant suggestions of opposition to Forster's proposals. One was the relatively isolated voice of Lord Robert Montagu. He felt that the extent of educational destitution was so slight that it could be resolved by mere tinkering with the existing system.[197]

The other, and much more significant, hint of dissent came from the 33-year-old Joseph Chamberlain, chairman of the NEL's Executive Committee. 'Out of Birmingham' came the ominous message, addressed to George Dixon: 'strong exception was taken to the first paragraph in your speech... in which you are alleged to have said that the country would receive the Bill with satisfaction'.[198]

It was a significant turning-point in Dixon's career. He was now fully alert to the problem that, if he thought that he could speak his own mind freely in Parliament without reference at virtually every turn to his followers in the NEL, he was mistaken.

---

196 Adamson, *Short History*, p. 310.
197 Raffell, 'Radical and Nonconformist Influences', p. 363.
198 Briggs, 'Introduction', p. lvii, fn.

CHAPTER FOUR

The Struggle for Legislation, 1870

FOR THE FIRST time there was revealed the extent to which the NEL was riddled with fissures, the most important of which was that which separated the Radicals, of whom Dixon was in the vanguard, from the Nonconformists.

Dixon's pivotal role had already been acknowledged in an 1869 editorial in *The Times*, which referred to the NEL as being 'Mr. Dixon's',[1] and just one month previously, the Mayor of Leeds, in concluding a conference of Nonconformist ministers held in the town, had opined that 'I believe of all the schemes that have been propounded, that of the League is the one likeliest eventually to work to the advantage of the religion which is so dear to us'.[2]

Now, three major obstacles lay ahead: the full scale of the NEL's demands were arguably unattainable, certainly in the very short term; the intensity of the religious divide was even more severe than anyone had earlier imagined; and Dixon was surrounded by colleagues with agendas and ambitions not his own.

---

1 See above, Chapter 3, p. 101.
2 [IoE], National Education League pamphlets Vol. 1, pamphlet 14, *NEL Report of a Conference of Nonconformist Ministers held at Leeds, 18 Jan. 1870* (1870), p. 60.

For more than twenty years, the English political scene had been relatively quiet, memories of Chartism fast fading, and the population reaping the benefits of lower food prices, following the campaign success of the Anti-Corn Law League (ACLL). In outline, the NEL owed something to both these: just as there were six points in the Charter, so the NEL had six objectives.[3] Moreover, not only did the NEL copy some of the ACLL's organisational methods, but it shared the name 'League'. In the simplest of terms, it could be argued that Chartism had failed to achieve its immediate objectives because, inter alia, its objectives for constitutional reform were too wide-ranging, whilst the ACLL, focused on just one objective, was completely successful. Like Chartism, the NEL's objectives were not narrowly focused. Years later, in 1905, Herbert Paul wrote that its 'platform of free, compulsory, secular education, with School Boards everywhere and voluntary schools nowhere, was quite beyond the range of practical politics'.[4] But this description of the platform was as it finally crystallised, for in its early days the NEL was arguing for unsectarian rather than secular education.

The existence of the 'religious difficulty' had been acknowledged as the major stumbling-block to educational reform for decades before 1870, but with an ecumenical Anglican like Dixon chairing an organisation, which had such widespread support nationwide at the beginning of the year, there was a feeling abroad that this time, things might be different.

Whilst the NEL's leadership did not reflect the very broad range of opinions held by the committee which ran the BES, nonetheless the NEL was in its early months at least far from being the predominantly Nonconformist body described by later historians. Furthermore, historians have often failed to note the significant shift in the balance of power within the NEL which took place in the weeks and months following the publication of the Bill. By 1872 the pattern was becoming more clear, and Sargant,[5] wholly supportive of what Dixon was trying to achieve, was able to write an *Essay* in which he described certain elements of the NEL as the 'Irreconcileables'.[6]

The *Essay* then went on to describe Dixon's leadership issues: 'Mr Dixon is a gentleman of moderate mind. He put himself into the hands of allies possessed of considerable ability and little discretion: of allies, friends to education but more friends to popular agitation: liberals in politics; bigots in religion. Mr Dixon, left to himself, would not have run into extravagances. But he got together and undertook to drive a team far too lively for his gentle guidance: he gave his cattle their heads, and they fairly ran away with him. He

---

3 See above, Chapter 3, p. 90.
4 H. Paul, *A History of Modern England* (1905), p. 218.
5 See above, Chapter 2, p. 52.
6 W.L. Sargant, *Essays of a Birmingham Manufacturer* (1872), Vol. 4, p. 4.

now appears as the nominal chief of a masterful and bitter faction'.[7] The *Essay* then proceeded to defend Dixon's overall strategy: 'Cunning men, to gain what they want, ask a great deal more',[8] before identifying (without mentioning any names) the Unitarians within the NEL as being a particular cause for concern – 'especially among themselves, [they] indulge in much scornful merriment at the expense of churchmen's superstitions and intellectual weaknesses'.[9] Dixon 'did not share the bitterness of their dissenting hatred',[10] and so it was with an air of some detachment that he continued to voice their considerable concerns in the weeks and months that followed.

This was all for the future. The immediate reactions to Forster's speech on 17 February 1870 were favourable, whilst opposition, when it emerged, came from those who believed that the government was not going far enough.[11] There was scarcely a voice to be heard denying that there was any need for action at this time. Indeed, a meeting of the Birmingham Education Union carried unanimously a motion 'that this meeting accepts with much satisfaction the general principles embodied in the Government Education Bill, and believes that in the main the proposals therein contained are calculated to meet the necessities of the country'.[12]

The change in attitudes within the NEL in the days immediately after Forster had presented his Bill was dramatic. The NEL's own *Monthly Paper*[13] recorded that Dixon attended an NEL meeting in London that very evening, where he was reportedly very pleased that a national and compulsory system was in prospect. Nevertheless, he regretted that the religious question had not been dealt with 'more clearly … he was jubilant that night, and they would not rest now till every child in England shared in the blessings of education – education for this world, and pre-eminently for another world, to the lasting benefit of his family and of the whole nation'. Other MPs who were present, including Charles Dilke, who was in the chair, and William Harcourt, did not appear to differ.

Yet just five days later, on Tuesday 22 February 1870, the London branch of the NEL executive passed a unanimous motion: 'That … the Government Bill is unsatisfactory'.[14]

Just a week after Forster presented his Bill to Parliament, the Executive Committee of the NEL met in Birmingham with Chamberlain in the chair.

---

7 Ibid., Vol. 4, p. 2.
8 Ibid., Vol. 4, p. 3.
9 Ibid., Vol. 4, p. 5.
10 Ibid., Vol. 4, p. 16.
11 W.H.G. Armytage, 'The Education Act 1870', *British Journal of Educational Studies*, 18 (1970), p. 124.
12 *Aris's Birmingham Gazette*, 26 Feb. 1870.
13 *Monthly Paper*, 1 March 1870.
14 Ibid..

Dixon was also present. In the eyes of Chamberlain and many of his colleagues, it transpired that Dixon's initial response in the Commons had been an embarrassment. It was obviously not politic to reveal the divisions in public, and a way had to be found of extricating him from the difficulty. It was argued that the defects of the Bill had not been apparent at the First Reading.[15]

But divisions there were as to tactics, with many within the League chary as to the wisdom of raising the religious issue at this very early stage, for it tended to suggest that they were more concerned with the rights of religious bodies, than with the cause of furthering children's education.[16] The course taken, with Chamberlain at the helm, was undoubtedly clumsy. Very shortly afterwards there was published a statement that other amendments would follow in Committee.[17] For Dixon this tactic was all rather awkward, acting as he was at the behest of his strident followers.

In his capacity of Chairman of the NEL's Executive Committee, Chamberlain had certainly not been resting on his laurels. As he wrote to Dixon on 26 February: 'I think we have anticipated all your suggestions. We have written to Mr Gladstone asking for an appointment before the Second Reading or as near to it as may be convenient to him. We have sent out an inflammatory circular to all the branches urging large delegations – also public meetings and petitions. We have set on foot a requisition for a Town's meeting and the Nonconformists are going to have a special meeting of their own'.[18] Indeed, the Executive Committee had met two days previously under Chamberlain's chairmanship, by which time 68 replies had already been received in response to the 'inflammatory' circular concerned, and concluded that numerous amendments were needed.[19] It also resolved to withhold the NEL's own Bill as already drafted.[20]

---

15 Taylor, 'Birmingham Movement', p. 119.
16 Raffell, 'Radical and Nonconformist Influences', p. 386.
17 Taylor, 'Birmingham Movement', p. 130.
18 Garvin, *Chamberlain*, Vol. 1, p. 109.
19 *[1] School Boards to be established in all districts, instead of only in those districts in which education is declared to be unsatisfactory after enquiry by the Privy Council. [2] Such Boards to be elected immediately on the passing of the Act, and to be required to provide, without delay, for the educational necessities of their districts. [3] In districts not included in boroughs, School Boards to be elected by the ratepayers generally, voting by ballot. [4] Compulsory attendance of children at school to be made imperative, instead of being left to the discretion of School Boards. [5] Admission to schools established or maintained by School Boards to be free. [6] No creed, catechism, or tenet peculiar to any sect to be taught in schools under the management of the School Boards, or receiving grants from local rates. [7] In all other schools receiving Government aid, the religious teaching to be at a distinct time, either before or after ordinary school business, and provision to be made that attendance at such religious teaching shall not be compulsory, and that there shall be no disability for non-attendance.* The story of the enactment of the legislation for the next six months was full of such minutiae, and whilst Dixon's background in the world of Chambers of Commerce was undoubtedly of great assistance in mastering the intricate detail of the debate, other such details are not repeated in this work except where of immediate relevance to Dixon's own involvement in events. The most authoritative account of the passage of the Bill is contained in Raffell, 'Radical and Nonconformist Influences'.
20 Adams, *History of Elementary School Contest*, p. 212.

Nationwide, the battle-lines were complex. Amongst the most significant issues was the question of whether there should be entirely secular education or, if religious education were included, whether its 'teaching must be eviscerated of every trace of institutional religion'.[21] Defining terms became a science in its own right. Already, Dixon had become irritated by some of the intricacies of the debate, when he declared that 'It was useless to teach children under thirteen years of age abstruse doctrines and creeds – they could not understand them'.[22]

So it was that in the first week of March 1870, several leading Non-conformists set up the separate Central Nonconformist Committee, with Dr. Dale and Crosskey as Honorary Secretaries, and the draper Schnadhorst operating secretary.[23] It was not as if there was any bitter personal animosity between them and Dixon. Far from it, as Dr. Dale was to prove a loyal friend some years later when significant difficulties emerged in the workings of the Birmingham School Board,[24] whilst Crosskey and Dixon thought along very similar lines as to the function of education. But at this juncture, with the prospect of imminent legislation, every special interest group was determined to have its say.

As many contemporaries pointed out, there were some 150 religious sects in Britain at this time,[25] and they did not speak with one voice. The Nonconformists' only common denominator was the self-evident one that they were disadvantaged, on occasion severely disadvantaged, by the prevailing laws and customs which favoured the established Anglican church, whose members were themselves far from agreed on many educational issues. Forster's Bill gave the Nonconformists common cause for complaint, and the Central Nonconformist Committee now focused on obtaining amendments, 'especially in those parts relating to the Conscience Clause and to the authority conferred upon school boards to establish denominational schools out of the rates, and to make grants to such existing schools'.[26]

The significance of all this for Dixon was that several of the leading figures in the Central Nonconformist Committee were also prominent members in the much better known NEL, and as the disputes became more bitter, so the reputations of the one began to impact the reputation of the latter, to the point where a couple of years later Dr. Dale had to defend his friend Dixon, whose personal reputation was being threatened.[27] As one commentator observed many years later, the NEL, through opposing many aspects of the Bill,

21 Adamson, *English Education*, p. 354.
22 *BDP*, 7 Dec. 1869.
23 Briggs, 'Introduction', p. xxix.
24 See below, Chapter 5, p. 160 and Chapter 6, p. 186.
25 Raffell, 'Radical and Nonconformist Influences', p. 370.
26 Ibid., p. 372.
27 See below, Chapter 5, p. 160.

'inadvertently turned themselves not so much into the Liberal Party at prayer, as the Nonconformists at politics'.[28] It is less surprising therefore that Dixon himself has occasionally been assumed to be a Nonconformist.

At this time, Chamberlain set out a new dimension to the debate in a letter to Dixon on 3 March 1870. The new divergence between the two men was clearly revealed: the latter intent on educational reform above all else, the former seeing it as part of a much larger political jigsaw. 'If Forster forces his Bill through the House there will be a tremendous revival of the agitation for the disestablishment of the English Church', stormed Chamberlain. 'If you see Mr Forster you may safely tell him that he has succeeded in raising the whole of the Dissenters against him, and if he thinks little of our power we will teach him his mistake'.[29]

In Parliament, the Conservative opposition fully supported Forster's Bill, a support which was seldom to waver until the Bill received Royal Assent in August. The Conservatives under Disraeli shared the virtually universal support for some form of legislation and, with the pace of extra-parliamentary agitation rising rapidly, they thought it best to support Forster's proposals – essentially a mixture of what the NEL and the rival National Education Union had been advocating – before the demands for change became even more radical. In fact, some Conservatives were relieved that the measures were less 'liberal' and less drastic than they had feared.[30]

Feelings outside the House were running high. On 9 March 1870, there descended on Downing Street 'probably the most numerous and representative [deputation] ever to have visited the place',[31] comprising 46 MPs and 400 League members. This was the meeting with Gladstone to which Chamberlain had referred in his letter to Dixon on 26 February.[32]

Dixon led the deputation, and set out the historical background. He emphasised that, in the very many meetings in the country organised by the NEL in the previous months, besides the Nonconformists who had attended in great force, there were many people from the working class. They had 'assembled in constantly increasing numbers'.[33] The fact that the NEL's muscle was flexing ever stronger was reason enough for the government to have introduced legislation now, rather than wait for another year, when the tide of public opinion might have flooded even further in the NEL's direction. After that veiled threat, Dixon made one more. After being refreshingly honest

---

28 Armytage, 'Education Act', p. 125.
29 Garvin, *Chamberlain,* Vol. 1, p. 109.
30 Raffell, 'Radical and Nonconformist Influences', p. 379.
31 Adams, *History of Elementary School Contest,* p. 215.
32 See above, Chapter 4, p. 113.
33 [IoE], National Education League pamphlets Vol. 1, pamphlet 18, *Verbatim Report of the Proceedings of a Deputation* (1870), p. 11.

that the League was not 'quite unanimous' on the issue of free schools,[34] he suggested that 'with reference to the religious question, there is only a section of the League that has any difference of opinion, and this section takes up a still more advanced opinion than the great body of the Leaguers. [Applause]'.[35]

Thereupon, Dixon left Chamberlain to expand on matters generally, followed by a variety of other speakers, on specific issues, including Dilke, Mundella – who, despite receiving a warm tribute alongside Dixon from Forster when the Bill had been introduced, played a significantly smaller role than him in the six months that followed – Applegarth, the trade union leader speaking on behalf of the working classes, and the Rev. Barham Zincke, who was the Queen's Chaplain. Chamberlain acknowledged that the NEL claimed to 'represent the great bodies of Nonconformists in this country; but inasmuch as they have established a separate organisation, I feel some delicacy in speaking for them'.[36] This warning indicated that a further deputation, organised by the Central Nonconformist Committee, was to attend the following month. Chamberlain evidently made a distinct impression upon Gladstone, who later in the meeting observed about Chamberlain 'who I may consider as in some sense being your chairman – the representative of you all ...'.[37]

Gladstone himself approached the educational issue with some ambivalence. Three years previously, before becoming Prime Minister, he had opined '... in affairs generally I follow others, Bruce for example on education, and wait for a breeze'. Indeed, it is difficult to determine whether at this particular time he had any strong views on the question of elementary education at all. Insofar as he did, it may well have been from the points of view of the Church and the Exchequer, to neither of which could national education appear attractive.[38]

In many respects, the deputation to Downing Street was something of a let-down for Dixon. It also marked a growing closeness between Chamberlain and Dilke, which became not only a professional relationship, but a close personal friendship. It later added a further twist to the relationship between Dixon and Chamberlain, for two years later, Dixon declined to support Dilke in the latter's criticism of the amount of public money being expended on the royal family: the rift between Dixon and Dilke also signalled Dixon's lack of enthusiasm for Chamberlain's stance too.[39]

There was also something irritating about the way in which Chamberlain failed to give Dixon full support in front of Gladstone. For example, Chamberlain quibbled about the accuracy of Dixon's figures: in his

---

34 Ibid..
35 Ibid..
36 Ibid., p. 13.
37 Ibid., p. 26.
38 J. Vincent, *The Formation of the Liberal Party, 1857-68* (1966), p. 222.
39 D. Nicholls, *The Lost Prime Minister: A Life of Sir Charles Dilke* (1995), p. 39; and see below, Chapter 5, p. 150.

introductory remarks, Dixon had said that the delegation had come from about 70 different localities; Chamberlain corrected him, and said that in fact there were representatives from 96 NEL branches.[40]

The campaigners, however, were making the running. And amongst their ranks, a new star was rising. The perception was clearly that NEL was no longer 'Mr. Dixon's' as it had been just a few months previously. He may have been the Chairman of the Council of the League. But Chamberlain was Chairman of the Executive Committee. Nominally, he reported to Dixon insofar as the latter's name always preceded the former's in NEL literature. Yet in reality Chamberlain was now in charge of the day-to-day running of the organisation and, most importantly, responsible for its publicity machine. The logistics of the situation demanded that it be thus, too. Dixon was in London for at least half the year for the Parliamentary season and, whilst speedy communications in the form of the railway and the telegraph were ever improving, the League's headquarters and support were firmly centred on Birmingham.

The meeting at Downing Street concluded with Dixon as the deputation's leader formally extending thanks, but not before he had answered one of Gladstone's concerns relating to the religious difficulty. The solution, Dixon suggested, was that in relation to the existing schools, 'there should be separate religious teaching, as a condition of the further grants which it is proposed under this Bill to make to them; and that with reference to the new schools which may be provided out of the rates, [i.e. the Board Schools] those schools should be entirely unsectarian'.[41] It is quite probable that this was the first time that Gladstone had to reflect in depth on two issues which had been concerning Dixon for some time. First, that there was going to be a fundamental divide between the old ('voluntary') and the new ('Board') types of schools, which would in name change to the private and state sectors. Interestingly, there was to be a subtle reversal of roles many years later, with the private sector taking on the role of filling perceived gaps in the public sector. Dixon had been quite clear as early as December 1869 that the two sectors would be in competition.[42] Second, there were very real practical problems with regard to the meaning of the word 'unsectarian', whose use Dixon had endorsed at the NEL's first Annual Meeting in October 1869. These issues were to be amongst a host of others which were to be debated in Parliament for more than twenty days in 1870.

---

40 [IoE] *Verbatim Report*, p. 10.

41 [IoE] *Verbatim Report*, p. 28. Interestingly, the problem has endured through the ages. R.A. Butler, in his Foreword to Marjorie Cruickshank's *Church and State in English Education: 1870 to the Present Day* (1963), p. viii, wrote that the objective through the ages has been to ensure 'that "religion is caught and not taught" in denominational schools and that council schools conduct their teaching on the non-denominational syllabus'.

42 See, for example, *Bradford Observer*, 1 Dec. 1869.

It was a deeply absorbing time for all closely involved in politics, with many twists and turns in the debates that raged in the following months. At the same time, it is worth remembering too that there was a world outside politics. In 1870 the new Football Association hosted the first international football match between England and Scotland; the British Red Cross was founded; the Married Women's Property Act was passed; and the reformer and novelist Charles Dickens died, his last novel *Edwin Drood* unfinished.

Meanwhile Dixon kept his eyes firmly upon educational reform. For most of the rest of his life, he was wont to use the phrase 'national system' in debates about the future of elementary education. To many contemporaries, this term implied that he envisaged that the vast majority of schools in the future would be run by the state sector,[43] and therefore the future of the existing schools was threatened. Indeed, from time to time Dixon also alluded to the 'painless extinction' of denominational schools, and it was the use of such language which could not but cause concern to the many who had contributed generously to the running of the voluntary system in the past.

Immediately after the Downing Street meeting, on 10 March 1870, Dixon gave notice of an Amendment on the Second Reading of the Bill, in the following terms:

> that this House is of the opinion that no measure for the elementary education of the people will afford a satisfactory or permanent settlement which leaves the question of religious instruction in schools supported by public funds or rates to be determined by local authorities.[44]

It was an unusual step, for as Forster rapidly pointed out, Amendments to Second Readings always had as their objectives the throwing out of the Bill – 'I will not suppose that it is the wish of my hon. Friend to throw out this Bill, for he is too earnest in the cause of education to entertain such a wish'.[45] Besides condemning the Amendment for its vagueness Robert Lowe, the Chancellor of the Exchequer, weighed in with the criticism that the religious difficulty was, 'as compared with the main scope of the measure, rather one of the minor principles'.[46] Hence he deemed it ironic that Dixon could be thought to be opposing the measure, since he was partly responsible – a tribute indeed – for awakening the zeal of the nation for a national system of education in the first place.[47]

43 Kenrick, 'George Dixon', p. 66.
44 Raffell, 'Radical and Nonconformist Influences', p. 385.
45 *Hansard*, Vol. 199, Col. 1932, 14 March 1870.
46 Ibid., Col. 2058.
47 Ibid., Col. 2064.

Dixon had now been in Parliament for slightly more than two years and, whilst he could have pleaded inexperience in such procedural matters, the responsibility for the manoeuvre lay with the Executive Committee of the NEL. As a Statement of the Officers read on 15 June at the only Council meeting ever held in the eight years of the organisation's existence proclaimed: '[following the deputation to see Gladstone] immediately afterwards it was decided that Mr. Dixon, our President [sic], should be requested, in the name of the League, to move an amendment…'.[48]

It is difficult to ascribe any one particular reason for taking such drastic, and tactically risky, action at this juncture. A charitable interpretation is that Dixon was fearful that the Act would create sectarian strife at elections (which, in the event, it certainly did), with the various denominations seeking to gain an ascendancy on the Education Boards so that they could control the use of school rates for their own particular ends.[49] Certainly there were members of the League who thought that the objections were precipitate, and pointed out that the decision to protest was made by a very few – it could be perceived that they were more concerned with the relative rights of religious bodies than with the cause of furthering children's education.[50]

In these unusual circumstances, Dixon's speech was described by Briggs as one which 'could not be said to have been good'.[51]

On the substantive issue, about half way through his speech, Dixon showed his true colours. 'He approached the religious question without any prejudice whatsoever. At least, as he was a Churchman, he approached it without any of the prejudices of the Dissenters'. So it was that he sought to play the role of the honest broker, but with a clear message to the Liberal government that, unless it heeded the views of the troops behind him, there would be trouble.

Dixon started his speech by setting out his stall of what he perceived to be the items on the agenda which were deficient, elaborating on his list of points made in the immediate aftermath of Forster's speech on 17 February.[52] He began with relatively minor points, and finished with the two issues which were fundamental to his agenda. He called for the formation of a separate Department of Education; he suggested that the number of training colleges should be increased; he opposed the idea of allowing a year to pass during which the voluntary sector could plan the construction of additional schools before decisions were made as to what gaps needed to be filled; he sought the appointment of School Boards everywhere; he urged that these Boards be

---

48 [IoE], National Education League pamphlets Vol. 1, pamphlet 22, *Statement of the Officers: Read at a Meeting of the Council and of Delegates, in London, 15 June 1870* (1870), p. 2.
49 D.W. Sylvester, *Robert Lowe and Education* (Cambridge, 1974), p. 127.
50 Raffell, 'Radical and Nonconformist Influences', p. 386.
51 Briggs, 'Introduction', p. xxx.
52 See above, Chapter 3, p. 108.

elected by ballot in rural areas, rather than appointed by vestries; he asked that a higher proportion of the cost of School Boards should be borne out of the Consolidated Fund, rather than from local rates; he demanded that compulsory attendance should be made immediate and universal; and finally he called for admission to all elementary schools to be made free.[53]

Dixon's list of demands was in many ways impressive in its grasp of the administrative as well as the political issues at stake. Of course, some of these agenda items were unattainable in the short term. How could there be compulsory attendance immediately if there were no schools in certain areas? His approach was certainly not dishonest, being completely up-front on the issue of costs: the NEL's programme 'would no longer rest on voluntaryism, it would rest on the national purse, and instead of hundreds of thousands of pounds being voted by Parliament, we should find that millions would have to be voted out of the rates and taxes for the education of the country'.[54] Dixon also identified that in certain circumstances, the Government was proposing that 'the minority would have to pay for the religious teaching of the majority', which would 'materially strengthen denominationalism'.

Then came a warning. 'It might be if this agitation should be continued for a lengthened period that a party would arise in this country with a great and growing influence that might ultimately prevail, which might demand that in every school aided by the government there should be exclusively secular education. This was not what he asked now; it was one of the possibilities of the future'.[55] This was an astute observation. If the government ministers had conceived that Dixon had proposed his Amendment as a means of destroying the Bill, they were wrong. Basically Dixon's agenda was to support the Bill as it stood, but with substantial modifications. Otherwise the world would move on, and the clamour would be for something much less acceptable to the government.

It was then time to elaborate on Dixon's own vision of the place of religion in the country's educational system. He stressed that the NEL comprised 'men of all creeds, and they [had come] to the conclusion to recommend to the country that education in our national schools should be unsectarian'. There were problems of definition, but to the NEL 'it meant that … there should be taught no creed, catechisms, or tenets that were peculiar to any sect; but no sooner had they furnished that answer than they received numberless questions as to what they meant about the Bible, and they answered that they were not prepared to ask for an Act to exclude from the schools only one book, and that book the Bible'.[56]

---

53 *Hansard*, Vol. 199, Col. 1919, 14 March 1870.
54 Ibid., Col. 1920.
55 Ibid., Col. 1922.
56 Ibid., Col. 1923.

The tightrope was getting ever more tricky. Certainly Dixon did not want any more religious instruction to be excluded from the schools than was absolutely necessary. 'The difference between an unsectarian and a secular system appeared to be this – that in both you would exclude all Christian dogmas, but in an unsectarian system you would not have to exclude Christian precepts. He had never been afraid of the bugbear about those awkward questions which exceptional children might put to a master asking the authority for such precepts; but if in the answer were involved the acknowledgment of a future state of existence or of a God, he still thought that would be unsectarian teaching'.[57]

Dixon was trying to appease all quarters. 'The League was assailed on both sides by the secularists and by the Churches'. The situation was not without considerable dangers, with a report from an Ulster school 'where reading the Bible after school hours was the only religious element, the boys would in the playground divide themselves into Bible and non-Bible boys, and pelt each other with stones; and even the girls took part in the affray'.[58] Dixon could speak with some authority on the subject of law and order – less than three years previously, his handling of the Murphy Riots in his capacity of Mayor of Birmingham had been the subject of Questions in the Commons on five separate days.[59]

Dixon aimed his next point squarely at Gladstone personally. Referring specifically to Clause 7 of the Bill, Dixon argued that many people believed that any Conscience Clause which allowed children to opt out of religious classes to which objection was taken would be inoperative. He pointed to the real prospect of 'fastening the teaching of religious dogmas upon every school in every district in which there was a dominant section', so that 'the children of the minority would be taught a religion to which the parents objected, and the minority would be forced to pay for the teaching of such doctrines'. 'Already the tocsin had been sounded and the forces were mustering; and it would be found that the Churches were on one side, and the Nonconformist bodies on the other'. 'It had already been whispered to him that if the clause should pass then, at every future election in the boroughs to be a Dissenter would be a qualification for a candidate, and to be a Churchman would be a disqualification in the eyes of the Liberal party'.[60] If that point were indeed true, his own position and that of Gladstone as Anglicans would both be in jeopardy. The point was not lost on Gladstone. Several days later, Kay-Shuttleworth referred to Dixon's fear. Moreover, *Hansard* reported that Gladstone exclaimed 'Hear, hear!', when Kay-Shuttleworth suggested that

---

57 Ibid..
58 Ibid., Col. 1924.
59 See above, Chapter 3, p. 81.
60 *Hansard*, Vol. 199, Col. 1925, 14 March 1870.

'In discussing this great question such matters, in his opinion, had better be left out'.[61]

Towards the end of his speech, Dixon highlighted the interests of the agricultural workers, with whom he was to start working so closely a few years later.[62] Elaborating on the weakness of the Conscience Clause, he suggested that 'Its inherent evil was that many parents would not dare to avail themselves of it; and it was not right in the agricultural districts to ask the people to say yes or no to this important question'.[63] He had little time for the employers of agricultural labourers, and did not mince his words when he later referred to them as being 'semi-feudal'.[64]

In winding up, Dixon acknowledged that he had taken 'the unusual and grave step of moving an Amendment to the second reading'.[65] He justified his action on the basis that the issues were so important that they could not be left till later. He pleaded that 'if he could only feel that the Government would deal with the religious difficulty in a manner more in accordance with the expectations of the Nonconformists, he should have the conviction that the Government would receive, as their well-merited award, a nation's gratitude'.[66]

On 18 March 1870, however, Dixon agreed to withdraw his Amendment after several days of intense debate. He had noted that Gladstone would consider sympathetically certain views expressed by Mundella, but without knowing for certain whether the religious clauses would be re-modelled.[67] Overall, Dixon concluded that: 'I do not think it will be supposed that in proposing it I have been doing anything that can be considered hostile to the Government....' [many would have differed on that point], and he ended with a final flourish 'I desire to add that, in my opinion, the result of the debate has fully vindicated me in the course I have taken'.[68] If by that he meant that he had been given adequate opportunity to ensure that the government knew the strength of public opinion, he was assuredly right. But Dixon was fortunate that his Amendment was never put to a vote, for in the next few months, he was frequently in a substantial minority.

Dixon had certainly furnished a comprehensive and measured summary of the League's overall position, without resorting to the flowery language of some of his parliamentary colleagues. Lowe, for example, likened the honourable

---

61 Ibid., Col. 2019.
62 See below, Chapter 5, p. 153.
63 *Hansard*, Vol. 199, Col. 1926, 14 March 1870.
64 See below, Chapter 5, p. 155.
65 *Hansard*, Vol. 199, Col. 1927, 14 March 1870.
66 Ibid., Col. 1928.
67 Gillian Sutherland described Gladstone's statement in the Commons on 18 March 1870 as being one of 'masterly vagueness': see G. Sutherland, *Policy-Making in Elementary Education* (Oxford, 1973), p. 120.
68 *Hansard*, Vol. 200, Col. 303, 18 March 1870.

Members [the Bill's critics] to a fine herd of cattle, which had tumbled into a bed of nettles. To that, William Harcourt[69] rejoined that the bed of nettles had been prepared for them by the herdsman, Gladstone.[70] Harcourt further suggested that the government had introduced a very dangerous commodity, religious nitro-glycerine, and proposed to export it to every parish in the country, to be experimented upon and handled by anybody who might happen to deal with it.[71]

Outside Westminster, there was much support for Dixon's approach. Lord Russell, for example, wrote to *The Times* acknowledging that the Dissenters did indeed have a point, and that Dixon's views 'underlined the complex, delicate and involved nature of the whole problem'.[72] There was also substantial support from J.S. Mill, in a speech at an NEL meeting in London on the same day.[73]

Too late for Forster's speech on 17 February, but in good time for the Amendment debate, the Fitch/Fearon Report, commissioned in the spring of 1869, had at last been published on 2 March.[74] On a key point – the accuracy of the figures produced by the BES, upon which Lord Montagu had earlier poured such scorn[75] – Dixon was completely vindicated. Fitch said of them: 'I judge from these that the enquiry thus made was conducted and recorded with scrupulous care and exactness, and without any desire to establish a foregone conclusion. … I regard the statistics collected by the Birmingham Education Aid [sic] Society as of the deepest significance, and eminently worthy of the attention of the House of Commons'.[76]

The BES remained a fundamentally impartial charitable body. That was evidenced in a statement in the Third Annual Report for the year to 31 March 1870: 'It is not for the Committee to give any opinion on the rival proposals which are now before the public, but they may justly congratulate the subscribers on having assisted to bring the educational question to a point at which a satisfactory settlement may now be hoped for'.[77]

The NEL was supporting the BES's criticisms of certain sections of society who were opposed to educational reform at the same time. The NEL *Monthly Paper* asked 'While the upper and middle classes get out-door relief in the form of gratuitous education at so many schools and colleges, what is the objection to giving free education to the poor?'[78]

---

69 For Sir William Vernon Harcourt (1827-1904), see *ODNB-online.*

70 *Hansard*, Vol. 200, Col. 213, 18 March 1870.

71 Ibid., Col. 215.

72 *The Times,* 25 March 1870, as cited in Raffell, 'Radical and Nonconformist Influences', p. 402.

73 Ibid., p. 405.

74 Ibid., p. 295.

75 See above, Chapter 2, p. 66.

76 [IoE], National Education League pamphlets Vol. 4, pamphlet 5, *Third Annual Report of Birmingham Education Society, 31 March 1870* (1870), p. 10.

77 Ibid..

78 *Monthly Paper,* May 1870, Question 9.

The Fitch/Fearon Report also identified a distinctive feature of Birmingham. Instead of the richer people being scattered around the town, nine-tenths lived in just one area, Edgbaston, but never far from the poor. This segregation had a pernicious effect in educational terms, for there was an abundance of voluntary Schools in two or three parishes, each benefiting from the existing 'Payment by Results' system. Elsewhere, in the absence of schools, there simply were no results, and hence no payments from central government.[79]

The BES Annual Report was starkly realistic in the spring of 1870. If a general scheme of elementary education were adopted by Parliament and brought into immediate operation, the work of the Society would now be of brief duration, but on that matter all is uncertainty. The Government Bill, as at present framed, could have no practical effect for two or three years. It is possible also that it may be withdrawn altogether. In either case, the necessity for the work which this Society aims to accomplish will continue for some time.[80]

The Report also made for depressing reading as to the limitations of its own ability to help. 931 children were so nearly unclad that it was considered useless to offer them School Orders;[81] whilst various reasons were given for non-attendance by those to whom Orders had been granted, including 331 at work, 319 who were wanting clothing, 212 who were ill, and 58 who, decisively, were dead. The litany went on.

The Third Annual Report of the Birmingham Education Society, 1870, contained the following statistics:

Total Number of Children to whom School Orders were granted	5226	
Number who used the Orders	3586	[68.6%]
Number by whom the Orders were not used	1640	[31.4%]
Number found still at School	1792	
Number found still at School – Fees paid by parents	10	

CAUSES WHY NOT AT SCHOOL

At work		331
Kept at home for housework		48
Dead	58	
In Workhouse	63	
In Reformatory	7	
In Orphanage	2	
In Blue Coat School	2	

79 R. Gregory, *Elementary Education* (1895), p. 117.
80 [IoE] *Third Annual Report of BES,* p. 13.
81 Ibid., p. 11.

Suffering from Illness	212	
Want of Clothing	<u>319</u>	663
Present address not to be found		1774
Not aware that Orders (which were granted for 3 months) could be renewed		114
Not to be found when Orders were delivered		71
Refused admittance, Schools being full		95
Discharged from Night Schools		155
Neglect of Parents		<u>173</u>	<u>3424</u>

Against this backdrop, the political arena was a strange contrast, at least to the world that was aware of the problems with which Dixon was contending. The NEL attracted 277,651 signatures to its March 1870 petitions.[82] At its 24 March meeting, the Executive Committee passed a resolution expressing satisfaction with the spirit of concession shown by Gladstone, but demanded again that 'no creed, catechism, or tenet peculiar to any sect shall be taught in schools under the management of School Boards, or receiving grants from local rates, and that in all other schools receiving Government aid the religious teaching shall be at a distinct time, either before or after ordinary school business, provision being made that attendance at such religious teaching shall not be compulsory, and that there shall be no disability for non-attendance'.[83]

The Liberal government was getting irritated. On 1 April, Forster wrote to Charles Kingsley, (historian and social reformer, author of *The Water-Babies,* a popular fairytale about the plight of a boy chimney-sweep)[84]: 'I wish parsons, Church and *other*, would all remember as much as you do that children are growing into savages while they are trying to prevent one another from helping them'.[85] Gladstone received a second deputation at Downing Street ten days later, this time from the Central Nonconformist Committee,[86] but until the end of May adopted a policy of silence, perceiving public opinion to be very confused.[87] Indeed, rumours were rife, including even one that the Bill might be withdrawn.[88] He then confided to his friend Lord Granville 'the subject of Education is so important and so arduous in regard to the "religious difficulty" '.[89]

---

82 Adams, *History of Elementary School Contest,* p. 220: there were only 18,822 signatures 'on the opposite side' [presumably the National Education Union], although Adams admitted that such figures were not conclusive.

83 Ibid..

84 For Charles Kingsley (1819-75), see *ODNB-online.*

85 Briggs, 'Introduction', p. xxix.

86 Ibid., p. xxxi; Adams, *History of Elementary School Contest,* p. 221.

87 Raffell, 'Radical and Nonconformist Influences', p. 409.

88 Adams, *History of Elementary School Contest,* p. 219.

89 Briggs, 'Introduction', p. xxxi: citing events on 30 May 1870.

Dixon meantime was finding favour in another quarter – the trade unions. Applegarth had almost since the inception of the NEL been in the forefront of union supporters, and in May the NEL published a pamphlet setting out his views, elaborating Dixon's own earlier case. The argument that the country needed better educated workmen to fight off foreign competition was fully accepted, but additionally 'education can and will do more than make them clever "hewers of wood and drawers of water" – that to be "complete men", and to enjoy life in its own most enlightened form, is what even working men may attain to'.[90] This concept of the 'complete man' was to remain a core part of Dixon's philosophy for years to follow.

Behind the scenes, Gladstone's government was planning its next step. On 13 May 1870, draft amendments were presented by Forster to the Cabinet (of which he was not yet a member). This was the first occasion when the Cowper-Temple Clause, the terms of which endured in educational history for decades, was discussed, but was not immediately introduced. It was to be a way forward, but its phraseology was tortuous: 'In all schools established by local rates, no catechism or religious formulary which was distinctive of any particular denomination should be taught'. In the event, the first round of official amendments was published a fortnight later, with three main provisions: where select vestries (which would otherwise have appointed the members of School Boards) were not popularly chosen, School Boards would be elected, using the ballot; a time-table Conscience Clause would be introduced for all schools receiving government or rate aid; and government inspectors would cease to examine religious teaching.[91]

These proposed changes were far from satisfying the NEL's wishes, for there was no reference to issues such as compulsion, nor free education. Hence it was clear to the Executive Committee that the public agitation needed to continue. Feelings were such that it was suggested that, if the NEL could not get what it wanted, it was desirable to postpone the legislation altogether.[92]

The response was to organise the only full Council meeting of the NEL in its entire eight-year history. It was held in London, and under Dixon's chairmanship. Its purpose was primarily presentational – a number of amendments had been introduced, but it was concluded that: 'It is desirable ... that a still more formal and impressive protest should be made'.[93] A history of the growth of the organisation was given: by now there were 138 branches; the *Monthly Paper* had a circulation of 25,000; numerous pamphlets, handbills, and other publications had been issued, amounting to some 800,000 copies;

---

90 [IoE], National Education League pamphlets Vol. 1, pamphlet 21 (May 1870) as reprinted from the *Sheffield Independent*.
91 Adams, *History of Elementary School Contest*, p. 223.
92 [IoE] *Statement of the Officers*, p. 2.
93 Ibid., p. 1.

and ordinary subscriptions were now very nearly £70,000, payable by annual 10% instalments. The latter would cover only Central Office and Branch Committee expenses, and there was a need for a further £10,000 Special Fund to extend the agitation. It was clear that the Executive Committee expected a long battle ahead.

Pamphlets written around this time heightened the tension. One made it clear that the NEL had agreed to the maintenance of two kinds of schools, denominational and national, only as a compromise. Now, 'Denominational education involves unjust monopoly in favour of one sect over a large part of the country; all conscience-clauses notwithstanding. ... It breeds Orangeism [support for the Irish Orange Order], Ribbonism [support for the Irish Ribbon Society], and sectarian bickerings in many forms. ... [It] is an anachronism; and Mr Forster, with a powerful Government behind him, needs little besides courage painlessly and pleasantly to extinguish it'.[94] Dixon may well have had such a plan in the very long term, but plainly in the short, if not the medium, term, this was impracticable, as the voluntary [and largely denominational] sector provided the majority of the existing educational infrastructure.

The following day, Gladstone presented what, in Disraeli's words, amounted to a new and entirely different Bill,[95] explaining that the Government had delayed as long as possible to enable as many opinions as possible to be expressed.[96] At one and the same time, Gladstone displayed examples of how he differed with Dixon, and how he agreed. On the one hand, Gladstone professed that he did not understand the meaning of the words 'undenominational' and 'sectarian'[97] – problems in the vocabulary of compromise over which Dixon himself had so often stumbled. On the other, Gladstone sought to address the concerns of the Catholics,[98] demonstrating, like Dixon, that he fully understood the controversy as one that existed in many dimensions. Here Dixon differed from some members of the NEL who tended to focus more exclusively on the divide between the Established Church, and Nonconformity. Gladstone, too, was professing a spirit of compromise: 'nothing except a general disposition to make sacrifices of cherished preferences, for the purpose of arriving at a common result, can enable us successfully to go through a work so difficult as that before us'.[99] The problem for Dixon would be whether the sacrifices would be sufficient to satisfy not only Radicals such as himself, but the host of Nonconformists behind him.

---

94 J. Leese, *Denominational Schools: Their Rights and Interests* (1870), p. 2.
95 Briggs, 'Introduction', p. xxxii.
96 *Hansard*, Vol. 202, Col. 266, 16 June 1870.
97 Ibid., Col. 268.
98 Ibid., Col. 278.
99 Ibid., Col. 267.

Dixon responded to the new draft legislation by calling for an adjournment, for further consideration of the position. His immediate concerns focused upon Gladstone's proposals to increase public grants to existing denominational schools by 50%, with a deadline of 31 December 1870 for applications, and upon the provision to permit the teaching of 'sectarianism, not only of twenty Churches, but of thousands of individuals'.[100] On this point, Dixon was supporting Disraeli, who had accused Gladstone of 'creating a new sacerdotal class' of schoolmasters.[101] There then followed no less than five days of debate on an Amendment tabled by Henry Richard, MP for Merthyr Tydfil, recorded in 265 pages of *Hansard*.[102] It proposed:

> That grants to existing denominational schools should not be increased, and that in any national system of elementary education the attendance should be everywhere compulsory, and the religious instruction should be supplied by voluntary efforts, and not out of the public funds.[103]

Richard himself was not a member of the NEL, but Dixon nonetheless supported his Amendment.[104] It was Dixon's second substantial speech in the course of the debate on the 1870 Bill, and was the clearest exposition of his views.

With a view no doubt to the overwhelming odds stacked against him,[105] Dixon had to justify his stance: 'The Amendment was not intended to catch the votes of the House; but to give an opportunity of expressing an opinion that the country might understand'.[106] As on a previous occasion, he was all too conscious that the act of opposing the detail of the proposals might frustrate his prime objectives. He understood Forster to have insinuated that the actions of Henry Richard and himself in putting forward the religious difficulty would keep the children of England uneducated for a further ten years. Yet Dixon could not understand such observations: 'They were, of all men, a portion of the most quiet and unobtrusive class'.[107] This comment was scarcely something that applied to some members of the NEL's Executive Committee.

Dixon also once again distanced himself from some of his followers: 'He was as tolerant of sects as any man. He had no prejudices against the

---

100 Ibid., Col. 293.
101 Adams, *History of Elementary School Contest,* p. 225.
102 Raffell, 'Radical and Nonconformist Influences', p. 430.
103 Adams, *History of Elementary School Contest,* p. 225.
104 *Hansard,* Vol. 202, Col. 799, 16 June 1870. Dixon did however have a tactical problem, for it was later said of Richard's speech 'Once more we are back in the seventeenth century': see Briggs, 'Introduction', p. xxxiv.
105 The amendment was defeated by 421 ayes to 61 noes: see Raffell, 'Radical and Nonconformist Influences', p. 437.
106 *Hansard,* Vol. 202, Col. 799, 16 June 1870.
107 Ibid., Col. 788.

Nonconformists, or in favour of them. He was not a Nonconformist himself'.[108] But it could scarcely be said that he spoke in punchy terms – 'He was not a religionist as contradistinguished to an educationist. He had no objects to serve apart from those that were involved in the education of the children of the country;'.[109]

But then Dixon got into his stride. On the subject of school attendance, he objected to the concept of 'permissive compulsion', with each district making up its mind on this subject. Whilst genuine compulsion would only happen in a few large towns, he feared that in the country agricultural labourers would oppose compulsion, because that would result in a withdrawal of part of the family income.[110] Given the immediate lack of schools in many areas, it might have been more sensible to have mentioned a target date for implementation, but this tactic was notably not mentioned throughout the debate.

These detailed concerns show how complex it was to create a national system from scratch. Later reforms were all simpler, in that the 1870 legislation provided, after many difficult debates, a starting-point.

Given the poverty which was all too abundant in certain areas in Birmingham, it was logical for Dixon to argue that compulsion, without addressing the parallel issue of free provision of schooling, would be tantamount to taxation, as poor parents were faced with the cost of schooling. Selective free provision would not work, he argued, on the basis that those parents unable to pay the school pence, would be pushed into becoming paupers. 'What they really preferred instead of it was that education should be made thoroughly national; that it should be under the control of the State; that it should be paid out of the national Exchequer'.[111] Little wonder that Dixon called himself an 'advanced Radical'. As if that were not enough, he went on: 'They [the people of the country] desired also that the middle-class schools, and even the Universities, should be opened free to all, without distinction of class, so that the poorest child might have the opportunity of obtaining advanced degrees in learning'.

This demand was most definitely not on the NEL's immediate agenda – the spirit of agitation was very much within him. It was not as if, to Dixon, the country could not afford the programme he outlined: 'The Government was rich, having an available surplus, which he suggested might be drawn upon for assisting the education of the masses of the people'.[112] Forster later disagreed, saying that the cost would be 'enormous', and adding that, if free primary education were offered, so secondary education would have to be

---

108 Ibid., Col. 795.
109 Ibid., Col. 789.
110 Ibid., Col. 791.
111 Ibid., Col. 792.
112 Ibid., Col. 793.

provided free too, although Forster did not explain why he came to that conclusion.[113]

In fact, a free and compulsory system emerged only in slow stages. Compulsion in England was introduced firstly with Sandon's Act in 1876, and then with Mundella's Act in 1880. Free education did not come until 1891, and even then the principle was not universally applied. The issues were deep-rooted. The Newcastle Commission in 1861 had reported: 'Almost all the evidence goes to show that though the offer of gratuitous education might be accepted by a certain proportion of the parents, it would in general be otherwise. The sentiment of independence is strong, and it is wounded by the offer of an absolutely gratuitous education'.[114] Other interpretations have been offered: some argued that a majority of the working classes could afford the school fees – indeed, if universal free education were not available, a stigma would be attached to those schools that did offer it. Furthermore, very few people indeed in 1870 conceived that the state itself had a duty to run an educational system from its own funds; an element of local funding was always assumed. 'To create a national system mainly out of the rates was to emphasise the parallel between education and poor relief'.[115] There were also those who held that free education would dangerously weaken parental authority. The belief was that, if the parents had to pay, they would be more concerned to ensure regular attendance.[116]

Ultimately, the NEL itself made a rod for its own back on this issue, on account of the religious difficulty. Since it failed to secure unsectarian education in the voluntary schools, it could not countenance the use of public money to compensate such schools for the income that would be lost by the abolition of fees.[117] It was therefore scarcely surprising that Dixon was defeated by 257 votes to 32 when the issue was the subject of a separate amendment at the Committee Stage, on 1 July.[118]

In his speech of 16 June, Dixon largely left the religious difficulty to other speakers, but he was quite clear as to the consequence of the new proposal to increase government grants to denominational schools by 50%. His warning was borne out by subsequent events, when there was a rush by the Voluntary sector to apply for grants before the deadline of 31 December 1870 expired. Dixon's fear was that, in areas without a large enough population to support two or more schools, the construction of a new denominational school would

---

113 E. Rich, *The Education Act 1870: A Study of Public Opinion* (1970), p. 90. For a fuller discussion of the meaning of the word 'secondary' at this time, see Chapter 6 below.

114 *Newcastle Commission Report* (1861), p. 73, quoted in E.G. West, *Education and the State: A Study in Political Economy* (1965), p. 170.

115 Rich, *Education Act,* p. 85.

116 Ibid., p. 92.

117 Sutherland, *Policy-Making,* p. 165.

118 Raffell, 'Radical and Nonconformist Influences', p. 441.

prevent the creation of an undenominational one.[119] However, the worst was over for the government, and for Forster in particular, with the significant victory in getting the Commons to reject the Amendment put forward by Henry Richard, MP for Merthyr.[120] But much detailed discussion remained at Committee Stage.

Through all these battles, Dixon attracted no strong personal enmity in London. But he remained a public figure of note: the *London Figaro* published a profile of him in June 1870, describing him as 'The General of those Dissenting Legions': Mr Dixon, like his predecessor, Mr Scholefield, was

> one of those quiet men with a purpose, who worked like warmth – noiseless, agreeable, and if so unusual a word is permissible – unbaffleable.
>
> Utterly unassailable in his own religious opinions – with a personal courtesy amounting to gentleness – and possessing a clear, generous, and honest quality of speech – he disarms hostility; or, better still, he does not awaken it. He excites neither suspicion nor distrust. The enemy must attack his proposals – they cannot the proposer. No invective on his part irritates them – no aspersion diverts public attention from the great principles to be fought out.
>
> He is minded to slay National Ignorance.
>
> In politics, he votes for equity in all things – for the political equality of men – the civil equality of women – for the equality of the elector at the polling booth, as the Ballot would secure it – for the representation of labour, as costless elections would make it possible – and against accumulation of landed property, the oldest and most prolific inequality of all.[121]

This was all very complimentary, and contrasted greatly with the reception that awaited Chamberlain when he was to arrive in the Commons six years later. The final paragraph is interesting, for during the course of 1870, whilst Dixon rose to speak in the Commons on very many occasions, all his speeches, with the sole exception of a trivial question on the minting of coinage,[122] were related to education. Evidently his voting behaviour was being noted: he was one of only 24 MPs who voted in favour of payment of Members;[123] and he was amongst a minority who voted for leave to bring in a Bill 'to relieve Lords Spiritual hereafter consecrated from attendance in Parliament'.[124]

---

119 *Hansard*, Vol. 202, Col. 796, 16 June 1870.
120 Raffell, 'Radical and Nonconformist Influences', p. 442.
121 Quoted in *BDP*, 22 June 1870.
122 *Hansard*, Vol. 201, Col. 273, 5 May 1870.
123 *BDP*, 7 Apr. 1870.
124 Ibid., 23 June 1870.

On 14 July 1870 there was a lengthy debate, with no less than fourteen divisions, on the issue of the manner of voting. Dixon fought for the secret ballot, but lost.[125] As on so many issues, he was somewhat ahead of his time: the secret ballot did not follow until 1872.

A few days later, the issue of who should elect members of School Boards was once again debated. The Bill as originally drafted contained provision for Town Councils to elect School Boards in municipal boroughs. The previous month Charles Dilke had resigned from the NEL over the issue of the Cowper-Temple Clause, and on 4 July 'as a guerrilla-fighter on the left … [Dilke] rose … to propose "that School Boards should in all cases be elected by the ratepayers" '.[126] This suggestion had initially been rejected, but was eventually accepted.

Yet Dixon opposed the idea, for three reasons. First, he disliked the turbulence and expense of a double set of contested elections in the wards. Second, it was felt that Town Councils would select a better class of men than the ratepayers, to whom it was too easy to appeal with cries of mere economy. Third, as suggested by one MP, against the backdrop of Town Councils being perceived as rather uninspiring institutions, 'The effect of imposing this duty on the Town Councils would be to raise the tone and character of these municipal bodies; … it would give them something more than matter of police to think of'.[127]

As if these issues were not enough, a further complication was also introduced. Lord Frederick Cavendish[128] proposed a system known as the cumulative vote. Immediately, in the words of the NEL's secretary 'Mr. Gladstone, with some impetuosity accepted on the part of the government'.[129] By this system, each voter was entitled to as many votes as there were seats to be filled, and the voter could 'plump' them (that is, restrict them to as few or as many) as they wished. In Birmingham, there were fifteen seats to fill on its School Board, and this rule was to have interesting consequences.[130]

In the background, those who opposed Gladstone's proposals were squabbling furiously. Mundella, whose name had been mentioned in the same breath as that of Dixon by Forster in such approving terms in February, was, by the time that the Bill had finished its passage through the Commons, writing to his friend Reader in Sheffield: 'There has been exceeding bitterness "sub rosa" on the Education question, Miall, Richard and Winterbotham uttering grievous things against Morley, Bright, Baines and all the moderate section, and much has passed that was downright uncharitable. Churchmen like myself

---

125 Raffell, 'Radical and Nonconformist Influences', p. 445.
126 Hennock, *Fit and Proper Persons*, p. 88.
127 Ibid..
128 For Lord Frederick Cavendish (1836–82), see *ODNB-online*.
129 Adams, *History of Elementary School Contest*, p. 227.
130 See below, Chapter 5, p. 138.

have been regarded with grave suspicion'.[131] Alas, no records survive to record how his fellow Churchman, Dixon, was feeling by this time. But if Dixon's hint to Gladstone[132] in March was anything to go by, he had been feeling uncomfortable for a while. Already there had been a fundamental division between Dixon and Mundella on the wisdom of seeking an Amendment on the Second Reading. Mundella took the view that the religious difficulty existed more within the House than out of it.[133] Yet Mundella, unlike Dixon, had been spared the problem of the NEL Executive Committee setting an agenda for him.

There were rifts everywhere. Amidst this confusion, somehow the infamous Clause 25 (whereby payments were made out of the rates to denominational schools) scraped through onto the Statute Book. It was clearly an oversight on the part of those who were otherwise scrutinising every detail with minute attention, and in Chamberlain's hands it was later to become the symbol of everything that was wrong with Forster's legislation, despite the very small sums of money involved. One educational historian later explained how the error came to pass: the original Clauses 23 and 25 had been taken together, the former providing for assistance out of the rates to existing (denominational for the most part) schools, a subject anathema to the NEL, whilst Clause 25 made similar provision, but in limited circumstances. Clause 23 having been deleted, the NEL had assumed, falsely, that Clause 25 would go as well.[134]

In the Commons, Dixon announced his intention to bring in an amending Bill the next session. In what were, for him, stern terms he announced: 'He thought it was a great disadvantage if not a positive evil, that those who had done so much to place the Government in the position which they now occupied should be accustomed to an attitude of opposition, and to make appeals which would be repeated to the great Liberal Party outside the House against the action of a Government which had hitherto received from them the most unvarying, loyal, and enthusiastic support'.[135] The enthusiasts for educational reform felt bruised and taken for granted – a state of mind that is not infrequently experienced by vanguard reformers.

For Dixon himself, his standing in Parliament had been changed by the bitter battles in the Commons. In the closing stages of the lengthy debate, Gladstone had spoken of him:

> I was very sorry to hear the Hon. Member for Birmingham issue a proclamation of war against it the moment it is about to pass. We shall be

---

131 Raffell, 'Radical and Nonconformist Influences', p. 442.
132 See above, Chapter 4, p. 121.
133 W.H.G. Armytage, *A.J. Mundella, 1825-97* (1951), p. 78.
134 Adams, *History of Elementary School Contest,* p. 227.
135 *Hansard,* Vol. 203, Col. 738, 22 July 1870.

compelled to put our trust in the good sense of the country. I must own I do not think the threatened blast of the trumpet will really rouse the land in opposition to the imperfections which mar such a measure as this. Far be it from me to say that this is a perfect measure.[136]

The mouthpiece of the rival National Education Union, the *Birmingham Daily Gazette,* was in gloating mood: 'This mighty regenerator of England's educational system found himself shivering in the lobby with a few score of avowed secularists – his [Dixon's] League in fragments, its work unaccomplished and its true principles discovered at last'.[137] How misconceived was this judgment in parts! The League was far from fragmented, and in the months that followed, it went from strength to strength. Even though there were secularists amongst its membership, they were not yet in the ascendancy. However, the newspaper did give credit where credit was due: the League's campaigning had laid the foundations for the Bill.

Of Dixon personally, it has been written: 'It is ironical that the League's founder, George Dixon, who had worked so tirelessly, if fanatically, should be observed in the guise of failure, when, in fact, his idea of universal elementary education was achieved'.[138] Dixon certainly did not portray himself a failure at the next Annual Meeting of the NEL, declaring realistically: 'unless there had been a League, in all probability there would have been little or no agitation on the question of education prior to the introduction of the Government Bill – while, if there had been no agitation, it was also extremely possible that there would have been no Bill'.[139]

Historically, the Act has been described as a compromise. It could scarcely have been otherwise, given the strength and variety of the views across the country. From Dixon's perspective, following his strategy of seeking to advance an inch by declaring that he wanted to advance a yard, it was a success. The most significant feature for him was the nationwide acceptance of the government's responsibility for the education of its people. The foundations had been laid for the later development of a system which would eventually become national, compulsory, non-sectarian, and free.

This success had been achieved despite the almost total lack of support from John Bright, Birmingham's senior MP. In the grand scheme of things, he 'did little enough for education'.[140] Some years after his death, one historian wrote cryptically of him: 'Mr Bright seldom remembered that he was in office except

---

136 Ibid., Col. 746, 22 July 1870.
137 13 July, 1870, as quoted in Raffell, 'Radical and Nonconformist Influences', p. 452.
138 Ibid., p. 451.
139 Meeting on 25 Oct. 1870, at Queen's Hotel, Birmingham: see Raffell, 'Radical and Nonconformist Influences', p. 464.
140 Vincent, *The Formation of the Liberal Party*, p. 194.

when he resigned'.[141] Whilst Bright was not well at the time, he managed to sit in the Liberal Cabinet to consider a Bill which made provision for permissive (but not absolute) compulsion, religious teaching in Board Schools, continuance of grants to Church schools, and even Clause 25. At the same time, 'he [Bright] saw no inconsistency in a Cabinet Minister taking up the policy of the Birmingham League, and patronising that Nonconformist revolt which had impaired the influence of Liberalism all over England'. However, his reputation as a campaigner against the Corn Laws and for parliamentary reform stood him in good stead to protect him from more vigorous criticisms.

Meantime, Joseph Chamberlain who was ultimately to be an even greater player on the Birmingham stage, but was still six years away from becoming an MP, took himself on holiday to Whitby. He wrote from there to Dixon: 'It [the Bill] is not National Education at all – it is a trick to strengthen the Church of England against the Liberation Society'.[142] He also feared that it was designed 'to pave the way for the *one* concession to Ireland which no English Parliament ought to make; and which, when made, will only prepare for that Repeal of the Union which I expect must come sooner or later. .... My feeling is that we must strengthen ourselves in the House of Commons at all risks. I would rather see a Tory Ministry in power than a Liberal Government truckling to Tory prejudices .... I expect to return to Birmingham in a week and bring my caravan (nine souls in all) back with me. Meanwhile, I hope to form a branch here and give the Prime Minister's son [William Henry Gladstone, MP for Whitby] some trouble at the next election'.[143] It was clear that Chamberlain, even at this early stage of his career, had a robustly more independent mind than most. It was also evident that the political arguments were far from over.

Dixon himself returned to Birmingham, ready to start implementing the provisions of the new legislation. His reputation at this stage in his life, now just turning the age of fifty, had reached its first peak some six months earlier, when Forster paid tribute to his campaigning skills. Since then it had not been seriously eroded in the course of the subsequent Parliamentary session. But the next six years would see a series of frustrations, amidst a number of diversions into other arenas, and the continuing education debates. 1870 was a great turning-point – but by no means a terminal one.

---

141 Paul, *A History of Modern England*, p. 317.
142 The Liberation Society was a pressure group campaigning for the disestablishment of the Church of England.
143 Garvin, *Chamberlain*, Vol. I, p. 118.

CHAPTER FIVE

Challenging Times 1870-76

W ITH ROYAL ASSENT granted in August 1870, and the spectre of war between France and Prussia looming just across the Channel, the focus of Dixon's involvement in the educational debate reverted to Birmingham itself. On the one hand, there was the urgent question of implementing the provisions of the new legislation, for which he had fought so hard for so long; and on the other, there was the continuing debate within the NEL, whose headquarters were based in the town, as to its future direction.

As ever, its history was turbulent, and became more so. Thus one local cleric wrote with a fair degree of irritation: 'Up to the passing of the Education Act he believed the labours of the League had been fraught with good, but since then they have been fraught with mischief, and had been a serious drawback to the spread of education'.[1]

The grounds for this assessment are revealed in the chapter that follows. And, as debates became more heated, so for Dixon personally, this moment marked the beginning of a steady deterioration in his relationship with Chamberlain.

---

1 *BDP,* 23 Oct. 1874.

With Dixon encouraging the Town Council to act, Birmingham was in the vanguard to form a School Board and to adopt compulsory bye-laws.[2] At the same time, the rush was on nationwide for the voluntary sector to apply for grants from the Government before the 31 December deadline. The spirit of competition was abroad, and in those areas of the country (mainly rural areas) which could not sustain more than one school, the formation of a denominational school to all intents and purposes precluded the formation of a non-denominational school; whilst in other areas, the driving force was the possibility that an insufficiency of educational provision would lead to the conclusion that a School Board school would have to be built to fill the gap.

This was an opportunity for the Birmingham School Board, of which Dixon was to be chairman for no less than twenty years from 1876 to 1896. The town's wealth, further assisted by Dixon's own philanthropy, enabled it to provide better and more up-to-date schools and to attract better teachers. At the same time, the impact of competition drove the costs of education higher and, as the old voluntary school buildings became more dilapidated, so the calls on the charitable sector increased.[3] In the final analysis, Board Schools simply had more resources upon which to call, and this provision enabled Birmingham under Dixon's control to be an innovator, pushing to the limits the meaning of the word 'Elementary' in Forster's Act.

On 7 September, the NEL's Executive Committee, under Chamberlain's chairmanship,[4] met to determine its own way forward, and passed a number of resolutions, which in effect would dictate Dixon's own future conduct in Parliament as the NEL's spokesman. The most significant of these were:

1. To assist in putting the Education Act in operation, so as to secure as far as possible, the establishment of unsectarian, compulsory, and free schools.

2. …

3. …

4. …

5. To influence public and Parliamentary opinion by meetings, publications, petitions, and all other available means in favour of a national, unsectarian, compulsory, and free system of education; and with this view to secure the return of members to the House of Commons pledged to support the principles advocated by the League.[5]

---

2 Adams, *History of Elementary School Contest,* p. 236.
3 Rich, *Education Act,* p. 100.
4 Garvin, *Chamberlain,* Vol. 1, p. 120.
5 [IoE] National Education League pamphlets Vol. 2, pamphlet 4, *Report of the Executive Committee Presented to the Members of the National Education League at Second Annual Meeting, Birmingham, 25 Oct. 1870* (1870), p. 8.

In parallel with this, Chamberlain also chaired a meeting of the Central Nonconformist Committee on 19 October, ominously declaring that 'the Committee were of opinion that they had previously been a little too moderate'. This group also set an agenda not dissimilar from that of the NEL. Nonetheless for the time being, the issue of secular (without religious teaching) as opposed to unsectarian (Bible-reading without note or explanation) education remained simmering just beneath the surface. As has already been emphasised, religious passions were not easily soothed.

Only nine months earlier, Dixon himself had written to *The Times* saying that 'The League might fairly be called the Reform or aggressive party…', indicating that moderation had never been contemplated.[6]

Dixon's speech as Chairman of the Council of the NEL at its Second Annual Meeting less than a week later was more measured, making the key point that 'They had gained an Education Act, which, notwithstanding its defects, would set the country in motion…'.[7]

It was at this meeting that an attempt was made to secure a significant change in the NEL's agenda, by substituting the word 'secular' for 'unsectarian' in the programme. The NEL had discussed this hot potato before. This time, Chamberlain led the resistance, on the pragmatic basis that 'the general body of subscribers were not prepared for it, and it would impair the efficiency of the organisation'.[8] This background debate did not help the Liberals in their election campaign for the School Board, where their unsectarian slogan was 'The Bible without note or comment'.[9] Indeed, it permitted the Church Party to declare that the true question was 'Bible or no Bible'.[10]

In that election, the Birmingham Liberals made a major mistake, which they were severely to regret for the next three years. Whilst at the General Election in 1868 they had maintained strict discipline and ensured that all their supporters voted as they were told,[11] and all three successful Parliamentary candidates were Liberals, in the School Board election of 1870 their self-confidence was such that they effectively left things to a free vote amongst their supporters. But, through spreading their votes, they secured only six seats out of the total of fifteen. The Church Party (led by Sargant, himself a Liberal, whilst Dixon himself, opposing him, was of course a Churchman) put forward only eight candidates, all of whom were returned, whilst the Catholic candidate – for whom the small Catholic population plumped nearly all their votes – came in as fifteenth out of the successful candidates.

---

6 *The Times,* 7 Jan. 1870.

7 Adams, *History of Elementary School Contest,* p. 239.

8 Ibid., p. 240: Garvin's version of events was more robust, recording that he said that secularism would 'break to pieces' the whole organisation: see Garvin, *Chamberlain,* Vol. 1, p. 121.

9 Cruickshank, *Church and State,* p. 38.

10 Adams, *History of Elementary School Contest,* p. 251.

11 See above, Chapter 3, p. 86.

TABLE ONE

SUPPORT SHOWN BY REFERENCE TO NUMBER OF VOTES

O'Sullivan, Very Rev. M (RC)	35,120 *
Lloyd, S.S	30,799 *
Burges, Rev. Dr.	21,925 *
Wilkinson, Rev. Dr.	19,829 *
Gough, J	17,481 *
Dale, Rev. F.S	17,465 *
Dawson, G	17,103 *
Dixon, MP, G	16,897 *
Dale, Dr. R.W	16,387 *
Vince, C	15,943 *
Hopkins, J.S	15,696 *
Sargant, W.L	15,683 *
Chamberlain, J	15,090 *
Wright, J.S	15,007 *
Elkington, A.J	14,925 *
Lloyd, G.B	14,642
Holland, Rev. H.W	14,359
Middlemore, W	14,332
Baker, G	14,101
Collings, J	13,873
Cooper, J.A	13,872
Crosskey, Rev. H.W	13,314
Sandford, Ven. J	13,202
Radford, W	12,515
Melson, Dr.	11,017
Kirkwood, D	7,095
Evans, Dr. S	5,351
Raffles, J	2,060

* = Successful candidate

TABLE TWO

SUPPORT SHOWN BY REFERENCE TO NUMBER OF VOTERS

Dixon, MP, G	14,435 *
Dale, Dr. R.W	14,394 *
Dawson, G	14,238 *
Vince, C	14,138 *
Chamberlain, J	13,861 *
Wright, J.S	13,567 *
Lloyd, G.B	13,461
Middlemore, W	13,446
Collings, J	13,432
Baker, G	13,399
Cooper, J.A	13,149
Holland, Rev. H.W	12,955
Crosskey, Rev. H.W	12,917
Sandford, Ven. J	12,790
Radford, W	12,284
Lloyd, S.S	11,134 *
Burges, Rev. Dr.	10,065 *
Wilkinson, Rev. Dr.	9,601 *
Dale, Rev. F.S	8,807 *
Sargant, W.L	8,520 *
Gough, J	8,461 *
Hopkins, J.S	8,344 *
Elkington, A.J	8,010 *
O'Sullivan, Very Rev. M (RC)	3,171 *
Melson, Dr.	2,651
Evans, Dr. S	2,002
Kirkwood, D	1032
Raffles, J	530

* = Successful candidate

TABLE THREE

VOTES WITHIN PARTIES

Party	Candidate	Voters	Ranking	Votes	Ranking
Liberal					
	Baker, G	13,399	10	14,101	10
*	Chamberlain, J	13,861	5	15,090	5
	Collings, J	13.432	9	13,873	11
	Cooper, J.A	13,149	11	13,872	12
	Crosskey, Rev. H.W	12,917	13	13,314	13
*	Dale, Dr. R.W	14,394	2	16,387	3
*	Dawson, G	14,238	3	17,103	1
*	Dixon, MP, G	14,435	1	16,897	2
	Holland, Rev. H.W	12,955	12	14,359	8
	Lloyd, G.B	13,461	7	14,642	7
	Middlemore, W	13,446	8	14,332	9
	Radford, W	12,284	15	12,515	15
	Sandford, Ven. J	12,790	14	13,202	14
*	Vince, C	14,138	4	15,943	4
*	Wright, J.S	13,567	6	15,007	6
Conservative					
*	Burges, Rev. Dr.	10,065	2	21,925	2
*	Dale, Rev. F.S	8,807	4	17,465	5
*	Elkington, A.J	8,010	8	14,925	8
*	Gough, J	8,461	6	17,481	4
*	Hopkins, J.S	8,344	7	15,696	6
*	Lloyd, S.S	11,134	1	30,799	1
*	Sargant, W.L	8,520	5	15,683	7
*	Wilkinson, Rev. Dr.	9,601	3	19,829	3
Outsiders					
	Evans, Dr. S	2,002		5,351	
	Melson, Dr.	2,651		11,017	
*	O'Sullivan, Very Rev. M (RC)	3171		35,120	
	Kirkwood, D	1032		7,095	
	Raffles, J	530		2,060	

* = Successful candidate

The two opposing groups in the first School Board did not, however, split neatly along traditional national party lines. The winning Church grouping in 1870 campaigned in the name of the 'Committee of friends of Scripture Education',[12] and over the years Dixon's NEL grouping usually campaigned as 'Liberals' (an arrangement continued even later when many were in fact joining the Liberal Unionists in national politics) or 'Secular'. The other group opposing the Liberals was termed variously as 'Conservative', 'Church', 'Scripture', or 'Denominational'. There was consistently one Roman Catholic candidate, always successful, and a scattering of Independents.[13]

Not surprisingly, there was total uproar amongst the Liberals as to the outcome in 1870 – not least because the winning party overall had attracted a significantly smaller number of supporters. The NEL shortly thereafter published a pamphlet, *The Cumulative Method of Voting: Its Nature, Operation and Effects as Exhibited in the late School Board elections,*[14] in which it vented its outrage. For Dixon personally, on the face of it, the outcome was a triumph – by a narrow margin, he had attracted votes from a larger number of electors than any other candidate. By contrast, to Chamberlain's undoubted chagrin, the number of votes plumped for him was such that he came thirteenth in terms of the number of votes cast.[15]

Dixon sought to have the issue of cumulative voting addressed in Parliament in the following Session, through the introduction of his own Bill. He was opposed, however, by some members of his own League, 'who belonged to the school of philosophic Radicals, and who were anxious to experiment in forms of proportionate representation'.[16] The Bill was withdrawn without a division.

Performing his parliamentary duties in London, well removed from his power base in the Midlands, entailed living in rented accommodation during the season from February through to August. For a couple of years, the family rented 16 Cromwell Place, just opposite South Kensington Station.[17] In 1870, the family rented the Fire-Proof House, so called for its experimental fire-proofing, at the top of Putney Hill, on the edge of Wimbledon Common.[18] In 1871, they rented the Boltons in South Kensington, immediately opposite

---

12 Taylor, 'Birmingham Movement', p. 160.
13 For full details of School Board election results, see A.F. Taylor, 'The History of the Birmingham School Board, 1870–1903' (Unpub. M.A. thesis, University of Birmingham, 1955).
14 [IoE] National Education League pamphlets Vol. 2, pamphlet 6, *The Cumulative Method of Voting: Its Nature, Operation and Effects as Exhibited in the Late School Board Elections* (n.d.).
15 Garvin, *Chamberlain,* Vol. 1, p. 123. It is interesting to note that in the elections in which Dixon and Chamberlain stood together under the cumulative voting system, Dixon always secured more votes than did Chamberlain. However, to what extent this accurately reflects more support for Dixon personally than for Chamberlain must be subject to substantial reservations.
16 Adams, *History of Elementary School Contest,* p. 251.
17 Rathbone, *The Dales,* p. 52.
18 Ibid., p. 54. The house was built in 1772-3 to demonstrate a system for preventing fire from spreading within a building; only a monument in the form of an obelisk, still stands: see D. Gerhold, *Villas and Mansions of Roehampton and Putney Heath* (Wandsworth, 1997), p. 67.

a church with a very loud bell.[19] And for the following five years, until Dixon applied for the Chiltern Hundreds, they took unfurnished accommodation at 46 Queen's Gate, also in Kensington. Not only did the family accompany George, but so did the carriage and horses, and a cow to make sure of good milk for the youngest child, Dora, born in 1871.[20] Additionally, within months of being elected, he had become a member of the Reform Club, his proposer being Stansfeld, and he remained a member until death.[21]

Socially, the family initially found itself a little isolated, although the Stansfeld family were in nearby Thurloe Square. Years later, after their respective wives had died within months of each other,[22] Dixon and Stansfeld began to share accommodation during the Parliamentary season, and this physical proximity almost certainly drastically reduced, if not obviated any need for correspondence between them. Just as there is no surviving correspondence between Dixon and George Cadbury, for the same reason, so with Dixon and Stansfeld.[23]

James's wife Caroline[24] laughed at Dixon's 'countrified and provincial ways' and the huge landau,[25] nicknamed the Ark. Despite Caroline's reservations about her relative by marriage, Caroline and Mary Dixon went shopping together, 'otherwise London life would have been very boring for Mary'.[26] Social life for George also appeared to be something of an uphill struggle too, as apparently he found 'the Parliamentary people he thought he ought to cultivate rather stodgy'.[27]

Katie also wrote about her mother Mary, that she 'had a delightful way of keeping my father in order and mothering him, and I thought that really, if any sex had the lead it was the female!'[28]

When the family moved to the suburbs of Putney in 1870,[29] they were near to the Rathbones. Just as Dixon was spending exhausting days in the Commons, his daughter Katie was playing marbles on the staircase,[30] or

---

19 Rathbone, *The Dales*, p. 55.
20 Ibid., p. 56.
21 The author wishes to thank Simon Blundell, Reform Club Librarian, for this information.
22 See below Chapter 6, p. 202.
23 There is no reference at all to his brother-in-law in J.L. Hammond, *James Stansfeld: A Victorian Champion of Sex Equality* (1932).
24 For Caroline Stansfeld, née Ashurst (1815-85), see J. Slinn, *Ashurst Morris Crisp: A Radical Firm* (1997), p. 5. Through this legal connection, Stansfeld enjoyed close contact with father William Ashurst's Radical enthusiasms, in favour of the co-operative movement, the political and social enfranchisement of women, the abolition of slavery in America, and the liberation of Italy. Hence the connection with Mazzini: see Stansfeld obituary in *The Times*, 18 Feb. 1898.
25 Birmingham Archives and Heritage, File MS 2239, Bundle 2, p. 44.
26 Ibid., p. 45.
27 Ibid..
28 Ibid., p. 29.
29 Rathbone, *The Dales*, p. 96.
30 Ibid., p. 54.

walking on Wimbledon Common.[31] Aerated bread had just become popular, and there were jars of blackcurrant jam on the shelves.

There were fairly frequent reports of illness, and when they moved to the Boltons, 'an unhealthy place, they all fell ill',[32] suffering from whooping cough. Thus it was only in 1872, in Dixon's fifth Parliamentary session, that any degree of permanence was established, at 46 Queen's Gate.

The family coped with these vicissitudes with a varying degree of equanimity. Katie's powers of observation were as astute as had been Charlotte Brontë's in a previous generation: 'my father was a perfect saint for never losing his temper, or even wanting to…'. By contrast, her mother could be hot-blooded.[33] Nor was the younger generation unduly perturbed by the niceties of social conventions: attending a Foreign Office reception where all the girls wore white, and Katie and her elder sister Maggie did not, the former mused, 'How were they to know? All the same I wasn't going to let any old duchess barge me out of her way, and stood firm'.[34]

Meantime, in 1871, George's elder brother Abraham Dixon moved south for the sake of his health to Cherkley Court, located in the Mole Valley between Leatherhead and Dorking. This substantial house had been rebuilt by Abraham in the years following its acquisition from Overend, Gurney & Co., which collapsed spectacularly in 1866.[35] It had a prominent site on the North Downs, not far from the site where was to be fought the fictional Battle of Dorking.[36] This event was imagined by one George Chesney, an army officer in the Royal Engineers. To the considerable consternation of the publication's readers, the ill-prepared British forces were defeated on the North Downs around Dorking by an invading Prussian army. The country became a province of Germany. If George Dixon had been warning of the dangers of increased German competition as a reason for improving English elementary education, Abraham Dixon would most certainly have been feeling that he was potentially in the front line of a military threat.[37]

Back in London, Dixon was not just 'the Hon. Member for Birmingham'; for a number of years he was 'THE Hon. Member for Birmingham'. The

---

31 This was a year before the area was regulated by the passage of the Wimbledon and Putney Commons Act in 1871.

32 Birmingham Archives and Heritage, File MS 2239, Bundle 2, p. 51.

33 Ibid., p. 10.

34 Ibid..

35 J.W. Dixon, 'Abraham Dixon's Involvement with Leatherhead: An Update', *Proceedings of the Leatherhead & District Local History Society*, 6 (2006), p. 289. See above, Chapter 2, p. 57.

36 G. Chesney, 'The Battle of Dorking', *Blackwood's Magazine* (1871), was the first of a new genre of science fiction in which a newly victorious German army invaded England.

37 George Dixon's own view was expressed in the course of a debate on Army Estimates, when he said that 'he did not believe in the probability of any invasion from abroad': *Hansard*, Vol. 205, Col. 494, 23 March 1871. In arguing for any increase in the Estimates, it would of course have been in the interests of Birmingham's armaments industry, but the prospect of substantially increased government expenditure on education was looming.

senior Member, John Bright, was for some years incapacitated by illness, and the third Member, Muntz, made very little contribution to the educational debate. However, such was Dixon's vexed relationship with Chamberlain and the NEL National Executive that he was becoming more of a delegate than a representative.

Thus the Third Annual Meeting of the NEL held in Birmingham in October 1871 passed a resolution calling for Dixon to give notice of a Commons motion in the following terms:[38]

That in the opinion of this House, the provisions of the Elementary Education Act are defective, and its working unsatisfactory, inasmuch as:

1. It fails to secure the general election of School Boards in towns and rural districts.
2. It does not render obligatory the attendance of children at school.
3. It deals in a partial and irregular manner with the remission and payment of school fees by School Boards.
4. It allows School Boards to pay fees, out of rates levied upon the community, to denominational schools, over which the ratepayers have no control.
5. It permits School Boards to use the money of the ratepayers for the purpose of imparting dogmatic religious instruction in schools established by Local Boards.
6. By the concession of these permissive powers, it provokes religious discord throughout the country; and by the exercise of them it violates the rights of conscience.

Dixon duly gave notice of this motion on 5 March 1872,[39] and it was a process that was repeated for the next few years.

On the other hand, there was a gulf fixed between him and the most vocal of his supporters on the all-important issue of religion. Time and again he had to remind the Commons of this fact, and only some ten weeks before he stood down as an MP in 1876 he referred to the Nonconformist difficulty as one which 'is not my difficulty, because I am not a Nonconformist, but I am closely allied to the Nonconformists, and I know what their feelings are upon this subject'.[40] The over-arching problem remained that Nonconformists emphatically did not want Anglicanism being taught to their children, especially if such teaching was financed through taxation. In one respect, though, Dixon's Anglicanism

38 [IoE] National Education League pamphlets Vol. 2, pamphlet 18, *Report of the Executive Committee Presented to the Third Annual Meeting, 17/18 Oct. 1871* (1871).
39 *Hansard*, Vol. 209, Col. 1395, 5 March 1872.
40 Ibid., Vol. 228, Col. 262, 5 April 1876.

was of advantage to the NEL, for it enabled the pressure group to present itself as being slightly less 'politically Nonconformist' than might otherwise have been the case.

Outside the confines of the educational debate, Dixon had very much a mind of his own. Having got into the habit of rebellion during the course of 1870, he continued in the spring of 1871. He notably participated in a Budget revolt on the specific issue of the proposed tax of a halfpenny on every box of Lucifer matches – and here he found success, leading a rebel party to join forces with the Conservatives.[41] It was a substantial defeat for Gladstone's government and the reputation of his Chancellor of the Exchequer, Robert Lowe, never recovered.[42]

In Birmingham, meanwhile, regular meetings of the Birmingham School Board now began. In the course of time they attracted not only intense local interest, but ultimately national notoriety. Always packed, meetings of the Board were likened to the Black Hole of Calcutta,[43] for there was from the start an inbuilt tension: the majority of eight members had been elected, however imperfectly, by a minority of the local population, and were dependent on funding from the Town Council, which had been elected by the majority. For Chamberlain, playing on such a public stage, this was a remarkable opportunity. In the course of a year, he had emerged from almost total obscurity, and there was nobody in the provinces to overshadow him – Dixon now being preoccupied with parliamentary concerns in London.

Within a couple of months of the inception of the School Board, there was controversy: mention was made of the payment of money out of the rates to Denominational Schools, with Chamberlain moving an amendment, seconded by Dixon, to the effect that this was 'an infringement of the rights of conscience'.[44]

This issue, best known as the 'Clause 25' controversy[45], centred on a piece of legislation which had somehow slipped on to the Statute Book. Seemingly an oversight,[46] it offended against the principle of no state investment in denominationalism. Significant amendments had been made to Forster's original Bill in the course of debate, but the principle endured in circumstances where there was no practical alternative but to send poor children to denominational schools which charged fees. Through some eyes, it was

---

41 Taylor, 'Birmingham Movement', p. 178.
42 R.C.K. Ensor, *England, 1870-1914* (Oxford, 1936), p. 20.
43 Taylor, 'Birmingham Movement', p. 168.
44 Birmingham Archives and Heritage, School Board Minutes, File SB/B1/1/1, p. 33.
45 Technically, the Clause became a Section after the passage of the 1870 Act, but the NEL preferred to talk of the 'Clause', and this word is used hereafter.
46 Years later, Dale confirmed this to be the case: the Clause had not attracted any opposition during debate. 'For once their "watchful jealousy" slumbered; they did not anticipate how it would work': see R.W. Dale, 'The Nonconformists and the Education Policy of the Government', *Contemporary Review* (Sept. 1873), p. 651.

possible to conceive this arrangement as a new form of Church-Rate, which had been abolished only a few years previously.[47]

Clause 25 came to be the symbol of the whole controversy between National and Sectarian education. Yet the sums were trifling, for in the year 1872 the total expenditure across the nation under this heading was just £5,070, of which £3,405 was expended in Manchester and Salford alone.[48] Contemporaneously, John Morley, then a Liberal journalist, described it as 'the smallest ditch in which two great political armies ever engaged in civil war'.[49]

What Dixon said, or rather, what he did not say on the issue was revealing. In Parliament he said very little, seemingly wishing to be disassociated from the controversy, and indeed in later years others were tasked to seek the repeal of the legislation. On 12 July 1871, he said in the course of debate 'he was certainly not in favour of constant strife on the subject of religion'. Then he revealed the bigger threat: 'The disestablishment of the English Church was a subject which would be kept permanently before the country ...'. So there would be agitation and opposition to Church institutions, 'that would hasten the great catastrophe which hon. Gentlemen opposite so much dreaded'.[50]

At the same time, it must have been unnerving for Dixon that already in 1871 there were those who supported the idea of Chamberlain standing for Parliament. Implicit in Chamberlain's public response to a speech at an 1871 meeting of the temperance movement, the United Kingdom Alliance, was the premise that he should represent Birmingham: he 'expressed his belief in the truth, honour, loyalty and good faith in Mr Dixon, ... yet he said that even he could not go into the House of Commons except by pushing his friend Mr Dixon out, [and] he would never go'.[51]

Chamberlain was beginning to make his mark in debates of the Birmingham School Board, and was also displaying his organisational talents, for the NEL was steadily expanding, with 150 new branches opened in the year to October 1871, when was held the Third Annual Meeting.[52]

At that meeting, Dixon left his audience in no doubt as to the antipathy to the government's support of denominationalism: 'the reports which the Officers of the League receive from all parts of the country induce me to believe that forces are now silently gathering which will undermine the power of the strongest Government, and overthrow the political fabric of the most time-honoured of Churches'.[53] For good measure, Dr. Dale added his voice to the Clause 25

47 Adams, *History of Elementary School Contest*, p. 258.
48 Murphy, *Education Act*, p. 72.
49 Cruickshank, *Church and State*, p. 42.
50 *Hansard*, Vol. 207, Col. 1529, 12 July 1871.
51 *BDP*, 22 Nov. 1871.
52 [IoE] National Education League pamphlets Vol. 2, pamphlet 17, *Report of the Executive Committee Presented to the Third Annual Meeting, 17/18 Oct. 1871* (1871), p. 11.
53 Adams, *History of Elementary School Contest*, p. 267.

controversy: 'This may lead to the breaking up of the Liberal party. When the Liberal party is false to its noblest principles, it is time that it should be broken up'.[54]

Around the same time, Dixon became embroiled in another issue where the fabric of the state was being questioned: the size of the annual grant to the monarch and her family for the performance of state duties, the Civil List. On such an issue, it was in the blood that he would take a radical stance. Charlotte Brontë in her portrayal of Dixon's uncle, Joshua Taylor (Hiram Yorke in *Shirley*) had clearly described the prudent Yorkshire lineage from which he was drawn, whilst Dixon's own brother-in-law, James Stansfeld, Financial Secretary to the Treasury, also had a strong belief in economy. In 1862, Stansfeld had moved a resolution in favour of a reduction in national expenditure, which had been rejected by 367 votes to 65.[55]

That the issue should have come to a head at around this time was triggered by a growing discontent with the failure of the Queen to perform many public duties, and the amount of public money expended on the wider royal circle, including the Prince of Wales. The Liberal-Whig historian G.O. Trevelyan[56] wrote a pamphlet demanding *What does she do with it?*[57]. And a great rash of Republican clubs sprang up around the country. Chamberlain was a member of the Birmingham one, his support being described as 'moderate in substance, but abrasive in expression'.[58]

In January 1871, a meeting of the working-class organisation, the Labour Representation League highlighted some of the detail. Dissatisfaction was expressed that Princess Louise was given a dowry of £30,000, as well as £8,000 a year from the Civil List, upon her marriage to the Marquis of Lorne. The Lord High Falconer was in receipt of a sinecure of £2,000 a year, yet he was only 18 months old.[59]

A few days later, Dixon and Muntz attended the annual meeting of their electors, Bright being absent due to ill-health. Dixon, supported by Muntz, did not oppose the granting of the dowry. There was uproar: 'an exciting scene ensued'.[60]

Away from the heat of the meeting, Dixon sought to defend his position. He agreed that there was need for economy, but noted that the Marquis of Lorne was, like him, an advanced Liberal, and supported the NEL. In any event, the Queen was being progressive in allowing her daughter to marry a subject.[61]

---

54 Ibid., p. 273.
55 *The Times,* 18 Feb. 1898: obituary.
56 For Sir George Trevelyan (1838-1928), see *ODNB-online.*
57 R. Jenkins, *Sir Charles Dilke: A Victorian Tragedy* (1958), p. 68.
58 Marsh, *Chamberlain,* p. 59.
59 *BDP,* 23 Jan. 1871.
60 Ibid., 31 Jan. 1871.
61 Ibid., 4 Feb. 1871.

Yet the issue preyed upon Dixon, for less than six months later, he began to ask a series of questions of Gladstone in the Commons.[62] Initially, he sought that inquiries be instituted into the appropriation of the Charges on the Civil List, to which Gladstone somewhat testily replied that 'we have no time to make' such inquiries.[63]

A week later, Dixon grew somewhat bolder. 'I must express my regret that there is not a working man present among us to state the views of his class upon the subject'.[64] Then, 'if there is one danger in this country greater than another, it is the existence, side by side, of these enormous incomes and that poverty which we are all so much in the habit of deploring, and seeking to remove'.[65] Finally, for good measure, Dixon did not deny that there was a large amount of republicanism, and that it was increasing – but it was of the vaguest possible kind. They felt that republican institutions would be less costly than Monarchy.

This implication was a ploy he had used to good effect in educational debates: he might deny that he was a Nonconformist, or a Republican, but there was the insinuation that unless his audience listened to him, forces less moderate than he would be unleashed '… there were millions of hard-working men engaged in a desperate hand-to-hand struggle with pauperism'.[66] '… I believe that if the people perceive a disposition on their part to practise economy in high places as well as low places, we shall be more likely to see a return of that loyalty among the working classes of this country which every hon. Member desires should exist'.[67]

As these examples showed, Dixon also expressed strong views on the issue of class. In December 1871, an advertisement appeared in the local paper, advising that Dixon was due to speak at a conference on the reform of the House of Lords, where he was due to propose the resolution: 'The hereditary principle in legislation is unwise, since it neither ensures wisdom in the individual, nor patriotism in the body; and is unjust, since it confers upon a class powers which ought to be exercised only by representatives of the nation'.[68] This resolution clearly showed that Dixon had few sympathies with the Establishment.

With Parliament in recess for the rest of the year, in those critical months Dilke delivered some very robust speeches on the subject, and the Prince of Wales fell seriously ill, with the same illness that had killed Prince Albert a decade or so earlier. In January 1872, however, he recovered. Public opinion, volatile as it has often shown itself to be in matters relating to the Royal Family,

---

62 *Hansard,* Vol. 207, 13 July 1871, Col. 1624; Ibid., Vol. 208, 24 July 1871, Col. 156; Ibid., 31 July 1871, Col. 583.
63 Ibid., Vol. 208, 24 July 1871, Col. 158.
64 Ibid., 31 July 1871, Col. 583.
65 Ibid., Col. 584.
66 Ibid., Col. 586.
67 Ibid., Col. 587.
68 *BDP,* 2 Dec. 1871.

swung dramatically in favour of those who only a few months earlier had been the subject of much disfavour.

Clearly there was a need for Dixon to re-assess his priorities: was he to jeopardise public support for the cause which was to be his life-long passion, education, by continuing to take the line which Dilke was now leading? Or should he follow the line taken by many of his fellow Radicals, and go to ground for the time being?[69]

It is a great pity that the record of what happened next is so badly chronicled. Dilke seemingly wrote to Dixon in late December 1871 saying that he intended to press a motion in the Commons on the issue. Dixon replied in early January:

> My mind has been a good deal exercised respecting the motion. I gave notice of a Committee on the Civil List, and as it was originally suggested to me by Trevelyan I consulted him on the subject. Indeed I had previously asked him to move it, and the whole matter was under consideration.
>
> The position of the question is now much altered – and you have so completely identified yourself with it, that we have come to the conclusion that our best course will be to leave it in your hands.
>
> I have never felt that I was the best man to take up such a question – though I still retain my old feeling that it ought to be taken up by someone: after the excitement caused by your speeches, there will be less chance of success, and it may be worth consideration whether it would not be prudent to wait for another Parliament.
>
> But of course I shall go into the lobby with you if you divide the house.
> With good wishes for the New Year.
> I remain. Yours faithfully,
> George Dixon.[70]

To which has been added a postscript, in different handwriting (probably that of Charles Dilke): ' *'Of course' he did nothing of the kind'* – for when it came to a division in the Commons, the voting was 276 to 2, and Dixon was not one of the defiant 2. As a result, Dilke became something of a social outcast in London society.

This episode brings to mind the young Charlotte Brontë's verdict upon Dixon as a man 'apparently constructed without a back-bone'.[71] Dixon had done not just one but two U-turns (the first having been his lack of opposition to the granting of a dowry to Princess Louise). But to have supported Dilke against the backdrop of the substantial swing in public opinion would have

---

69 Fawcett was actually to oppose Dilke's stance in Parliament, refusing 'to link the lofty ideals of republicanism with a mere haggling over a few pounds': see Nicholls, *Lost Prime Minister,* p. 56.
70 British Library, Gladstone Correspondence files, MS 43909, f. 241.
71 See above, Chapter 1, p. 23.

been severely to jeopardise Dixon's chief cause. Furthermore, there is also the suggestion that Gertrude Tuckwell, Dilke's first biographer (and niece), excised material so as to portray her uncle in the most favourable possible light.[72] Of what might have been excised in this particular instance can only be a matter for speculation. Perhaps Dixon had warned Dilke in the previous few weeks that his conduct was foolhardy?

In essence, Dixon in politics was Mr Compromise himself. Throughout the 1870s he was involved in arbitration in one way or another. When the lockouts in agriculture in eastern England in 1874 were causing great distress to the members of the National Agricultural Labourers' Union, it was Dixon who was in the forefront seeking a solution.

The first major arena in which he had advocated the concept was in early 1871, as the Franco-Prussian War was raging. Addressing his constituents, he suggested that 'England should join other nations, and encourage other nations to join her in elevating law above force'. He went on to suggest that there should be a Council of Nations in Europe.[73]

The esteem in which Dixon was held was shown in 1874 when he presided over a meeting of the Midland International Arbitration Union. He argued that, with more than 2,000,000 men under arms in Europe, more than £100 million of extra wealth would be created if these armies were abolished. Wars were made by governments, he explained, and the governments often consisted of just one individual; by settling disputes through arbitration, the people of the world would increase enormously their material interests, and 'raise their moral and intellectual natures'.[74] It was a line of thought that harmonised well with Dixon's support for free trade, itself a powerful force for peace.

Dixon's views on the drink question were yet again very much middle-of-the-road. Here there was a clear conflict between his two relatives who were also Liberal MPs. On the one hand, his brother-in-law Stansfeld owned the Swan Brewery in Fulham. On the other, Rathbone in Liverpool was a supporter of the temperance movement. Dixon's position was one of compromise – a position that is sometimes more difficult to hold than being firmly in one or other camp. An example of his fence-sitting was his address to his constituents just before the start of the new Parliamentary season in 1871. Dixon declared that he was going to support the proposed Licensing Bill, where he agreed with the objectives of the UK Alliance, but not with some of the detail of its proposals. He was sympathetic to legislation which would enable licences to be withheld from public houses which promoted and encouraged excessive drinking.[75]

---

72 Nicholls, *Lost Prime Minister*, p. ix.
73 *BDP*, 31 Jan. 1871.
74 Ibid., 9 May 1874.
75 Ibid., 31 Jan. 1871.

Meantime, back in the Birmingham School Board, Chamberlain was devising a new strategy. From 1869, NEL policy had been in favour of unsectarian religious education. Adams as Secretary of the League described the backdrop: 'The School Boards were the arenas in which solemn questions of religion and delicate matters of doctrine were made the shuttlecock of debate. No better device could have been imagined for encouraging a spirit of irreverence. … The doctrines of the Trinity, the Atonement, the Inspiration of Scripture, of Eternal Punishment, of the Actual Presence, became subjects of debate'.[76] In this arena, Chamberlain publicly quizzed teachers on appointment on subjects such as the teaching of the Trinity and the Atonement, in order to demonstrate from the variety of their interpretations the futility of trying to secure undenominational teaching.[77] One of the key weaknesses of the NEL's early adherence to 'unsectarian' teaching was difficulty of interpretation of its meaning. Whatever that meaning, 'undenominational' teaching was taken to be the same.

Nationally, Chamberlain's bizarre behaviour attracted much sharp criticism: the *Daily Telegraph* suggested that as Birmingham had a Bull Ring, it should use it for future interviews of candidates for posts in its schools.[78] Working closely with Dr. Dale, who had led a large conference of Nonconformists convened to debate the subject,[79] Chamberlain now argued for ending the Board's existing policy that the Bible should be read and taught daily. Instead, he proposed that religious teaching should be left to the various denominations, outside core school hours.

To what extent Dixon was involved in the change of policy is totally unclear, but it was sudden. As late as November 1871 he had been writing to Earl Russell to assure him that the League did not favour secularism,[80] but this stance could have been either because he was then 'toeing the line', or because he had been left in the dark.

The arguments went on and on, and Dixon was hard put to see a way forward in finding a compromise that did not entirely cost him his credibility.

In the Birmingham School Board, no less than four separate days were given over to debating the topic of religious instruction in Board Schools, spread over a period of eight weeks.[81] Dixon's performance was totally unconvincing. He confessed that he would not have addressed the meeting but for the suggestion that there had been a change of direction.[82] He confirmed that the Liberal

---

76 Adams, *History of Elementary School Contest,* p. 252.
77 Cruickshank, *Church and State,* p. 44.
78 Taylor, 'Birmingham Movement', p. 196.
79 Marsh, *Chamberlain,* p. 52.
80 Taylor, 'Birmingham Movement', p. 186.
81 [IoE] National Education League pamphlets Vol. 2, pamphlet 32, *Religious Instruction in Board Schools* (1872).
82 Ibid., p. 65.

minority continued to support the policy of Bible-reading without note or comment, 'so long as their present term of office, which was three years, lasted'. However, he recognised that this policy had led 'to those very discussions and heart-burnings which they had always honestly desired to avoid', so 'they now thought it would be much better if there was now an entire separation' between religious and other teaching.[83] He went on to plead that the change was 'a very small change', on the grounds that the majority on the Board thought that mere reading of the Bible was a mockery in any event.

The Liberals were not to win control of the School Board until the following year, and the Minutes of that series of 1872 meetings recorded the votes of just 14 members. Dixon 'was absent, attending an important meeting at St. Helens'.[84] Given that the nature of the 'important meeting' was not specified, it is tempting to suggest that this excuse was no more than a pretext to avoid becoming embroiled in the debate any further. Again, he had significantly failed to make his own views abundantly clear.

Dixon was far from being preoccupied with educational issues at this time, for the plight of the agricultural workers was giving cause for concern. At first sight, it might appear strange that an advanced Radical MP, representing one of the largest towns in the country, should take such a passionate interest in the affairs of the countryside. But the position should be seen against the backdrop of significant unemployment in the countryside and consequent migration of agricultural labourers into the towns, where they increased competition for often scarce jobs. Dixon was not alone in this regard: his close Birmingham colleague, Jesse Collings, for example, is best remembered by the nickname 'Three Acres and a Cow', advocating policies to keep the labourers on the land.

As a young man, George Dixon and his elder brother Abraham had frequently taken rides in the adjoining countryside.[85] In his thirties, the younger brother had a prolonged period living in the rural environment of the antipodes, where he had first hand experience of the opportunities that awaited those who had the initiative to make the long and often perilous journey half way round the world.

Living conditions in the countryside were often more wretched even than those in the towns, and if emigration was too daunting a challenge, then migration into the towns was ostensibly an easier alternative. Those already living there were distinctly unenthusiastic about having their own problems made worse, although as many were themselves recent migrants from the country, they had many friends and relatives who still lived there. The strength of support for their rural brethren was exemplified by the demonstration

---

83 Ibid., p. 67.
84 Ibid., p. 77.
85 See above, Chapter 1, p. 20.

backing striking labourers that took place in Manchester in 1874, when 300,000 people took part.[86]

Geographically isolated the agricultural workers might have been, but recent changes in the law were to come to their assistance. The *Hornby versus Close* judgment of 1867 had thrown the legal status of trade unions into considerable doubt,[87] but after a Royal Commission, the Trade Union Act of 1871 was passed. Dixon had made it clear on earlier occasions that he was supportive of trade unions in general, but he was not willing to oppose some of the government's measures relating to criminal clauses with penalties.[88]

The first proposal for the formation of a National Union of Agricultural Workers was made by Canon Girdlestone at a meeting of the British Association in Norwich in 1868.[89] There were some prospects for success with the new legislation in place: better communications in the 1860s meant closer links between branches, and news and newspapers (and expressions of support) could easily reach the labourers;[90] whilst the fact that they had been neglected by the 1867 Reform Act gave them a bond of unity, stiffened by Nonconformist resolve, a factor emerging from the parallel protests of the League. Indeed, the backbone of the movement was Nonconformist, with an element of millenarianism.[91] Taylor, secretary of the National Agricultural Labourers Union (NALU), said that it 'had a higher and nobler aim than that of increasing the wages of the labourers; it aimed at raising them intellectually, morally and politically'.[92]

Into this world Dixon made his first move in late 1871 when he was invited to Brampton Bryan, to chair a meeting of the North Herefordshire and South Shropshire Agricultural Labourers Improvement Society, whose watchword was 'emigration, migration, but not strikes'. Dixon 'promised liberal aid to a fund which it proposed to raise to enable some of the men to emigrate'.[93] This union was the first large-scale, more than local, organisation, and the moving spirit was the vicar of the village.

A few months later, the NALU was formed in Warwickshire amidst a general revival of unionism.[94] Its leader was Joseph Arch, who himself declared that he had been inspired by the speeches of John Bright.[95] The movement

86 O.J. Dunlop, *The Farm Labourer: The Story of a Modern Problem* (1913), p. 161.

87 H. Browne, *The Rise of British Trade Unions* (1979), p. 44.

88 W.H. Fraser, *Trade Unions and Society: The Struggle for Acceptance, 1850-80* (1974), p. 160.

89 F.G. Heath, *The English Peasantry* (1874), p. 189.

90 Browne, *Rise of British Trade Unions,* p. 61.

91 A belief in a coming major transformation of society.

92 J.P.D. Dunbabin, ' "The Revolt of the Field": The Agricultural Labourers' Movement in the 1870s', *Past and Present*, 26 (1963), p. 69.

93 *Loughborough Advertiser*, 14 Dec. 1871, as quoted in P. Horn, *Joseph Arch, 1826–1919: The Farm Workers' Leader* (Kineton, 1971), p. 19.

94 Dunlop, *Farm Labourer,* p. 146.

95 R. Quinault, 'John Bright and Joseph Chamberlain', *Historical Journal*, 28 (1985), p. 632.

appealed to middle-class Radicalism, for it was in opposition to Tory farmers and landowners.[96] For Dixon, this might indeed have been a factor, for by his normally exceptionally mild and moderate standards, his speeches on occasion took on a distinctly robust hue. Whilst there may well have been a calculation that by helping to secure an extension of the franchise he was thereby aiding the Liberal cause in the long term, what does shine through as events unfolded is a genuine sense of philanthropy for a sector of the population for whom there seemed little hope.

Along with Mundella, Dixon sent a letter of support to a preliminary meeting of the NALU in Leamington Spa on 29 March 1872.[97] Chamberlain, Collings and Wright were also named as supporters.[98] Dixon himself was invited to preside over the inaugural meeting a couple of months later.[99] The *Daily News* sent the 'famous' war correspondent Archibald Forbes[100] to report on proceedings, whilst Arch recorded in his autobiography: 'A labourers' friend at Birmingham sent us a donation of £100, through Mr Dixon, MP. When this was announced there was a tremendous outburst of cheering, and, when a note from the unknown friend was read out, the cheering was louder than ever'.[101]

Dixon was realistic: 'this conference is a commencement of a very great work, which will take all your energies, and all your patience and tolerance; and not only yours, but also those of the men who come after you, for the work which you have undertaken will not be completed in this generation'.[102] Evidently his efforts were appreciated, as he was invited to chair the second conference a year later. By then, he was able to announce the establishment of 23 district unions, with 982 branches, covering 24 counties, and with 71,835 members.[103] This rapid growth was achieved despite the fact that Dixon was not able to devote as much time as he would have wished to their cause, for which he apologised. His devotion to the cause was appreciated despite the verbosity of some of his sayings. What did the farm labourers make of the following sentence: 'he was not sure that there would not be an advantage in their not being united in one body'?[104]

Generally, Dixon urged a measure of caution, for labourers would be getting rid of a 'semi-feudal and semi-parental relationship' and replacing it with a commercial one. He urged the provision of better allotments; he mentioned

---

96 Fraser, *Trade Unions*, p. 96.
97 Horn, *Joseph Arch*, p. 55.
98 Ibid., p. 52.
99 *BDP*, 27 May 1872.
100 Dixon and Forbes evidently got on well, as Forbes was Dixon's guest some years later when Forbes visited Birmingham to talk about the Russo-Turkish War: see *BDP*, 23 April 1878.
101 J. Arch, *The Story of His Life* (1898), p. 51.
102 Bob Scarth, *We'll All be Union Men: The Story of Joseph Arch and his Union* (Coventry, 1998), p. 20.
103 Ibid., p. 26.
104 *BDP*, 29 May 1873.

the benefits of education; and he extolled the benefits of emigration. He spoke highly of Canada, Australia and New Zealand: having referred to the dread of going across the seas, 'if any portion of those extensive countries could be possibly detached and tacked on to Land's End, so that emigrants had only to pass over a bridge to gain possession, thousands and thousands would leave and go over at once...'.[105] He had a message for the farmers and landlords: 'put aside all those old-fashioned notions about looking after your labourers, and treating them as you do your cattle – look upon them as men, and place them in a position of independence, and take care that they shall be educated, so that they will be able to do your work better, with better machinery'.

There was an immediate task to be accomplished: he must press for an extension of the franchise, and a few weeks later was to be found speaking in the Commons in favour of the Household Franchise (Counties) Bill,[106] having presented a petition from 80,000 farm labourers.[107] It was all to no immediate avail, however, and farm labourers had to wait a further eleven years until the passage of the Third Reform Bill under Gladstone's government in 1884.

Years later, a Conservative MP who represented a nearby rural constituency, described his dislike of 'Birmingham's' involvement in rural affairs: 'I felt a righteous hatred for the demagogues who come out of Birmingham at election time, black-coated, gamp-umbrellaed [sic], cotton-gloved à la Stiggins, and interfered with the farm hands. This they called farmyard canvassing'.[108] In the context, the writer may have been describing events after the 1884 Act had come into force, but the description is of a man very similar to Dixon. From Dixon's point of view, the dislike was almost certainly mutual.

The spring of 1874 saw industrial relations between farmers and labourers deteriorate further, with widespread lock-outs in Lincolnshire and East Anglia; Dixon acted as secretary of the London Relief Committee and was given a mandate by the NALU to mediate a settlement. Whilst in East Anglia attempts at mediation were rejected out of hand by the farmers, there was more success in Lincolnshire, where the farmers agreed on union recognition, in return for the dropping of a claim for a minimum wage of eighteen shillings per week.[109]

Dixon had tried hard to improve the lot of the agricultural labourer, and there was little to show by way of achievement. However, contact with Arch and his colleagues may well have influenced him in a different course of action. One such colleague was Arthur Clayden, who in 1879 was to give a lecture entitled *The England of the Pacific: Or New Zealand as an English middle-class emigration*

---

105 A. Clayden, *The Revolt of the Field* (1874), p. 160.
106 *Hansard*, Vol. 217, Col. 830, 23 July 1873.
107 Arch, *Story of his Life*, p. 101.
108 J.A. Bridges, *Reminiscences of a Country Politician* (1906), p. 127.
109 Scarth, *We'll All be Union Men*, p. 46.

field.[110] In the course of his delivery, he said 'I shall experience a new joy in life if I am able to induce English capitalists to make it possible for tens of thousands of working classes to go out and realise its bliss'. Was this the spark that was to ignite George Dixon and his elder brother Abraham into incorporating the Dixon Investment Company six years later?[111]

As a Radical, George Dixon also supported moves to lift some of the disabilities upon women. He supported protecting the property of married women, and opposed the ban on marriage with a deceased wife's sister.[112] Just over a year later, he presented a petition to the Commons in favour of the removal of the electoral disabilities facing women.[113] Moreover, just as his brother-in-law James Stansfeld provided frequent support for Dixon's educational campaigning, Dixon provided consistent support for Stansfeld's campaigning on the Contagious Diseases Act.

Shared family interests did not end there. Cousin Mary Taylor had now returned from New Zealand, and was beginning to make a name for herself as a writer of articles, with a collection published in 1870 as *The First Duty of Women*.[114] There is no evidence of any contact between Dixon and Mary in these years, but they certainly shared one great enthusiasm, walking in the mountains.[115] Such diversions must have come as a welcome relief from his travails in the battle for educational reform in Parliament, for the 1872 session was to be described as 'a dismal one'.[116]

Dixon's focus was, as it was to remain for the next four years, upon the issues of universal School Boards and compulsion. However, he did on occasion enter the fray on the vexed question of Clause 25. Here, he threatened the government with the troops behind him. Unless Clause 25 were amended or repealed that Session, 'the grievance would increase, and every one would admit that Birmingham knew how to make the most of a grievance'.[117] All too well they did. Beresford Hope, MP for the University of Cambridge, responded:

> The hon. Gentleman, in effect, said – "We Nonconformists [overlooking the fact that Dixon was an Anglican] give you on the Treasury bench notice that you exist – not 'for the benefit of the Liberal party,'" for that party includes Churchmen as well as Nonconformists, nor even "for the benefit

---

110 A. Clayden, *The England of the Pacific: Or, New Zealand as an English Middle-Class Emigration Field* (1879), p. 13.
111 See below, Chapter 7, p. 203.
112 *BDP,* 31 Jan. 1871.
113 Ibid., 30 April 1872.
114 J. Bellamy, *'More Precious than Rubies': Mary Taylor: Friend of Charlotte Brontë, Strong-Minded Woman* (Beverley, 2002), p. 82.
115 Mary Taylor led a walking party of four lady friends to Switzerland in 1874, an account of which was published anonymously a year later as Anon., *Swiss Notes by Five Ladies* (1875).
116 Adams, *History of Elementary School Contest,* p. 287.
117 *Hansard,* Vol. 210, Col. 1727, 23 April 1872.

of Nonconformists", for they number among them a great many earnest religious men who respect the rights of conscience; but – "You exist for us, a select committee of political Nonconformists, sitting somewhere in Birmingham – Birmingham, which knows so well how to make itself disagreeable – and if you do not act as our small political clique tells you, you will soon know the reason why".[118]

The machinations of Chamberlain and his close colleagues were certainly beginning to make themselves felt in Westminster.

By the following winter, *The Times* was publishing a rather disdainful view of Dixon's position in an editorial: 'What strikes us most in Mr Dixon is the complacency with which he goes on repeating commonplaces, the shallowness of which has been exposed over and over again... Mr Dixon is an excellent man, a worthy man, but he belongs to a type very well-known, and more liked as friends than followed as leaders'. It then went on to accuse him of following the Birmingham headquarters and echoing its very words.[119] Indeed, it was certainly true that Dixon had proposed a motion in Parliament that had been agreed, word for word, at the previous autumn's NEL annual meeting. And members of the Conservative opposition expressed irritation with the manner in which he appeared to lecture to them, on matters with which they were already familiar.

1873 was the last full year in which Gladstone's Liberal government was in power. The NEL's objectives were now to urge compulsion. 'The power of enforcing this attendance, and of expending the money of the ratepayers, cannot be entrusted to irresponsible or self-elected bodies, but must be provided for by the establishment of fairly elected School Boards in every district of the country'.[120]

On the question of how much educational reform was going to cost, nobody could accuse Dixon of not being honest, nor did it seem that such honesty cost him unpopularity. His colleague George Kenrick, speaking more than a third of a century later, specifically dates 1873 as the year in which Dixon pronounced: 'There is no greater loss of wealth to a country than an uneducated people; never therefore let the idea of economy come between you and a high class and universal education'. A year later, he went further, supporting high rates and in almost Biblical terms said: 'Whatever we are called upon to pay we shall receive

---

118 Ibid., Col. 1734.
119 Reprinted in *BDP*, 18 Jan. 1873. The fact that material of this nature was being published in the *BDP* at this time was a foretaste of its support for Chamberlain in his quest to succeed Dixon as a Birmingham MP in 1876.
120 [IoE] National Education League pamphlets Vol. 3, pamphlet 5, outlining policy following the Fourth Annual Meeting (1873). Clause 25 remained firmly on the agenda as always: see Adams, *History of Elementary School Contest*, p. 290.

back again'.[121] But Dixon stayed clear on the precise detail of costs, and thereby avoided any criticism of being found wrong on that account.

1873 was a year in which the Liberal government was to come to a head-on clash with its Nonconformist supporters. And Bright re-emerged onto the political scene, proclaiming the 1870 Act as 'the worst Act passed by a Liberal Government since the Reform Bill of 1832'.[122]

Right at the beginning of the session, the government introduced its Agricultural Children Bill, providing for compulsion, albeit indirect.[123] Dixon did not support this measure, on the basis that it would be ineffective.[124]

7 March 1873 was provisionally booked for the introduction of Dixon's own NEL-inspired measure, but Gladstone appealed to him to postpone it until the government brought in its provisions.[125] Dixon agreed, but he was then faced with new government thinking on the subject of Clause 25: the fees of children of indigent parents should be paid by Boards of Guardians rather than by the School Boards. The NEL objected, pointing out that contests then confined to School Boards would be extended to Boards of Guardians. Dixon promptly led a deputation to see Gladstone. For once, their criticism was taken on board, and the proposal did not long survive, in the short term.[126]

The government's proposals on what Dixon had hoped would be the substantive issues, universal school boards, compulsion, and the repeal of Clause 25, were, when they came, a 'slap in the face'.[127] The Executive Committee of the NEL met on 23 June, strongly objecting.[128] Indeed, at a meeting of the Central Nonconformist Committee three days later, Dr. Dale pronounced that 'the government and the Nonconformists have for some time parted company'.[129] On 1 July, Dixon chaired a joint conference of the NEL and the Central Nonconformist Committee[130] (possibly the only time when Dixon came into direct contact with the latter body) at the Westminster Palace Hotel.[131] In the ensuing Commons debate, Dixon was in a quandary, his difficulty concerning children in rural areas, where there was a predominance of Church schools. In the long run, the education of such children might 'be

---

121 Kenrick, 'Dixon', p. 67.
122 [IoE] National Education League pamphlets Vol. 4, pamphlet 13, *Report of the Executive Committee Presented to the Members of the National Education League at Fifth Annual Meeting, Birmingham, 23 Oct. 1873* (1873), p. 9.
123 The essence of indirect compulsion was that children could not be employed if they were of an age when they should have been at school, subject to certain exemptions. Direct compulsion by contrast implied enforcement of attendance by a designated authority.
124 *Hansard*, Vol. 214, Col. 698, 19 Feb. 1873.
125 [IoE] National Education League pamphlets Vol. 4, pamphlet 13, p. 7.
126 Ibid., p. 5.
127 Marsh, *Chamberlain*, p. 55.
128 [IoE] National Education League pamphlets Vol. 4, pamphlet 13, p. 8.
129 Ibid., pamphlet 9, p. 3.
130 Garvin, *Chamberlain*, Vol. I, p. 138.
131 [IoE] National Education League pamphlets Vol. 4, pamphlet 13, p. 8.

placed in the hands of those who had confessed their own incompetency', but at the same time he did not wish to oppose a measure introduced for the purpose of educating a large number of then neglected children.[132] In the event, he abstained from voting. He could scarcely have done otherwise.

Around the same time there was also the unpleasant episode of the Bath by-election, which hit the headlines not only on account of the eventual outcome, but also because of the degree of violence which emerged: cayenne pepper was hurled at the NEL's candidate Cox, who was nearly thrown out of a window. Cox agreed to withdraw his candidature after the Liberal candidate Hayter agreed to support the aims of the NEL. But the damage was done: the Liberals were divided, so that the Tory won by 51 votes.[133]

Dixon certainly had an inkling of the controversial nature of the NEL's strategy of fielding its own candidates in by-elections. Mundella, always on the fringes of the NEL, but sharing above all else the objective of compulsion, wrote to a colleague in Sheffield on 20 June: 'I appealed to Dixon to stop Cox's proceedings at Bath, but he is weak and powerless. Chamberlain and the fanatics have the mastery, and mean to gratify their vanity and magnify their importance by showing their power to do mischief'.[134]

Shortly after, the Executive Committee of the NEL decided to suspend its electoral policy, purportedly because Gladstone had asked Bright to re-enter the Cabinet, and it was considered best not to jeopardise efforts on behalf of education reform.[135] Nonetheless, this excuse may have been no more than a pretext, as there is evidence that the NEL had exhausted its resources.[136]

Around this time, Dr. Dale entered the fray, perhaps conscious that not only were School Board elections due before the end of the year, but also a General Election at a date yet to be fixed. Dixon would be a candidate in both. Perceiving that Dixon's image needed some support, Dr. Dale leapt to his defence, making it crystal clear in a significant article[137] that Dixon was a Churchman who had 'been thrown very much among the Nonconformists. … Except on one occasion, I never heard of his being present at a Nonconformist service. He has contributed largely, and within very recent years, to the building of churches; he has never contributed to the building of chapels. [Whilst] he believes that disestablishment would be an act of political justice … he has never been present at a meeting of the Liberation Society'.[138]

---

132 *Hansard*, Vol. 217, Col. 575, 17 July 1873.
133 Taylor, 'Birmingham Movement', p. 215.
134 Armytage, *Mundella,* p. 130.
135 [IoE] National Education League pamphlets Vol. 4, pamphlet 13, p. 11.
136 P. Auspos, 'Radicalism, Pressure Groups, and Party Politics', *Journal of British Studies*, 20 (1980), p. 195.
137 Dale, 'The Nonconformists', p. 643 et seq.
138 Dr. Dale also stressed the number of other Anglicans in the upper echelons of the NEL; in fact, only four out of the eight executive officers were Nonconformists: see Marsh, *Chamberlain,* p. 39.

The Dales, Augustus Road, Birmingham.

A TOUGH JOB

Gladstone's favourite hobby was tree-felling. Following the split in the Liberal party over Irish Home Rule, he is depicted attacking the Birmingham Liberal Unionist tree, but spares the highly esteemed Bright tree in the background. By courtesy of the Birmingham and Midland Institute.

Cherkley Court, near Leatherhead, Surrey.

A late nineteenth century postcard of Cherkley Court.

Both George and Abraham Dixon were keen gardeners. Inside the huge Conservatory at Cherkley Court stands an unidentified young man, probably a family member. By courtesy of Hugh Lohan.

The obelisk that stands beside the slip road from the A3 at Tibbets Corner, Putney Hill, all that remains of the Fireproof House.

The distinctive tower of a School Board school. By courtesy of Joe Holyoak.

THE WOLF & THE LAMB

A cartoon which appeared in The Dart during the spat between Chamberlain and Dixon in 1878. By courtesy of the Birmingham and Midland Institute.

THE COVENTRY COACH

Mr J–S–PH CH–MB–RL–N (Reading a Telegram from Birmingham):– "George Dixon has carried his motion for a New Code of Morality." He exclaims "Oh! and has it come to this? A Brummagam Bible! Oh, Horror! Oh, Tempora! Oh, Moses! Oh, why did I ever leave the Chair of the Board!

There was widespread working class support for Dixon in his clash with Chamberlain in 1878. Euphemistically, Chamberlain was being sent to Coventry. By courtesy of the Birmingham and Midland Institute.

Dixon's proposals for moral education were the first stage in the abandonment of Chamberlain's earlier policy of secular education. By courtesy of the Birmingham and Midland Institute.

THE BELL WETHER OR FOLLOW MY LEADER

With Dixon alongside him, John Skirrow Wright leaps into the fold of those who favoured Bible-reading. By courtesy of the Birmingham and Midland Institute.

Again with Dixon alongside him, Wright confirms that Bible-reading is now permissible. By courtesy of the Birmingham and Midland Institute.

A BOARD SCHOOL BOY *(with Bible)* "Please Sir, may Master read the bible to us?"
Mr. J.S.W. – "Yes my lad, NOW he may."

There was a view that it should have been Chamberlain rather than Dixon who apologised for the Aston Park riot of 1884. By courtesy of the Birmingham and Midland Institute.

EATING THE LEEK.

JOSEPH:– It's got to be eaten George. I shan't do it, so you had better George, there's a good boy. [George does as he's told].

Prominent Birmingham politicians in 1886. Extract of original cartoon. Reproduced with the permission of Birmingham Libraries & Archives.

A POLITICAL BEAUTY SHOW.

OLD FACES: NEW PHASES.
[MR. GEO. DIXON, M.P., THE FATHER
OF FREE EDUCATION.]

A view of Dixon's role in the introduction
of free education. Reproduced with the
permission of Birmingham Libraries &
Archives.

THE TOWN CRIER

Chamberlain confirms a change of heart in
supporting the voluntary sector of education.
Reproduced with the permission of Birmingham
Libraries & Archives.

Close to the M6 stands the joint headstone of
George and his wife Mary Dixon on the left, whilst
that of his elder sister Mary is on the right. Witton
Cemetery.

Plaque on the wall of the George Dixon
International School and Sixth Form
College.

Dixon had to go more and more his own way in order to ensure his own political survival. Chamberlain was certainly not going down the same road. For him stretched forth a broader highway, built on a Free Church, Free Land, Free Schools and Free Labour.[139] His scheme was to organise a pool of candidates, known as the Irreconcileables. They were 'determined to smash up this gigantic sham called a Liberal Party and to secure organisation on a new basis'.[140] He had justified his strategy in a letter to Morley in August 1873,[141] shortly after the decision to 'suspend' the NEL's electoral policy: 'I have long felt that there is not force in the Education question to make it the sole fighting issue for our friends … the assistance of the working classes is not to be looked for without much extension of the argument'.[142] Dixon was plainly not of the same mindset.

In the dying days of the first Birmingham School Board, tensions were rising. Across the nation, distraints were being levied on goods belonging to all manner of people who were protesting against Clause 25.[143] The problem had not yet arisen in Birmingham itself, of course, because the School Board had come to an agreement with the Town Council not to use any part of the precept to pay fees.[144] But the agreement was for one year only, and in 1873 the School Board returned to the fray. The Town Council once more refused, so the Board applied to the High Court for a writ of *mandamus*, which it duly won, thus giving them powers of enforcement.[145] The victory was however a hollow one. With the threat of riots,[146] the Court order was not enforced, elections being imminent.[147]

The autumn of 1873 saw the second triennial School Board elections. The Birmingham Liberals were far better organised than they had been the first time around, having appointed Francis Schnadhorst[148] to manage them. No longer was there the complacency of 1870, in which the lack of discipline had led to just six Liberal candidates being elected, a minority of the total. Just eight candidates' names were put forward for the 15 seats. Initially, Dixon indicated some reluctance to stand because of a potential conflict with his Parliamentary duties. But he eventually agreed to continue on the basis that his membership would give him a valuable insight into the workings of the Boards. However he was crystal clear that his favoured option was not secular education, as then

---

139 Respectively, these were the campaigns for disestablishment, reform of Land Laws, NEL objectives, and freedom of workmen to combine in trade unions: see Read, *The English Provinces*, p. 175.
140 Auspos, 'Radicalism', p. 192.
141 For John Morley (1838-1923), see *ODNB-online*. At the time, he was editor of the *Fortnightly Review*.
142 Garvin, *Chamberlain*, Vol. 1, p. 146: letter dated 19 Aug. 1873.
143 Adams, *History of Elementary School Contest*, p. 295.
144 Taylor, 'Birmingham Movement', p. 188.
145 Cruickshank, *Church and State*, p. 43.
146 Taylor, 'Birmingham Movement', p. 192.
147 Garvin, *Chamberlain* Vol. 1, p. 126.
148 For Francis Schnadhorst (1840-1900), see *ODNB-online*.

advocated by Chamberlain and others, but Bible-reading without explanation, on the basis that secular teachers were not sufficiently qualified to elaborate on the message of the Bible.[149]

John Bright, who was returning to better health, advised Chamberlain to abandon the call for secular education, observing that 'on a clear issue of excluding the Bible from the schools I suspect you would be beaten in Birmingham'.[150] And just beaten he was. Among the Liberals, for what the figures were worth, Dixon led with 39,447 votes, and Chamberlain came second with 38,901.[151] *The Daily Telegraph* described Dixon as the 'veteran Reformer', and the outcome overall as 'remarkable'.[152]

Nonetheless, as the new Chairman of the School Board, Chamberlain moved fast to effect changes. Amongst other things, teachers were now forbidden to give any religious teaching whatsoever, or even to hold the usual assembly to begin the day with a hymn and a prayer.[153] Religious education was now to be given out of school hours and not by the schools' teachers. This secular experiment lasted just six years, from 1873 to 1879. But it failed, through a combination of factors, including the refusal of the Anglicans to participate, divisions of opinion among the Nonconformists, and the incompetence of the inadequate number of experienced instructors.[154] This failure was an embarrassment in the Liberals' heartland, and it ultimately needed Dixon to retrieve the situation.[155]

As 1873 drew to a close, expectations were mounting as to the date of a General Election, and when it was announced in January 1874, the timing took all parties by surprise.[156] The NEL was ill prepared, although out of 425 Liberal candidates in England and Wales, over 300 had pledged their support for the repeal of Clause 25.[157] Gladstone by contrast had earlier disquieted Chamberlain by speaking locally in favour of the voluntary school in Hawarden, close to his country retreat at Hawarden Castle in north Wales. He added that 'the parish should exert itself to the utmost to close the gap and prevent the formation of a School Board'.[158] By this comment, Gladstone was clearly hoping that the voluntary sector would expand the provision of elementary education

---

149 *BDP*, 8 Oct. 1873.

150 Quinault, 'Bright and Chamberlain', p. 630.

151 *BDP*, 19 Nov. 1873.

152 *BDP*, 21 Nov. 1873.

153 Taylor, 'Birmingham Movement', p. 201.

154 J. Murphy, *The Education Act 1870* (Newton Abbot, 1972), p. 71. Of 15,690 children in Board schools in 1876, religious instruction could be given to only 9,354: see Dale, *Life of Dale*, p. 480.

155 See below, Chapter 6, p. 188 et seq.

156 [IoE] National Education League pamphlets Vol. 4, pamphlet 26, *Report of the Executive Committee Presented to the Members of the National Education League at Sixth Annual Meeting, Birmingham, 25 Nov. 1874* (1874), p. 4.

157 Ibid., p. 5.

158 Taylor, 'Birmingham Movement', p. 218.

to the point where there was no longer a gap to be filled under the provisions of the 1870 Act. That attitude was far from acceptable to Chamberlain and the activists of the NEL.

Although Dixon had been prepared for a general election many months previously, it was not entirely plain sailing. The Conservatives were not going to contest the three-member constituency, so considerable responsibility rested with the BLA. It nominated Bright and Dixon unanimously, and Muntz by a very large majority.[159] However, the working men were disquieted, and threatened to nominate a Radical republican, named Mr Gilliver.[160] With the prospect of now four Liberals contesting three seats, there was a risk that the Conservatives might change their minds and nominate a candidate too. Dixon decided to test the waters, and threatened to resign. Dr. Dale quickly came to his aid, and spoke up strongly for Bright and him, but not Muntz. The following day, the name of Gilliver was withdrawn.[161]

Meantime, Chamberlain was rebuffed by the electors in Sheffield.[162] He apparently could not accept the concept of Conservative working-men, referring to them as a 'monstrous anomaly and abortion'. Feeling alienated by such attitudes, he no longer attempted to put himself forward primarily as a working man's representative.[163] Therein lay Dixon's political strength: he never forgot the interests of the working man in his educational reforms, and by and large, they seldom forgot him.

A few months later, it became apparent why Muntz was not at this time universally popular. The occasion was a Town Hall meeting on the subject of the Licensing Act Amendment Bill. Neither Dixon nor Muntz were able to attend, due to attendance in the Commons. Both wrote letters of apology. Dixon trod warily, saying that he wanted to improve the condition of the people, and thought that the Liberal party would give an almost unanimous vote on the side of temperance. By contrast, Muntz's letter, couched in terms of considerable detachment, stated only that he would watch the progress of the Bill 'carefully in the interests of all whom it may concern'.[164] This caution was greeted publicly with hisses.

The overall electoral outcome nationally was a resounding defeat for the Liberals, and the NEL Executive Committee recognised that this result was

---

159 *BDP,* 27 Jan. 1874.
160 Ibid., 30 Jan. 1874.
161 Ibid., 31 Jan. 1974. Gilliver was a Republican, demanding the release of Irish political prisoners, and even in Radical Birmingham such a platform was too extreme. Little wonder that there was a closing of ranks against him. *Birmingham Historian,* 31 (Winter 2007), p. 11.
162 Taylor, 'Birmingham Movement', p. 224.
163 Marsh, *Chamberlain,* p. 74.
164 *BDP,* 12 May 1874.

in substantial measure due to the educational issue.[165] It was not the complete story, however, for the Temperance issue, amongst others, also featured strongly. The Liberal defeat was the end of an era in some people's eyes. As one of Chamberlain's biographers expressed it: the electorate's decision meant 'the ardent Nonconformist dream of political supremacy in England went down for ever as it proved, though for many years this historic fact was not fully realised by the larger body of Dissenters'.[166]

Now back in Parliament for a third time, but once more on the Opposition benches, Dixon faced a different atmosphere with regard to educational reform. Much of the heat seemed to have gone out of the religious complications; and, although Clause 25 remained on the Statute Book, attempts were being made around the country to implement the provisions of the 1870 Act. As a result, the scale of educational deprivation nationwide was not as bad as it had been.

Dixon was still Chairman of the NEL, and that summer he yet again presented a Bill for compulsory education. Yet again it was thrown out, quite probably because it was coupled with the proposal to introduce universal School Boards. 'Men were tired of the acrimony and expense they [the Boards] caused, and they were prone to apathy, incompetence and jobbery'.[167] The League's Bill fared little better in 1875, but at least the minority was reduced, with support from both Forster and Lord Hartington, who by then was leader of the Liberal party.[168]

John Bright, however, was still none too supportive. He was a minimalist, and on one occasion pronounced: 'It was possible to give too much education and to too high a level: teach a lad to read and write and do his sums, and if he has any talent he will get on'.[169] If George Dawson had been asked, he would no doubt have repeated his quip about the fire engine and his pitiful wet blanket.[170]

Nonetheless, spirits were high in Birmingham. Schnadhorst had become the secretary of the BLA in 1873 and, as the *Birmingham Daily Post* commented, thus began the missionary era. 'Birmingham had revolutionised political organisation in the United Kingdom'.[171] Dixon went slightly overboard. Addressing his local supporters in Edgbaston in 1874, he described the BLA as 'one of the most magnificent political organisations existing in any part of

---

165 [IoE] National Education League pamphlets Vol. 4, pamphlet 26, *Report of the Executive Committee Presented to the Members of the National Education League at Sixth Annual Meeting, Birmingham, 25 Nov. 1874* (1874), p. 5.

166 Garvin, *Chamberlain,* Vol. 1, p. 146.

167 Taylor, 'Birmingham Movement', p. 229.

168 Ibid., p. 233. For Lord Hartington, Eighth Duke of Devonshire (1833-1908), see *ODNB-online.*

169 Ibid., p. 237.

170 See above, Chapter 3, p. 81.

171 *BDP,* 24 March 1885, in a report of a speech by Schnadhorst which gave the history of the BLA.

England or the world', for it enabled everyone to participate in the decision-making process.[172]

A new government meant an opportunity for a reappraisal for the NEL. By now, it was precisely half-way through the ten-year period which the founders had originally estimated might be required to complete their task.[173] In some respects the NEL could congratulate itself: 78% of the country's borough population lived in districts where compulsion was now operative, thanks to the permissive provisions of the 1870 Act; but the situation was still dire in the countryside where, of some 13,000 parishes, only 594 had elected School Boards, and of these, only 183 had made provision for compulsion.[174] That fact in itself justified some of the agitation of recent months. However, there was a hint of apology in the air when the NEL declared: 'We never at any time were so unreasonable as to expect that the Ministry should immediately adopt the whole of the League scheme; but there was no unreasonableness in protesting against Retrogression'.[175]

The political outlook was also more straightforward: 'they now had to contend against avowed enemies [the Conservatives] rather than professed friends'.[176] The battle for compulsion was all of a sudden gaining a momentum of its own, for managers in the voluntary sector were waking up to the fact that at a stroke, their flow of income would rise.[177]

Where the NEL could be faulted was its strategic linking of compulsion with universal School Boards.[178] School Boards were unpopular for a variety of reasons, from the most basic point that they cost money – a powerful weapon in the hands of the NEL's opponents, who often exaggerated the size of the rate[179] – to Conservative fears, that 'They will become the favourite platforms of the Dissenting preacher and local agitator...'.[180]

There was also a fault-line developing at the very top of the NEL itself, which was clearly revealed in a debate on the Endowed Schools Acts Amendment Bill. The issue for Dixon was the manner in which the Governors of the King Edward VI's Grammar School should be appointed. He alluded to his own Town Council, of which Chamberlain was by then Mayor, as holding an 'extreme view', namely that the whole power of electing Governors

172 Ibid., 2 Nov. 1874.
173 [IoE] National Education League pamphlets Vol. 4, pamphlet 26, *Report of the Executive Committee Presented to the Members of the National Education League at Sixth Annual Meeting, Birmingham, 25 Nov. 1874* (1874), p. 16.
174 Ibid., pp. 17-18.
175 [IoE] National Education League pamphlets Vol. 4, pamphlet 23, outlining its policy following the 1874 election (1874), p. 1.
176 Adams, *History of Elementary School Contest*, p. 302.
177 Ibid., p. 308.
178 Sutherland, *Policy-Making*, p. 25, makes the point particularly well.
179 Adams, *History of Elementary School Contest*, p. 309.
180 Sutherland, *Policy-Making*, p. 131.

should be thrown into the hands of the Town Council itself.[181] He himself had long been the chairman of the Free Grammar School Association, and it proposed a middle course, 'suggesting that the majority of the board should be representative men – [who] should elect the remainder'. On the other extreme was the view that the existing Governors should self-elect, filling vacancies in their own body.

Typically, here was Dixon seeking a position of compromise, as a potentially realistic way of moving forward. In his own words, 'He did not wish to advocate any views which should be merely in the interests of any particular sect or section of the community'.[182]

The fault-line among Birmingham's leaders became even more marked at the time of the leadership crisis following Gladstone's resignation in 1875. Chamberlain supported the candidature of Lord Hartington, and Dixon supported his educational ally-cum-jousting partner, Forster.

Mundella at that point exchanged correspondence with the editor of the *Sheffield Independent,* the latter writing: 'I am disappointed that you will have to give up Forster in deference to Birmingham dictation'.[183] To which Mundella responded that 'Dixon's speech at Birmingham was decidedly against Hartington and for Forster, and Bright, whom the Leaguers had hoped would smite him, *carefully refrained*'.

Dixon persevered in the Commons with his attempts to enact compulsory attendance at schools. In a broad-ranging speech full of optimism in 1875, he fully recognised the heavy defeat he had suffered in 1874 on this question, and had subsequently researched the issue fully. There simply was no alternative to the School Boards, the Boards of Guardians in many parts of the country having shown a great disinclination to act. He claimed that support for the proposition came from all quarters, even from the agricultural workers of Dorsetshire [sic] and Somersetshire, who had pleaded 'So that the disgrace of so many men and women being unable to read or write, and believing in witchcraft, ghosts, and fairies, may not continue in this so-called Christian country'.[184]

Dixon once more threatened the Conservatives with Chamberlain's Radicalism. 'There is a party springing up in this country, and increasing in power – a party which is of opinion that wherever the Government grant is given, there should be the management of the representatives of the ratepayers: and who hereafter, unless something is done, will be prepared to say that the annual grant shall be withdrawn in the cases of all schools which are not controlled by the ratepayers'.[185]

---

181 *Hansard*, Vol. 221, Col. 519, 20 July 1874.
182 Ibid., Col. 331.
183 Armytage, *Mundella*, p. 156.
184 *Hansard*, Vol. 224, Col. 1565, 9 June 1875.
185 Ibid., Col. 1573.

He tackled the question of cost head-on, acknowledging the existence of the problem. As an advocate of rigid economy, however, he believed the problem to be containable, with relief from the Education Department in certain cases.[186]

Then Dixon made a tactical error, reviving memories of a phrase he had used some years previously, in which he had forecast that there would be a 'painless extinction' of the existing voluntary sector, simply through the powerful competition of Board schools. Referring to such schools already formed, in the future it would be that much easier to transfer other schools which were short of funds, to Board management.[187] In the words of the following speaker, 'the cat was out of the bag'.[188] Dixon sought to retrieve the situation in his closing speech, somewhat inadequately denying that he had intended to vex or annoy the voluntary schools. But he noted that no government had found any alternative machinery to School Boards for ensuring attendance.[189]

Despite this *faux pas*, the majority against Dixon's case was considerably reduced by comparison with 1874 (91[190] as opposed to 164[191]).

Public opinion at large was also swinging, helped on by the appearance of new Board schools in ever-increasing numbers. Architecturally, they set new standards prescribed by the Education Department. Purpose built, the institutions were a far cry from many older schools, which were simply big rooms, ill adapted to their special purpose, and often defective in ventilation, lighting and heating.[192]

For the very last time, in the autumn of 1875 the annual cycle of events was starting again: Dixon was once more being asked by the Executive Committee to reintroduce his Bill.[193] Yet this time there was a difference. Dixon's wife was ill, and for some time he had been talking about resigning.[194] Life was pretty uncomfortable for him politically, with the powerful rivalry of Chamberlain in his home base. Indeed it was his brother-in-law's opinion that 'There is no doubt that he [Chamberlain] is *King* in Birmingham but whether there will be a vacant seat [as MP] is another matter'.[195]

---

186 Ibid., Col. 1576.
187 Ibid., Col. 1579.
188 Ibid., Col. 1583.
189 Ibid., Col. 1610.
190 Ibid., Col. 1611.
191 *Hansard*, Vol. 220, Col. 849, 1 July 1874.
192 Adamson, *English Education*, p. 359.
193 [IoE] National Education League pamphlets Vol. 4, pamphlet 32, *Report of the Executive Committee Presented to the Members of the National Education League at Eighth Annual Meeting, Birmingham, 8 Nov. 1876* (1876), p. 5.
194 Marsh, *Chamberlain*, p. 110. Just how ill Mary Dixon was at this stage is impossible to determine, but she survived until 1885, eventually dying from a cancerous growth.
195 Armytage, *Mundella*, p. 167.

Given Muntz's less than total popularity with sections of the Birmingham Liberal Association, particularly with regard to temperance matters, it might well have been wondered why Chamberlain and his friends did not seek to suggest that Muntz, rather than Dixon, should stand down in Chamberlain's favour. Muntz had, however, played a significant part in the process of securing the town's Charter of Incorporation in 1838. There was thus an element of long-standing respect for Muntz, who was to receive the Freedom of the Borough in 1888. Dixon by contrast was a relative newcomer, although he had become a successful businessman and MP – as was acknowledged when he became a Freeman of the City (as it by then was) in 1898.

When Dixon raised the topic of resignation in early 1876, Chamberlain was ill from overwork, so the inner group at the Arts Club[196] who controlled the political fortunes of the town arranged for Dixon to defer his resignation for two or three months until Chamberlain's situation improved.[197] However, this was not quite how Dixon relayed the news to a wider audience, for on 23 January at a speech in the Town Hall he announced his intention to fight a future Education Bill [ultimately Sandon's Act of the same year] through all its stages.[198] Thus there was increasing restiveness amongst Chamberlain and his supporters as the spring progressed.

Despite the announcement in the Queen's Speech of a forthcoming Government measure, there was no immediate sign of one, and on 5 April 1876 Dixon's familiar proposals were presented once again. Without a shadow of a doubt, he was pertinacious.

But he was not yet winning the argument, and this time the majority against him rose to 155, Sandon having mentioned in the concluding moments of the debate that, when his own Bill came, the principles of compulsory attendance and universal School Boards would be separated;[199] and in the following month, indeed they were.

Writing from an address in Bayswater, Dixon was liaising closely with Chamberlain in mid-May about their respective future plans: 'Some months ago you told me that June would be the most convenient time for you. But things have not shaped themselves for maturing that month. The Second Reading of the Educ. Bill will be on the 12th June – & we shall not be thro' committee until the latter half of July, all of which I mention for your guidance. … My present feeling is to try to improve and not to throw out the Bill. Mrs Dixon's convalescence is very slow, if it be convalescence at all'.[200]

---

196 For membership details, see W. Wilson, *The Life of George Dawson* (Birmingham, 1905), p. 127.
197 Marsh, *Chamberlain,* p. 110.
198 Taylor, 'Birmingham Movement', p. 236.
199 *Hansard*, Vol. 228, Col. 1300, 5 April 1876.
200 University of Birmingham, Chamberlain Papers, Special Collections, File JC5/27/1: letter dated 21 May 1876.

Meantime Chamberlain, impatient as to his own position, was writing to Collings: 'Everything must have an end, even his [Dixon's] indecision'.[201]

Just over three weeks later, Dixon was in Eastbourne, from where he wrote to Chamberlain:

> 'You know how much I have wished to take an active part in the struggle over the Gov. Educ. Bill – and yet now that the time has come I find I cannot do so: Mrs Dixon's state is such that I ought not to leave her, & if I were to do so my heart & mind would be elsewhere, & I should have neither pleasure nor success in my work. I understand that by taking measures at once the writ could be moved for early next week. To-morrow I shall talk matters over with Stansfeld. If you wish delay, telegraph me at the above address. So far as I am concerned it matters nothing when retirement takes place – the only object of speed being to get you in in time for you to take part in the discussions on the Educ. Bill. If I receive no telegram to-morrow I shall assume you wish all haste to be made'.[202]

Things then happened very rapidly. It was evident that Dixon never received any telegram, on this subject. His old friend J.S. Wright presided over a meeting of the Management Committee of the BLA that same day,[203] and so was set in train the process whereby Chamberlain very quickly succeeded Dixon as one of the town's three MPs. A passing comment in the *BDP* indicated that consideration had been given to allow Dixon time away from Parliament whilst his wife was so ill (Bright had been away for more than two years due to ill-health), 'but George Dixon was not agreeable to that course of action'. A report in *The Times* indicated that Dixon had decided to stand down 'on the conclusion of the debate on the Government Education Bill'.[204]

On 16 June, a leader in the *BDP* proclaimed that directly the resignation of Dixon had been announced, the town 'turned instinctively' to Chamberlain.

An editorial in the same paper was flowing in its tributes to Dixon – and well it might, given that Bunce, the editor, had played a part in Dixon's departure. Comments included

> It is no secret to those who are intimate with him that Mr Dixon never had a strong desire to enter Parliament. Personal ambition, which is entirely wanting in his character, had no place in his acceptance of the position

---

201 University of Birmingham, Chamberlain Papers, Special Collections, File JC5/16/53: letter dated 26 May 1876.

202 University of Birmingham, Chamberlain Papers, Special Collections, File JC5/27/2: letter dated 13 June 1876.

203 *BDP,* 14 June 1876.

204 *The Times,*14 June 1876.

offered to him in 1867. He took it less as an honourable distinction than as a trust. He was felt to be the fittest candidate to represent Liberal opinion of Birmingham…

… [it is to be hoped] that at some future period Mr Dixon may be enabled to resume the Parliamentary duties which he now feels himself obliged to relinquish.

To his exertions, in a great degree, we owe the defeat of the insidious measure by which, in the first session of the present Tory Government, an endeavour was made to undo the work of the Endowed Schools Act passed by Mr Gladstone's Administration. His, again, with strict impartiality, was the first voice raised in the House of Commons against Mr Lowe's famous match tax, which Mr Dixon promptly denounced as a tax upon industry, and therefore as a violation of the principles of free trade.

Other incidents in Mr Dixon's public course will be fresh in the minds of our readers – his keen and practical sympathy with the agricultural labourers; his interest in all questions affecting the social progress and material well-being of the poorer classes; his honest and self-sacrificing work as a member of our School Board; his deep interest in our public educational and charitable institutions; his liberal-minded gifts to deserving objects; and his unfailing courtesy and kindness to all, from the highest to the humblest…. It is a great thing to say of a public man that he has no enemies; but as regards Mr Dixon we may go further, and say with truth that in public and private, in his representative and personal character, he has none but friends.[205]

Meantime, the *Birmingham Daily Gazette* was highly critical of Dixon's conduct in the educational debate. Nothing could be in worse taste than his 'direful threats against the wholly un-offending Church of England if the Birmingham League ideas of national government were not adopted by the government. … It is hardly reasonable to expect that the whole kingdom should forego its views in favour of the Radicals of Birmingham'.[206]

On 19 June, the paper *BDP* announced (without giving its authority)[207] that Dixon would not wait for the Committee Stage, and on the same day Chamberlain booked Bingley Hall for an election meeting. On the following day, he resigned the mayoralty. Two days after that, Dixon resigned, by applying for the Chiltern Hundreds. On 27 June, Chamberlain was elected to Parliament, unopposed.

---

205 *BDP,* 17 June 1876.
206 *Birmingham Daily Gazette,* 17 June 1876.
207 Briggs suggests that Bunce, the editor of the *BDP* and a supporter of Chamberlain, 'appears to have forced Dixon's decision to retire': see Briggs, 'Introduction', p. lii.

The *Birmingham Daily Gazette* reproduced a number of items from other papers. One was an article from *The Daily Telegraph*: 'while we regret Mr Dixon's secession from public life, we shall have more calls for sorrow if his probable successor, Mr Chamberlain, reproduces in the House of Commons the tone, temper and verbiage he thinks good enough for the Birmingham School Board'.[208] There was also an article from *The Globe* stating that: 'we shall scarcely be accused of undue partiality for the peculiar tenets professed by Mr Dixon when we express an opinion that the change is to be regretted. His political opinions may be of far too advanced a school to receive a general acceptance. Nevertheless, we heartily wish that he would remain member of Birmingham for many years, sooner than see that important borough represented by its present Mayor. Of these two enthusiastic Radicals, Mr Chamberlain is apparently somewhat the cleverer. There, however, his superiority seems to stop'.[209]

It was an understatement that Dixon 'might fairly have complained that he was being rushed'.[210] But he remained upright and congratulated Chamberlain with warmth, wishing him luck in relation to the parliamentary debates on the education Bill.[211]

These developments came as no surprise to colleagues. There was much muttering in the wings. On 20 June, Mundella had told the editor of the *Sheffield Independent*: 'Muntz tells me *confidently* that Chamberlain has warned Dixon out of his seat and that he had thrown it up rather than lead such a *dog's life*'.[212] As a measure of compensation, it was agreed that Chamberlain would surrender the chairmanship of the School Board to Dixon at the next elections in November. Dixon let it be known that he had been harried out of office, and his friends resented his treatment. Chamberlain too felt some resentment, although with less logic, for he had been obliged to resign his office as Mayor, a job he loved, in order to enter parliament. Suffering from gout, he snapped at a School Board meeting, denouncing Disraeli 'as a man who went down to the House of Commons and flung at the British Parliament the first lie that entered his head'. There was a general outcry, and Chamberlain was forced to apologise, pleading over-work, but not before Disraeli had described this attack as what 'you might expect from the cad of an omnibus'.

Local resentment at the treatment of Dixon then surfaced. Moving a resolution of thanks to him at the meeting of the BLA that approved Chamberlain for the Parliamentary vacancy, Dr. Dale observed that in the heat of conflict Dixon had never uttered 'words which either he or his friends had

208 *Birmingham Daily Gazette,* 19 June 1876.
209 Ibid., 20 June 1876.
210 Taylor, 'Birmingham Movement', p. 240.
211 Briggs, 'Introduction', p. lii.
212 Armytage, *Mundella*, p. 167.

occasion to regret or apologise for'.[213] That this should have come from the mouth of someone who disagreed profoundly on the issue of secular education showed not only that Dixon had many good friends; but also the general disgust at Chamberlain's conduct.

Even a year later, amongst Dixon's former parliamentary colleagues, feelings were not soothed. Holidaying with Mundella, John Gorst,[214] and Lord Edmond Fitzmaurice,[215] they heard the latter's views on Chamberlain: 'Full of overweening ambition, destined to a considerable degree of disappointment, but so clever and intriguing withal, that he will sacrifice party interests to his own'.[216] Whilst the name of Dixon could certainly not be upheld as the most loyal member of the Liberal party, given his revolt on the subject of Lucifer matches and his conduct on educational issues for so many years, here was a perceptive comment of an entirely different dimension.

After Dixon stood down in June 1876, the NEL played very little part in the remainder of the debate on Sandon's Bill, which soon reached the Statute Book. In essence, it was now encumbent on the parents of children to cause their children to receive efficient instruction, with penalties for those whose children worked for wages under the age of ten. Where there was no School Board, enforcement was put in the hands of new School Attendance Committees,[217] and the Poor Law Boards after all took on the responsibility previously assumed by the School Boards under the 'Clause 25' provisions. The NEL Secretary suggested sarcastically that the Act should have been titled 'An Act for compelling attendance in denominational schools, under private management, supported out of the rates and taxes'.[218]

To its end, Dixon retained the formal title of 'Chairman of Council' of the NEL. The Executive Committee under the Chairmanship of Chamberlain, however, had the task of explaining events at the Eighth Annual Meeting in November, and did so in the following terms: 'In concluding their reference to a measure with which Mr Dixon's name has been so long and so honourably associated, your Committee desire to record their appreciation of the noble and unselfish efforts made by him in the cause of education during his Parliamentary career, and their keen regret that he has been compelled by the pressure of domestic anxiety to retire from the House of Commons before witnessing the complete success of the cause which he has so deeply at heart. In his enforced retirement Mr Dixon takes with him the gratitude and the

---

213 Marsh, *Chamberlain*, pp. 110-11.
214 For Sir John Gorst (1835-1916), see *ODNB-online*.
215 For Lord Edmond Fitzmaurice (1846-1935), see *ODNB-online*.
216 Armytage, *Mundella*, p. 179.
217 Adamson, *English Education*, p. 357.
218 Adams, *History of Elementary School Contest*, p. 319.

sympathy of vast numbers of his fellow-countrymen, whose condition he has so arduously striven to improve'.[219]

Given that compulsion, albeit in a form that was widely despised as ineffective, the *raison d'être* of the NEL had now disappeared, and with only £308 of cash left, the decision was made to wind it up, with the final meeting on 28 March 1877.[220] Chamberlain had written the previous summer: 'When this Bill has passed my impression is that the Education fight is over for the next seven years',[221] and he was right. For a good while, the country was exhausted by the issue.

---

219 [IoE] National Education League pamphlets Vol. 4, pamphlet 32, *Report of the Executive Committee Presented to the Members of the National Education League at Eighth Annual Meeting, Birmingham, 8 Nov. 1876* (1876), p. 7.
220 Adams, *History of Elementary School Contest*, p. 329.
221 Sutherland, *Policy-Making*, p. 145: letter dated 11 July 1876.

CHAPTER SIX

Leading the Birmingham School Board 1876-85

I N THE NEXT decade Dixon moved from being a medium-sized fish in a large pond, to become a very big fish in a medium-sized pond. His work at this time put Birmingham firmly on the national education map.

A considerable workload was involved. Of the 129 meetings to which he was summoned in the year to 5 December 1878, he attended 111.[1] Five years later, the figure was 157 out of 167.[2] And the figures remained consistent until he reduced his commitments in Birmingham following the death of his wife and his return to Parliament in 1885. This commitment was spread over very many years. School Boards were in existence from 1870 until 1902, and Dixon was a member of the Birmingham Board from its inception until his death in 1898, being Chairman for nearly twenty of these years. It was a record which his fellow Board member, Rev. MacCarthy, believed was 'unprecedented in the whole country'.[3] Although the opposition could complain that the Liberals in

---

1 Birmingham Archives and Heritage, School Board Minutes, File SB/B1/1/3, p. 557.
2 Ibid., File SB/B1/1/4, p. 688.
3 *BDP,* 5 Nov. 1894.

their uninterrupted majority from 1873 to 1900 ruled 'despotically',[4] Dixon's personal leadership was characterised by great goodwill. Indeed there were periods, especially around 1890, when his opponents on the Board proclaimed that, if elected, they would have continued almost exactly the same policies as he. There was however the exception of the ever-divisive matter of religious teaching, a problem that outlasted him.

Dixon was described as 'the most active municipal administrator of his day',[5] and his strongest talent as, effectively, a very capable senior civil servant shone forth.

It was a period of constantly rising standards in every field. Indeed the story of this period revolves around how the Birmingham School Board addressed issues that were never foreseen when Forster's Education Bill reached the Statute Book in August 1870.

The focus of Dixon's endeavours was recorded in the scarcely impartial history of the family firm, Rabone Bros., written in the middle of the twentieth century. This tome observed that 'As Chairman of the School Board he was … moving heaven and earth to obtain secondary education for the country'.[6] The same brief publication, however, made no reference at all to his work with the NEL. It could be that memories of the internal wrangling in its later days lingered on.

At the heart of educational change in these years was the definition of 'elementary', and, in the same breath, of 'secondary'. Neither word had the same meaning as it does today. In 1870 'Elementary Education' was a euphemism for 'Education for the Children of the Poor'.[7] The statutory definition of an elementary school was 'a school or department of a school, at which elementary education is the principal part of the education there given, and does not include a school or department of a school at which the ordinary payments in respect of the instruction, from each scholar, exceed ninepence a week'.[8] With no reference to the age of children attending, in the years immediately after 1870 the Board was using its resources to teach the 3Rs even to those of more mature years, until the backlog of illiteracy dwindled.[9] The word 'primary' scarcely featured. Elementary education was thus a term which defined a social function, that of educating the working classes, and its minimum content was

---

4 S. Wright, 'The Struggle for Moral Education in English Elementary Schools, 1879-1918' (Unpubl. Ph.D., Oxford Brookes University, 2006), p. 142.

5 *Daily Argus*, file clipping Jan. 1898: obituary of George Dixon.

6 [Promotional Handbook] Anon., *Rabone, Petersen and Company Ltd.* (c.1950): copy in author's possession. This was by the middle of the twentieth century the name of the original Rabone Bros. business, later merged with others.

7 E. Eaglesham, *From School Board to Local Authority* (1956), p. 7.

8 Rich, *Education Act*, p. 90.

9 Birmingham Archives and Heritage, *Birmingham School Board Annual Report 1879*, File SB/B1/4/2, p. 116.

narrowly prescribed by the codes of the national Education Department.[10] 'Secondary education' by contrast was taken to mean the education of the middle classes. Only at a much later date was 'secondary education' taken to mean in England what it means today, namely the education of children over the age of 11.

One-seventh (or fourteen percent) of the population was assumed to be either middle or upper class. For Dixon, the challenge was how to create an educational ladder within Birmingham that would enable each child from the remaining six-sevenths to reach the limit of his or her own abilities. The masses were his first concern, but the elite was not overlooked in the course of his endeavours.

There was an obvious need for an integrated system overall. As late as 1886 (and matters were to get worse before they eventually got better) Mundella commented: 'At present education in this country is divisible into two parts: one, elementary education organised by the State; two, university controlled by the State; and all between was chaos'.[11] In Parliament, there was a debate in 1883 as to the possible establishment of a separate Department of Education.[12] Towards the end of the century, no less than eight central authorities were involved in educational matters, the three most significant being the Education Department (elementary schools), Science and Art Department (technical and art schools), and the Charity Commissioners (endowed schools). It was only in 1899, a year after Dixon's death, that a national Board of Education was established – something he had been advocating for almost 30 years.

One area in particular where the Birmingham School Board was well ahead of central government was trying to create a comprehensive system of free schools in which all classes could mingle, not as a charity but as a natural right of the citizen.[13] It had a unique opportunity here. Although there had been a rush of new building by the voluntary sector nationwide immediately after the 1870 Act, the sector struggled with a legacy of smaller and sometimes inappropriate school accommodation. By contrast, the Birmingham School Board had the perceived competitive advantage of apparently unlimited funding. And, except where it was assuming the management of former voluntary sector schools, all its buildings were new.

If Dixon's ladder were to be implemented in its entirety, there was a long-term need for an infrastructure in which the elementary schools could pass their brighter pupils to local university colleges, or to grammar schools, and then university. It might have been a pipedream in 1870. Yet, within twenty-

---

10 S. Maclure, *One Hundred Years of London Education, 1870-1970* (1970), p. 14.
11 Ilersic, *Parliament of Commerce,* p. 133.
12 *Hansard*, Vol. 280, Col. 1933 et seq., 29 June 1883.
13 Taylor, 'History of the Birmingham School Board', p. 3.

one years, a former Birmingham Board school pupil became a Fellow at Cambridge.[14]

In the very short term, however, there was the problem of the education of his own daughters. He could not possibly send them to the King Edward's Foundation Grammar School, given his past stance in the Free Grammar School Association. That would have deprived poorer members of society from the places to which they were entitled. Whilst he was still an MP, the solution was to send them to school in London, but that solution no longer applied from June 1876. Instead, he took a broader view.

Thus in December 1875, Dixon sent round yet another printed circular:[15]

PROPOSED HIGH SCHOOL FOR GIRLS IN EDGBASTON. A MEETING OF LADIES and GENTLEMEN will take place at THE DALES, on the evening of Monday, January 10th at Eight O'Clock p.m., to take into consideration the propriety of establishing a HIGH SCHOOL FOR GIRLS in Edgbaston.

GEORGE DIXON

The timing was certainly interesting. It was only a few weeks later[16] that he began to intimate that he would eventually have to leave Parliament on account of his wife Mary's ill-health. The location of the proposed meeting was also interesting, for it was by now the third significant occasion on which his house was used as the base for initiating new movements, the previous occasions being the Birmingham Education Society in 1867, and the National Education League in 1869.

The circular was sent to 52 local families, including many colleagues: Chamberlains, Collings, Dales, Dawsons, Frys, Kenricks, Lloyds, Matthews, Martineaus, Sturges, Wilsons.[17] Whilst the School's constitution was modelled on that of the recently formed Girls' Public Day School Trust, exception was taken to there being any degree of control from London. Furthermore, Chamberlain threatened to withdraw his support unless all mention of religious instruction were omitted.[18]

Nonetheless, a meeting duly took place, which Chamberlain addressed, although Dixon's 'subsequent speech was neither so eloquent nor so aggressive'. Dixon seemed to have handled the meeting well and secured full agreement. Hence he congratulated it on being "homogeneous ... not divided by religious bitterness or strong political strife". He was enhancing his reputation in

---

14 *BDP,* 6 Nov. 1891.
15 J. Whitcut, *Edgbaston High School, 1876-1976* (Edgbaston, 1976), p. 30.
16 See above, Chapter 5, p. 167.
17 Whitcut, *Edgbaston High School,* p. 30.
18 Ibid., p. 36.

the process and, many years later, Chamberlain spoke of the much earlier establishment of the BES 'which was started by Mr George Dixon, as almost everything else that is good in connection with education has been started'.[19]

The foundation of the Edgbaston High School for Girls was undoubtedly a matter of enlightened self-interest, although it was a second, albeit small, rung in his educational ladder. Dixon said: 'It must be remembered that those who subscribe the money will have a reasonable expectation of a dividend of 5% p.a., which is a rate of interest not now obtainable on the highest class of securities, and that the object in view is not merely the education of other people's children, but of our own!'[20]

Dixon was formally appointed Chairman of the School Board on 7 December 1876,[21] at the commencement of its third three-year session. There had been no election on this occasion, but a new member was W.J. Davis, General Secretary of the National Society of Amalgamated Brassworkers, standing as an Independent. W.J. Davis had stood in the only contested by-election in Board history the previous year, and lost, but Dixon ensured his nomination a year later. He was to prove a useful ally. All subsequent Board vacancies were filled through co-option, with Dixon pursuing a policy of filling each vacancy by an individual from the same party as the previous incumbent. Dixon himself and Chamberlain had switched their respective positions as MP and School Board Chairman; and, whilst Chamberlain remained an Alderman on the Town Council until 1880, he was no longer a member of the School Board.

That switch did not mean that Chamberlain was no longer to cause Dixon problems. Their views of the role of education in society differed. Chamberlain saw things mostly as a politician,[22] at this time justifying expenditure as a means of reducing the cost of pauperism and crime in the town.[23] Dixon, by contrast, viewed education more as a philanthropist. Indeed, upon his death in 1898, Chamberlain fairly said this:

'I do not think that he [Dixon] concerned himself greatly with the political or the sectarian side of the question. He did not want any gain for the party with which he was connected, or for the church to which he belonged, but he thought it to be of the first importance to save the children from ignorance, and he believed that if this were done, if they were educated, they would certainly become better citizens and better men and women'.[24]

The major costs were those needed for buildings and staff. Whilst progress on the first front had been slow during the first three years of the Board's

---

19 *BDP*, 25 April 1891.
20 Whitcut, *Edgbaston High School*, p. 40.
21 Birmingham Archives and Heritage, School Board Minutes, File SB/B1/1/3, p. 30.
22 Taylor, 'History of the Birmingham School Board', p. 99a [sic].
23 Ibid., p. 87.
24 *School Board Chronicle*, Vol. 59, 29 Jan. 1898, p. 150.

existence, the pace changed radically under Chamberlain on becoming Chairman in 1873. This dynamism was continued by Dixon. However, there was a change of direction within a few years with the introduction of the German classroom system (setting the children into groups by age), which meant that many of the early schools had to be rebuilt.[25]

There was a fundamental policy difference between the parties on the size of buildings. Churchmen generally wanted smaller buildings, so that they would not compete unduly with their voluntary counterparts, whilst the Liberals preferred large buildings, ostensibly because they were cheaper per head to build and maintain, but also because they were more impressive.[26] Since the early Board schools relied heavily on pupil teachers, it was felt necessary to fit glass partitions so that they could be observed by the headmaster.[27] Most schools were designed by the architects, Chamberlain & Martin,[28] and featured a distinctive tower, part of the 'air-conditioning system', felt to be vital for the combination of healthy body and mind.[29] Dixon was proud: 'he doubted whether greater perfection had been attained in any other town in the kingdom'.[30]

By law, School Boards were required to provide eight square feet per child,[31] but School Boards generally aimed at ten square feet. Dixon took this matter so seriously that even the family back in leafy Edgbaston felt the impact. Katie complained about her 'vast, high nursery', so cold in winter and so hot in summer. 'I think … he must have been already ruminating over the number of cubic feet of air necessary for each child, which played a great part in Board School management later'.[32] Aim they might, but the Birmingham Board was not able to provide ten square feet at all times. It had passed a bye-law on compulsion soon after it came into existence, but this rule could not be generally enforced until there was basic accommodation for all. So many children had to be squeezed in. The Board was regularly required to calculate the deficiency of accommodation, and even in 1881 it was calculated that 4,000 more places were still required.[33]

Dixon was extremely fortunate in having a devoted Clerk, George B. Davis. Although Dixon had not initially supported his candidature as a nominee of the Church party, the two men subsequently developed a notably harmonious

---

25 Ibid..

26 G.T. Rimmington, *The Rise and Fall of Elected School Boards* (Peterborough, 1986), p. 12.

27 Taylor, 'History of the Birmingham School Board', p. 126.

28 The architectural firm Chamberlain and Martin had no connection with Joseph Chamberlain.

29 C. Upton, *A History of Birmingham* (Chichester, 1993), p. 162.

30 *School Board Chronicle,* Vol. 37, 30 April 1887, p. 448.

31 *Hansard*, Vol. 259, Col. 1803, 24 March 1881.

32 Rathbone, *The Dales,* p. 14.

33 [G. Dixon], *An Address Delivered to the Birmingham School Board by the Chairman, George Dixon, Esq., JP, 20 January 1881* (1881), p. 12.

relationship over a period of twenty years, Davis dying in office in 1897.[34] Their *modus operandi* was not fully appreciated by everyone, as Katie Rathbone somewhat pompously recorded: her father 'loved having School Board people up to dine and talk, especially the clerk, a truly valuable little man, but not popular with the rest of the family'.[35] Diligent he was, as the Board Minute Book recorded on 6 November, 1879: 'The Clerk had been requested by the Board to spend his holiday in Germany, with partial reimbursement of his expenses, in reporting on how German elementary schools compared with their English equivalents'.[36] Largely as a result of this visit, the Board resolved to emulate the German classroom system.

As for Dixon, there is no doubt that one of the secrets of his success as a leader was not only his ability to get on well with people as individuals, but also to use hospitality to oil the wheels of everyday life.

Around this time, Dixon first began to make pronouncements on the ideological import of the debates about 'socialism'. The first press report on this topic was on the occasion of a Sunday school opening, a rather unlikely occasion. Dixon's key point was that 'socialism was a name that covered a great variety of opinion', but it was evident that he perceived his audience might be fearful of its rise. He was happy to report that socialism did not affect the English in the same way as it did in Germany, where there was a rapid growth of support. 'The question was what steps they were to take "to prevent its growth"'. He himself felt on the defensive because the Birmingham Radicals were vulnerable to the accusation that their system of education encouraged the growth of socialism.[37]

'Socialism' of course was a term with many gradations of meaning, which were deployed very loosely in this period. In Dixon's case, he used it to indicate a political philosophy of collectivism, but without specifying anything like a state-directed redistribution of income or collective ownership of the means of production.[38]

It was an inconclusive discussion, as reported, but a topic to which Dixon reverted in later years. Indeed he changed his stance as the meaning of the word itself changed with the times.

George Davis's report on his visit to Germany also confirmed Dixon's belief that there was no long-term future in the pupil-teacher system. It did not have the potential to deliver the results that he was seeking. Before 1870 the best voluntary school in Birmingham had had one head and seven pupil teachers.

---

34 Taylor, 'History of the Birmingham School Board', p. 112.
35 Birmingham Archives and Heritage, File MS 2239, Bundle 26, p. 1.
36 Birmingham Archives and Heritage, School Board Minutes, File SB/B1/1/4, p. 26.
37 *BDP,* 20 June 1878.
38 Guides to the debates are available in the following: S. Mukherjee, *A History of Socialist Thought: From the Precursors to the Present* (2000): and G. Lichtheim, *The Origins of Socialism* (1968).

But many years later Dixon described the newly-created Board's attitude: 'we are not going to entrust the education of these children to other children. We will have adult teachers, and, if possible, they shall be certificated and trained'.[39] Throughout his period as Chairman, he strove to improve matters, sometimes pursuing policies which were arguably outside the framework of the legislation, such as the unsuccessful Hope Street training centre from 1881 to 1886.[40] Yet by modern standards, the statistics still left much to be desired, with 118 pupils per adult teacher in Birmingham in 1876. The ratio, however, was reduced by 1900 to a more reputable 43 pupils per teacher.

One way of linking the Board schools with other institutions further up the ladder was to offer scholarships to bright pupils. In 1876 Chamberlain initiated such a scheme, offering £500, with the hope that others would follow his example.[41] One of the scholarships was tenable at King Edward's School.[42]

After winding-up the NEL in 1877,[43] Chamberlain broadened his agenda and in particular helped to create the National Liberal Federation [NLF]. The organisation of this body owed much to the earlier structure of the NEL.[44] Dixon's involvement in the NLF in its early days was minimal at most. A cartoon in *The Dart,* the Birmingham weekly publication, sub-titled *A Journal of Sense and Satire,* displayed an NLF fancy ball at the Town Hall and an accompanying verse quipped about those present, but eventually remarked on Dixon's absence:

> Schnadhorst, Baker and Muntz you discern at this party,
> With DIXON and others to memory dear;[45]

Dixon did attend the Conference held in Birmingham on 31 May 1877, at which he seconded a resolution that certain local Liberal Association Presidents be requested that they accept office as Vice-Presidents of the Federation, but he did so with considerable reluctance. The Report of the Proceedings indicated that 'he did not come to make a speech, and it was merely by accident that he was at that end of the room; but when the resolution which he was about to move was put into his hands, he felt bound, as a good Liberal – which he hoped he was – to move it'.[46] A meeting was held after the Conference, at

---

39 *Hansard*, Vol. 15, Col. 967, 31 July 1893.
40 Taylor, 'History of the Birmingham School Board', p. 242.
41 Ibid., p. 193. See also Birmingham Archives and Heritage, School Board Minutes, File SB/B1/1/3, p. 31.
42 Taylor, 'History of the Birmingham School Board', p. 194.
43 See above, Chapter 5, p. 173.
44 Francis H. Herrick, 'The Origins of the National Liberal Federation', *Journal of Modern History, 17* (1945), p. 120.
45 *The Dart,* 22 Dec. 1877. From 1881, the publication was titled *The Dart and Midland Figaro.*
46 Proceedings Attending the Formation of the National Liberal Federation; with Report of Conference held in Birmingham, on Thursday, 31 May 1877 (Birmingham, 1877).

which Gladstone thanked the Mayor for chairing the proceedings, and Dixon seconded the motion.

At this time, Chamberlain was in far from good humour. In the spring of 1878, he wrote to his old confidant Collings that he was fed up with Westminster, and said of the atmosphere in the Commons: 'It is a miracle to me that Dixon was not suffocated long ago'.[47] Dixon had certainly not found Westminster congenial,[48] but he had in the past managed to survive nine years there. A major dispute was about to erupt between the two men.

Earlier, the governance of the King Edward's Foundation had been the subject of debate in the Commons, with Bright pointing out that in 1866 the Schools Inquiry Commission had found that scarcely a child of the poorest was to be found in the school, 'but almost the whole benefit of this great charitable educational institution was given to the superior classes'.[49] The immediate problem was a proposal that three of the Governors would be nominated by the Universities of London, Oxford and Cambridge, and arguably they knew very little of what Birmingham actually needed.[50] A number of other Governors were to be nominated by the Town Council.

On 1 May, Dixon's name was passed over by the Town Council. Chamberlain had pursued the policy that all the Council-nominated Governors should be drawn from amongst the ranks of the Councillors, of whom Dixon was not one.[51] He, however, was outraged. On the following day, he announced his intention to retire at a Board meeting.[52] The Minutes recorded that the Regulations of the Board were temporarily suspended 'in order to afford facility for discussion'.[53]

Details of this discussion were printed in the *School Board Chronicle,* and revealed the nearest that Dixon ever came to losing his temper. The voting in the Town Council had been nine votes for Chamberlain's proposals, 44 neutral, and none against.

> Mr Joseph Chamberlain is a remarkably clever man, but he is undertaking a great work; he is undertaking to create the public opinion of the Town Council and of Birmingham – [hear, hear] – and also to be its public exponent. In fact, it seems as if the terms of Mr Joseph Chamberlain and Birmingham were becoming synonymous. Mr Joseph Chamberlain is Birmingham, Birmingham is Mr Joseph Chamberlain. He represents himself in the Town Council and he also represents himself in the House of Commons.

47 Chamberlain Papers, JC5/16/82: Chamberlain to Collings, 5 April 1878, p. 5.
48 See above, Chapter 5, p. 143.
49 *Hansard*, Vol. 238, Col. 778, 5 March 1878.
50 Ibid., Col. 782.
51 *BDP*, 1 May 1878.
52 Birmingham Archives and Heritage, School Board Minutes, File SB/B1/1/3, p. 398.
53 Ibid., p. 399.

Dixon's rant continued at some length: decisions were being made behind closed doors; the Chairman of the School Board was a truly representative individual, since the Board was in much closer contact with the needs of the children than were the Grammar School governors. He continued more calmly:

> What is required is this – that each body should know what is in the mind of the other, what it is that they are projecting in the immediate or distant future, and that each one should cordially, harmoniously, with good will and feeling towards each other, work up to the same point. What we require … is a proper system of graded schools that should have application to every child in the town and to any one child who wishes to rise gradually upwards; but how is that system of graded schools to be filled and properly established unless there be continual communication of the most friendly character between this Board and the governors of the Grammar School?

And Dixon concluded:

> 'I find myself thwarted'.[54]

The Dart was rather more graphic, reporting that 'Mr Dixon was greatly moved in making his long personal statement. So deeply affected was he that at times he almost broke down, and he appeared to have been wounded to the quick by the cavalier treatment of the Council'.[55] A number of other members offered to resign in sympathy.

After this appeal, the School Board fully agreed with Dixon. A unanimous resolution earnestly appealed 'to him to reconsider the decision which he has announced this afternoon of retiring from his position'.[56]

The Dart had a field-day in exposing the controversy. The Chamberlain Memorial which still stands today in Chamberlain Square, was in prospect, and the publication was quick to debunk: 'Some new suggestions for the talked-of Chamberlain memorial are being made. Would a statue of J.C. as "Alexander sighing for New Worlds to Conquer" suit the popular taste? Perhaps Mr George Dixon will kindly furnish a few hints!'[57]

A one-line joke also pulled Dixon's leg: 'A "School" Bored Official. Mr G. D-x-n'.[58] But a poetic effusion revealed real affection for him, as well as much suspicion of Chamberlain's ambitions.

---

54 *School Board Chronicle,* Vol. 19, 11 May 1878, p. 445.
55 *The Dart,* 11 May 1878.
56 Birmingham Archives and Heritage, School Board Minutes, File SB/B1/1/3, p. 399.
57 *The Dart,* 11 May 1878.
58 Ibid..

Poor Georgie he cries -
These provoking young boys
Have stolen my toys,
Have embittered my joys
  And now I must go into exile.
Oh, was it not sad?
It was really too bad
For that 'Forward' lad
To drive me so mad
  And now I must go into exile.
I gave him my seat,
I laid all at his feet;
With his Statue and Street
His tri-umph was complete,
  And for me I was left a poor exile.
I must really resign
The political line;
The fault is not mine
If the fates combine,
And my star decline,
I must not whine,
  But cheerfully go into exile.

After which it was Chamberlain's turn:

But Joseph he sings –
How poor Georgie clings
To those baubles of things?
All this fame may take wings,
And what trouble it brings;
  You're better by far in exile.
Poor Georgie, my boy,
Have I taken your toy?
Then pray do not cry,
I'll tell you "for why",
  You need not very long be in exile.
I'm a very bold man,
I've a Federal plan,
And I think that I can,
From Beersheba to Dan,
  Make MP's of all you poor exiles.
I'll find you a seat again,
You'll fall on your feet again,

184

*Your tri-*umph *be complete again,*
In St Stephen's we'll meet again,
     We exiles, and I'll be Prime Minister.[59]

The strength of Dixon's popularity within the town, first apparent with his handling of the Murphy Riots as Mayor in 1867,[60] came to his aid. The correspondence columns of the newspapers stirred, notably with a letter from 'One of Mr Dixon's Political Opponents' on 7 May:

> Sir, I humbly suggest that the working men of Birmingham answer Mr Dixon's question, and answer it in such a manner that it will make his heart beat a little faster than usual, when he hears it. I would suggest that the answer to the question should take the form of a requisition asking him to reconsider his determination to resign. I trust that all who have admired the noble efforts he has made to improve our educational system will sign it. Let the requisition be presented by a few working men, and I trust that there will be one or two on the deputation who are Mr Dixon's opponents, because the requisition will be signed by hundreds who differ from him in politics.[61]

This initiative infuriated Chamberlain, who promptly wrote to Collings:

> I note today in the *Post* the letter suggesting a requisition to Dixon and the Resolution of St George's Club. Now once for all <u>I am not going to stand this.</u> A requisition to Dixon is inferentially a vote of censure on me, and if this is to go on I see only one course open viz. to summon the 600 [the BLA] & challenge a decision between Dixon and me. If it is for Dixon, I will either resign at once, or hold my seat till the General Election for the convenience of the Party, but I am not going to pretend to be a representative of Birmingham, if there is the least colour for the statement that an unprovoked and gratuitous attack on me is approved and sustained by my constituents.[62]

This correspondence revealed Chamberlain's touchiness with regard to Dixon, as well as indicating the close relationship between Chamberlain and Collings. Whilst the Liberals were in the majority within Birmingham, the BLA was seen as the arbiter of political fortunes. A further letter two days later,

---

59 Ibid..
60 See above, Chapter 2, p. 68.
61 *BDP,* 7 May 1878.
62 University of Birmingham, Chamberlain Papers, Special Collections, file JC5/16/85: Chamberlain to Collings, 7 May 1878.

also to Collings, spoke of Chamberlain's contempt for Dixon's 'weakness',[63] but also some nervousness.

The next edition of *The Dart* offered further musings

> The Liberal Schism. We are not inclined to blame Mr. Chamberlain for the recent contretemps so much as his advisers – his Cabinet, as Mr. Dixon so cleverly put it. But is it to be tolerated that the whole thing is to be determined by twenty-three members (eight of them personally interested) closeted in the banqueting room of the Queen's Hotel, and promulgating therefrom a decree which the Council must ratify?[64]

Followed by:

> The best evidence of a public man's popularity is the manner in which he is referred to by the populace. This is an axiom against which must be set the old proverb, "familiarity breeds contempt". Last week the *Dart* was eagerly and recklessly bought up, and, sharing the general excitement, the itinerant newsvendors yelled vigorously: " 'ere y'ar for the *Dart*, Joey Chamberlain a-pitchin' into Mr. Dixon". Gentle reader, riddle me this![65]

And finally a cartoon depicting Chamberlain being conveyed to Coventry.[66] Yet Dixon was in a stronger position than Chamberlain at this point. Events moved swiftly. W.J. Davis chaired a meeting of Working Men, and eventually a memorial bearing nearly 12,000 signatures was presented to Dixon.[67] He at once withdrew his threat, reassured that there was at least some formal connection between the Board and the Governors of the school. That link was established as his fellow Board member Dr. Dale was nominated as the University of London's representative.[68] A compromise was achieved.

Chamberlain had done himself no favours by this outburst. One comment from a member of the public deplored '… the apparent policy of repression which was beginning to show itself in this town'. Other criticisms were circulated.[69] Whilst the Conservatives were not strong in the town, the President of the Birmingham Conservative Association wrote to *The Times* a while later:

> If this is not caucus government, it is very nearly allied to it. It has, perhaps, a nearer resemblance still; for when a presumed member [Dixon] is

---

63 Ibid., file JC5/16/86: Chamberlain to Collings, 9 May 1878.
64 *The Dart*, 18 May 1878.
65 Ibid..
66 Ibid..
67 *BDP*, 6 June 1878. See also W.A. Dalley, *The Life Story of W.J. Davis, J.P.* (Birmingham, 1914), p. 50.
68 *BDP*, 7 June 1878.
69 Ibid., 6 June 1878.

refractory, or shows too much independence, the whole machinery of the Liberal Association is put in force to teach the moral of party obedience. … the interesting feature in these events is the fact that private meetings were held at the Queen's Hotel, or elsewhere, and the matter settled, as many other matters have been in Birmingham, long before it came before the Town Council.[70]

The incident put Dixon back on the map in the larger arena of parliamentary politics. Presenting the issue in the form of a horse race, *The Dart* commented that

> Critics think that one of the Liberal stable should be scratched this year. Philip Henry [Muntz] has done some good work in his time, and it is expected that he will retire on his laurels in favour of a younger horse, probably John Skirrow [Wright], or Dixon St George. …

In whimsical mood, *The Dart* quoted odds of three to two against 'Bright John', five to two against 'The Chamberlain', four to one against 'John Skirrow', and five to one against 'Dixon St George'. Dixon in this instance had got a new lease of life as an 'Independent Horse'.[71]

Shortly before Christmas, it seemed that Dixon 'retired to private life' – albeit 'varied by duties at the School Board'.[72] Chamberlain never did summon a meeting of the BLA. But in the words of his biographer, he 'remained in an ugly humour'.[73] *The Dart* mocked him thus:

> *Come screw up my pluck, quite too amiable muse,*
> *Help me, while I acrostic the king of all screws,*
> *And screw out of Chamberlain's name, a big goose.*
> *Made a councillor first, – ('Twas for 'Artemus' Ward).*
> *Brum soon made him Mayor – still upward he soared*
> *Elections came on – then our member he's dubbed,*
> *Returned vice Dixon – poor Dixon he snubbed,*
> *Gas and water came next – then for something to do, he*
> *All the publics would buy – he alone could be* screwy.[74]

Dixon's position meantime was getting stronger. In March 1879 he once again had frequent contact with W.J. Davis, having been asked to arbitrate in

---

70 *The Times*, 30 Aug. 1878.
71 *The Dart*, 22 June 1878.
72 Ibid., 7 Dec. 1878.
73 Marsh, *Chamberlain*, p. 123.
74 *The Dart*, 21 Dec. 1878.

a pay dispute between his National Society of Amalgamated Brassworkers and the Chandelier and Gasfitting Trade Employers' Association. Reports of the proceedings revealed the respect in which Dixon was held by Davis.[75]

In April, a report of a Conservative soirée bemoaned the activities of the Mayor, Chamberlain's friend and confidant, Collings, whilst regretting that 'the most respectable men of his own party, the trusted men, are conspicuous by their absence. Of course, I allude to Mr George Dixon and men like him, who made Liberalism respectable …'.[76]

On 1 May Dixon was further emboldened. From a practical point of view, Chamberlain's policy of secular education, announced in 1873, was not working. In essence, that policy comprised setting aside time on Tuesday and Friday mornings, during which religious instruction was given by voluntary agencies.[77] But there was a problem of insufficient teachers,[78] among whom there were some who could not maintain discipline.[79] There may have been sufficient teachers when the policy was introduced, but since then the number of Board schools had mushroomed, and continued to do so, as the population expanded and as the deficiency of places was remedied.[80] Years later, the policy was described as 'about the most melancholy farce ever perpetrated in political annals. … amiable individuals, who undertook a task like that of mopping up the Atlantic'.[81] Most crucially, too, both the Anglicans and the Wesleyans remained aloof, so there was no critical mass of support.[82]

Dixon's solution was to move a resolution 'that … it is desirable that systematic Moral Instruction be given in all the Birmingham Board Schools'.[83] Birmingham was not the first town to go down this route, Burton-on-Trent having set the precedent the year before.[84] Dixon was, however, a pioneer working in relative isolation,[85] and the policy was controversial, with both main parties divided on the issue.[86]

In mature form, moral lessons comprised the teaching of good manners, punctuality, order, neatness, obedience, perseverance, courage, temperance, truthfulness, honesty, industry, kindness, consideration for others, and the

---

75   *BDP,* 24 March 1879. See also Dalley, *Life Story,* pp. 50, 74.
76   *BDP,* 22 April 1879.
77   Taylor, 'History of the Birmingham School Board', p. 177.
78   *The Times,* 19 Jan. 1877.
79   *School Board Chronicle,* Vol. 19, 16 March 1878, p. 263.
80   Dale, *Life of Dale,* p. 480.
81   *The Dart and Midland Figaro,* 27 July 1888.
82   N.J. Richards, 'Religious Controversy and the School Boards, 1870-1902', *British Journal of Educational Studies,* 18 (1970), p. 192.
83   Birmingham Archives and Heritage, School Board Minutes, File SB/B1/1/3, p. 660.
84   Wright, 'The Struggle', p. 156.
85   Ibid., p. 188.
86   Ibid., p. 156.

idea of duty.[87] In a circular to head teachers, after the Board had ratified the policy two months later, its introduction was linked to the national Education Department's Code. Accordingly, instructions were issued to school inspectors. But, as Dr. Dale conceded, these regulations said nothing 'about the necessity of making special provision in the timetable for definite moral instruction'.[88] Again, *The Dart* waxed satirical:

> *I stick me fast by our old text –*
> *A stolid, firm, neutrality*
> *Respecting creeds, and questions vexed –*
> *But can't we teach 'Morality'?*
> *An hour on 'Truth', an hour on 'Greed',*
> *Say half an hour on 'Bigamy',*
> *Without a tinge of Bible creed;*
> *If this is wrong – Why, jigger me!*
> *I feel 'tis awkward, and no doubt,*
> *We're like to come a cropper;*
> *God's 'fear' we may not talk about,*
> *'Fear' only of 'the copper'. [Policeman].*
> *'Morality' down at 'The Dales'*
> *We teach; ourselves the teachers;*
> *I know not if the plan prevails*
> *With these poor little creatures.*[89]

For good measure, *The Dart* waggishly attributed to Dixon a naïve but politically charged gospel, which the senior teacher was bidden to read every morning.

> *All children have a conscience. Sometimes consciences are elastic, sometimes the other. It is nice to be good. It is very unpleasant to be bad. To be naughty is not nice. Be virtuous and you will be happy. Honesty is the best policy. Good boys always live to be old men. Naughty boys die at the age of ten, invariably. Good little boys generally marry (when they grow up) ladies with immense fortunes. Naughty boys marry for love, and always come to grief, and end their days in the workhouse. To be a good Liberal covers a multitude of sins. The wages of Toryism is death.*[90]

The policy of moral instruction was sufficiently novel for a question to be asked in the Commons, especially as to whether the 1870 Conscience Clause

---

87 *BDP,* 6 Nov. 1891.
88 Wright, 'The Struggle', p. 152.
89 *The Dart,* 10 May 1879.
90 Ibid..

would be applicable.[91] The issue was raised because Dixon had reportedly observed that 'the children should be taught that there were moral laws, and that those laws should be enforced, and that if in the course of instruction the name of God was mentioned he saw no harm in it'.[92] Some MPs construed this move as a 'step in the right direction'. The Conservative *Birmingham Daily Gazette* observed that: 'We cannot but think that in due time the conviction will gain ground that religious instruction is the best and most solid basis for moral teaching and training'.[93] Others saw in the situation another Dixon trait: compromise. 'There are only two courses to be followed on the question – religious instruction, or the absence of religious instruction', stated the *National Schoolmaster.* 'This bastard system of some unknown "Code of Moral Ethics" will satisfy nobody'.[94]

The Birmingham Liberals were by then divided on the question of excluding the Bible from schools. Whilst the Conservatives felt themselves sufficiently strong as to be able to field eight candidates for the next Board elections, they offered to withdraw a number of them (so that there would be no contest), if the BLA were to re-consider. Amidst considerable discord, it was eventually decided that the Liberals on the Board might vote as they individually thought fit on the question of Bible reading.[95]

In the event, Dixon's Liberal colleague Wright proposed on 4 December 1879 the motion that 'the Bible be read daily in the Board schools'.[96] He was supported by Dixon, and by five Conservatives. All the other Liberals and the solitary Catholic did not vote. Only Davis opposed, on the grounds that ratepayers had not been consulted. Provisions were made for the Bible to be read, without note or comment. 'The portion to be read shall be suitable to the capacity of the children, and shall be selected by the Head Teacher, who shall, at the close of each reading, make a record of the portion read in a book to be provided for the purpose'. For those who opted out, secular instruction was to be provided in a separate classroom.[97]

Dixon praised the stance of the BLA, 'that their bowing to the voice of the majority outside when they could have carried the vote showed a magnanimity from which others might learn a lesson'. However, his Board colleague Crosskey declared grumpily that, having made one concession, 'they were perfectly determined not to consent to anything beyond that in the shape of religious teaching'.[98] Dr. Dale added that he 'was sorry Birmingham had lost

---

91 See cartoon of Chamberlain sitting on a chair, holding his head in his hands.
92 *Hansard*, Vol. 246, Col. 125, 12 May 1879.
93 Wright, 'The Struggle', p. 166.
94 Ibid., p. 186.
95 Taylor, 'History of the Birmingham School Board', p. 63.
96 See cartoon of Wright [a sheep] jumping over a fence with Dixon [a sheep] behind, to join the Bible fold.
97 Birmingham Archives and Heritage, School Board Minutes, File SB/B1/1/4, p. 64.
98 *BDP*, 5 Dec. 1879.

heart and courage after six years' endurance'. As a realist, however, he did not expect a reversal of this policy in the future.[99] Religious instruction would be permitted on school premises, but this would have to be outside school hours, which was 'the least objectionable system' possible, according to Dixon many years later.[100] So from 1879 until at least the end of Dixon's period in office as Chairman, the Board's policy on religious education remained unchanged, although subject to very frequent discussion and occasional challenge.

Just before Christmas 1879 Dixon personally suffered a slight accident,[101] and several weeks later he was forced to tell the Board that, on his doctor's advice, he was going abroad for a few months.[102] On his return, he found that Chamberlain had decided to mend his fences. Dixon thus wrote from The Dales on 30 April 1880:

> My Dear Chamberlain,
> I have received your note of yesterday with great pleasure.
> It shall be as you wish. We will forget the past.
> The estrangement has been one of the most painful episodes of my life.
> I remain in great haste
> Yours faithfully
> George Dixon.[103]

What precisely Chamberlain had written to trigger this reply has long since been lost in the mists of time. It may have related to rumours that Dixon might stand as a candidate in North Warwickshire.[104] Or, perhaps Chamberlain had been goaded into action by a ditty which appeared in *The Dart*, at a time when he, Muntz and Bright were the Liberal candidates for the next election:

> *Forward! Sons of Birmingham*
> *Liberty and Right*
> *Love and honour vote for*
> *Dixon, Muntz and Bright*
> *Bear our standard proudly*
> *As in days of yore*
> *O'er the host assailant*
> *Onward to the war.*[105]

---

99 *Daily News,* 5 Dec. 1879.
100 *Hansard,* Vol. 15, Col. 968, 31 July 1893.
101 *BDP,* 18 Dec. 1879.
102 Birmingham Archives and Heritage, School Board Minutes, File SB/B1/1/4, p. 93.
103 University of Birmingham, Chamberlain Papers, Special Collections, file JC5/27/4.
104 *BDP,* 27 March 1880. It was observed that he was currently in the South of France, so his views were unknown.
105 *The Dart,* 20 March 1880.

Certainly Dixon was mentioned in April 1880 as a possible candidate as MP for Nottingham to succeed his friend and former Board colleague Wright, who had died suddenly.[106] In the event, however, Dixon did not stand.

Better relations with Chamberlain had been restored and on 4 June Dixon was elected Treasurer of the BLA.[107] Thereafter Chamberlain did very little to disturb Dixon's supremacy over the Birmingham educational world.[108] Indeed, by November 1880 a new era was dawning. At a banquet Dr. Dale felt able to observe about Dixon that he had 'reigned over a Board which had its rough and stormy times, but which was now as calm and peaceful as an Italian lake under a July sun. What the explanation of the change might be, he would not venture to suggest. It was possible the Board was a spent volcano. It was possible the tranquilising influence of Mr Dixon's own gentle and kindly spirit might be seen in the better manners and conduct of his colleagues'.[109] What a contrast with the spirit of ten years previously, when the Conservative leader Sargant had commented on the Liberals that 'Garrulity is their natural element'.[110] The change was just as significant as had been the conduct of the Birmingham Chamber of Commerce in 1863 under Dixon's calming leadership.[111]

There then followed several years when the Birmingham School Board faded from the national headlines. A Liberal Government had returned to power under Gladstone, and across England and Wales compulsory education was now the order of the day. Mundella's 1880 Act sought to take care of the inadequacies of Sandon's 1876 Act, by enacting specifically that the authorities were directly responsible for ensuring attendance, rather than indirectly placing responsibility on the parents.[112] Boards nationwide grappled with the problem of making good the deficiency of places. In Birmingham by 1880 there were 28 new Board schools, providing places for 28,827 children. But what satisfaction was that when there was still such a great shortage of accommodation?

For Dixon personally, this was a period of consolidation, punctuated by acts of characteristic philanthropy. Thus in July 1880 he was thanked for £100 which had been spent on cricket bats. The Board appreciated 'the many ways in which the Chairman [was] constantly manifesting his great anxiety to promote the welfare and happiness of the children in the Board schools of this Borough'.[113] Not for him the narrow constraints of the 3Rs.

---

106 *The Times,* 21 April 1880. The health of Dixon's wife Mary, which had been the occasion of so much concern in the early months of 1876, was by this time no longer an issue.
107 *BDP,* 4 June 1880.
108 Just before Dixon's death, the two once more differed substantially: see below, Chapter 7, p. 231.
109 *BDP,* 10 Nov. 1880.
110 Taylor, 'History of the Birmingham School Board', p. 48.
111 Editorial in *The Times,* 3 Aug. 1863: see above, Chapter 2, p. 49.
112 See above, Chapter 6, p. 172.
113 Birmingham Archives and Heritage, School Board Minutes, File SB/B1/1/4, p. 159.

What would have pleased Dixon still more were favourable comments about the reduction of crime. Thus Mundella quoted a Birmingham Inspector's report that the effect of compulsion had been 'to get rid of the young ruffians who used to stand at the street corners, and whose coarse language and manners caused a scandal in all our large towns. There was a great diminution in that respect and in juvenile crime, and the same thing was reported from all parts of the country'.[114] Nonetheless, there was the occasional hiccough. In 1884, the Mayor of Birmingham complained about the number of children on the streets. Dixon's initial suggestion to the Board was that a deputation should go and see the Mayor. His colleagues were more robust. Dixon was overruled, and the Mayor was promptly informed 'that the Board is fully aware of the necessity of providing for the elementary education of the children of school age, and is taking measures to accomplish that end'.[115]

In 1881 Dixon was elected to fill a vacancy as a governor of the Grammar School,[116] Dr. Dale having stood down from the School Board.[117] From around this time there was a reorganisation in the Foundation's own affairs. It was becoming obvious that there was an overlap: the 'Lower Middle Schools' of the Foundation became a new set of schools intermediate between the elementary school on the one side and the High School on the other.[118] Dixon also became a trustee of the recently founded Sir Josiah Mason's Science College. Out of this College grew Birmingham University, which received a Royal Charter in 1900, just two years after Dixon's death.

With the passage of time, educational standards in the Board elementary schools were rising rapidly, and children were reaching and passing the Sixth Standard at an ever-earlier age. The problem was what should happen to them then? In 1882 the issue was resolved nationally by the creation of a Seventh Standard.[119] It was a point that Dixon pondered, for even whilst engaging with Chamberlain at the time of his own threat to resign as Chairman, he had noted developments elsewhere: 'I read the other day in a newspaper that in Bradford they had determined to build a second school for what we might call higher education … We are here alive to everything that is going on'.[120] Leeds too was moving in the same direction.[121] Time was needed for Dixon to turn his aspirations into action.

---

114 *Hansard*, Vol. 264, Col. 1222, 8 Aug. 1881.

115 Birmingham Archives and Heritage, School Board Minutes, File SB/B1/1/4, p. 722.

116 *BDP*, 7 Dec. 1881.

117 Taylor, 'History of the Birmingham School Board', p. 65.

118 Dale, *Life of Dale*, p. 490.

119 J. Lawson and H. Silver, *A Social History of Education in England* (1973), p. 329; Eaglesham, *From School Board*, p. 32; Rimmington, *The Rise*, p. 35. The words Standard and Grade were interchangeable.

120 *School Board Chronicle*, 19, 11 May 1878, p. 445.

121 A. Morton, *Education and the State from 1833* (Kew, 1997), p. 24.

The early 1880s saw Dixon and Bright in closer political alignment than at any other stage of their long mutual association in Birmingham. 1882 was the critical breaking point between Bright and Chamberlain over the issue of British intervention in Egypt. Bright resigned from Gladstone's Cabinet in July over an incident which he regarded as a deplorable blunder.[122] Dixon supported Bright robustly, on one of the few occasions that Dixon delved into foreign affairs. Thinking in financial terms, as was his wont,[123] he wrote upon his return from a holiday in the Dolomites: 'My own opinion of the Egyptian war is that every step of the government which has led up to it has been a mistake – and that the objects to be gained by it will not give to the world at large a return equal to the cost of the war, using the word cost in its widest sense, including therein the violation of that principle of non-intervention which I hoped had become a plank of the Liberal platform'.[124] A week later, Bright responded, expressing his intention to give up public life: 'Recent events tend to hurry me to this conclusion'.[125] Dixon replied very hastily, pleading to him to stay in office: 'My dear Bright, you must <u>die</u> in harness'.[126]

Bright took due notice of Dixon's plea, but the matter was still causing him concern. On Christmas Day 1882 Bright again wrote from his home in Rochdale, suggesting that Dr. Dale and Dixon should visit Chamberlain. But then Bright realised that such an intervention might not succeed: where would it lead? 'I do not see how I can with advantage take part in a meeting at which it will be impossible to avoid a discussion of the Egyptian question, on which Mr Chamberlain and I are far as the poles asunder'. Chamberlain had apparently spoken of the 'ignoble doctrine of non-intervention'.[127] Despite it being the Christmas period, Dixon would seem to have replied by return, for on 27 December Bright thanked him for an invitation to come and stay at the Dales.[128]

Come and stay he did, at a later date in the summer following, after which he wrote a letter of thanks: 'I must send a special message of kind remembrance to the very young lady who acted as "boatman" for me on your small garden lake'.[129] By Christmas 1883, however, relations between Bright and Chamberlain had

---

122 Quinault, 'Bright and Chamberlain', p. 637; Marsh, *Chamberlain*, p. 159.
123 The prospects for capital investment were to be one of the key issues in Dixon's opposition to Irish Home Rule.
124 University of Birmingham Special Collections, George Dixon file: letter GD5, 10 Sept. 1882.
125 Ibid., letter GD8, 17 Sept. 1882.
126 Ibid., letter GD9, 20 Sept. 1882.
127 Ibid., letter GD10, 25 Dec. 1882.
128 Ibid., letter GD11, 27 Dec. 1882.
129 Ibid., letter GD12, 25 Aug. 1883. A later manuscript entry on the letter indicates that the very young lady could well have been Dora, Dixon's youngest daughter. A water colour reproduced in Rathbone, *The Dales*, p. 40, depicts the boat in question, the caption suggesting that Gladstone, not Bright, had visited. This would seem to be in error, for there is no record of Gladstone ever having visited the house, although the previous summer, 30 May 1882, the Gladstone Diary at St. Deiniol's, Hawarden, indicates that Gladstone did go to see Abraham Dixon's 'solemn wood of yews' at Cherkley Court.

improved, with Bright declining a further invitation to stay at the Dales, as he was going to stay with Chamberlain.[130]

On a broader front, this episode revealed a more fundamental issue for Dixon and his allegiance to the Liberal Party leadership. Although at the time he was not an MP, it demonstrated that, once again, he was his own master, and was not afraid to express views which ran counter to those of many Liberal colleagues. Dixon and Bright were far from being alone in opposing the party leadership on this question. But party discipline was relatively relaxed and two years later Dixon was re-elected to Parliament without his dissension being an issue.

Meantime, Harris, the President of the BLA, stood down due to ill-health, and Dixon was chosen to succeed him.[131] The wheel had come full circle, for he had been involved in its creation in 1865. Yet it was a very different body now by comparison with then. From the point of view of Dixon's educational agenda, there were two ramifications: it involved a considerable addition to his workload, while his close supporters wanted him to return to parliament as well.

Dr. Dale in particular regretted that Birmingham had not as yet a fourth seat to offer him. However, with a wry reference to the power of what was commonly called the Liberal Caucus, Dixon had been offered 'a position [President of the BLA] which, in the judgment of many of their enemies at least, was one of far greater authority and power than the seats which most constituencies were able to give to their representatives'.[132] Slightly more than a year later Dixon was moaning, denying that he wanted to return to Parliament. 'He had found that there was more work in these two offices than his poor abilities enabled him adequately to perform'.[133] Indeed, he was by now approaching his 63rd birthday.

Sadly, there were some children whom even the School Board could not help – the 'street arabs', children whose condition had been so wretched in the days of the Birmingham Education Society that it had been pointless to provide them with vouchers to attend school, for they lacked even the clothes in which to go. In May 1882 Dixon attended the annual meeting of the Middlemore Emigration Homes, which under the auspices of Mr Middlemore had helped 640 children to emigrate to Canada, to avoid a life of crime. Whilst Dixon believed that it was the role of government to intervene to assist in such instances, he praised Mr Middlemore for the work he had done in complementing it,[134] as government had not been up to the task.

---

130 University of Birmingham Special Collections, George Dixon file: letter GD13, 28 Dec. 1883.
131 *BDP*, 28 April 1882.
132 Ibid..
133 Ibid., 26 June 1883.
134 Ibid., 25 May 1882.

At the end of 1882, there followed a contested School Board election, for the first time in nine years. Dixon this time fared only moderately well, coming fifth out of the usual fifteen places. He was inevitably beaten by the Catholic candidate, for whom the local Catholic community plumped all their fifteen votes. And now, at the head of the poll, was the Borough Coroner, Hawkes, standing as an Independent, pledged to economy and retrenchment. The cost of all the new schools was imposing a substantial burden on the rates,[135] but Hawkes did not endear himself to the teachers, whose salaries he sought to reduce. He also opposed compulsory attendance. His support had come from 'an unholy alliance of the affluent, who always resent paying rates, and the very poor who were opposed to compulsory schooling'. His popularity, however, was only transient.[136]

Feelings yet again were running high in another local sphere. In 1884, there was furious rioting when the Conservatives, unwisely, decided to hold a rally in Birmingham's Aston Park, where Sir Stafford Northcote and Lord Randolph Churchill were scheduled to speak. Punches and chairs were thrown, as an estimated 40,000 blaspheming 'roughs' attempted to oppose a few hundred Conservatives, against a backdrop of accusations that the Radicals had issued forged tickets to gain admission to the meeting. It was left to Dixon, as 'the mouthpiece of the radical view' to address these accusations.[137] Accusations of libel were in circulation subsequently, and a cartoon appeared bearing the caption 'Eating the Leek' (that is, eating humble pie). Dixon was depicted having his arm twisted by Chamberlain, who was saying 'It's got to be eaten George. I shan't do it, so you had better George, there's a good boy'. An accompanying article was firmly of the view that, as it was Chamberlain who had made so much capital out of the riots, it was he who should have apologised.[138]

Also in 1884, Dixon unveiled his own plan for complementing the work of the government, and with minimal burden on the rates: the promise of a Seventh Grade Technical School in Bridge Street. Continuing in his tradition of innovation, this school differed from all earlier higher grade schools by offering tuition only at the Seventh Grade. Earlier schools, by contrast, had taken children through all Standards, whilst the Bridge Street School was essentially a central school to which were drafted the brightest pupils from other local schools who wanted to progress beyond the Sixth Grade. Logistically, therefore, it was a formula that could only work in a large conurbation. Its experimental

---

135 The Board's precept on the Town Council had risen to £48,000 by this time: see Taylor, 'History of the Birmingham School Board', p. 65.
136 G.J. Barnsby, *Birmingham Working People: A History of the Labour Movement in Birmingham, 1650-1914* (1989), p. 165.
137 Bridges, *Reminiscences*, p. 144.
138 *Birmingham Dart and Midland Figaro,* 27 Feb. 1885.

nature was emphasised in papers submitted to the Education Department by the Clerk, George B. Davis:

> The object of opening the School is to try what is believed to be an important experiment, viz. that of collecting together the boys who have passed the 6th Standard in order to give them more complete and effective instruction than they are able to receive when scattered in twos and threes over the Board Schools.[139]

It immediately attracted national attention. Its affairs were discussed in detail in the Commons and before a Royal Commission, and its lineal descendant, the *George Dixon Academy* still survives today.

Its premises in Bridge Street had formerly been a cocoa factory but, when Cadbury's enterprise moved to Bournville,[140] it was surplus to the requirements of Rabone Bros. Dixon made the building available to the School Board, rent free, for five years. He also offered to make all the very considerable structural alterations and to provide heating apparatus at his own cost.[141] The Education Department in London looked on with great interest, as this 'obviated the raising of the difficult question of a loan for so high a type of school', – as civic funding for buildings was considered as illegal.[142] That left the Board with the responsibility for the furniture and fittings, and paying the teaching staff. The Board did in fact seek permission from the Education Department to take out loans for the purchase of items such as cupboards,[143] demonstrating the extent to which central government intervened in matters of local detail. The burden on the rates was contained since, while the pupils, aged from 12 to 14, were studying the syllabus prescribed by the Education Department at the Seventh Standard (and this necessarily involved an element of the 3Rs), they were also going on to take examinations prescribed by the rival Science and Art Department, so that the school was also in receipt of grants from this alternative source. Paying no rent, the school's expenditure in 1886 was £1,479, whilst its income comprised grants from the Science and Art Department of £963, from the Education Department £105, from fees, calculated at 3d per week, for a roll of 250 pupils over 40 weeks, approximately £125, and a contribution from the rates of £238, leaving a minimal loss of £48.[144]

---

139 National Archives, file ED21/575.
140 See above, Chapter 1, p. 28.
141 Birmingham Archives and Heritage, School Board Minutes, File SB/B1/1/4, p. 726. The cost was £5,000: see Taylor, 'History of the Birmingham School Board', p. 106.
142 National Archives, file ED24/38, 'Higher Grade Schools in England, with their Origin, Growth, and Present Condition', p. 7.
143 National Archives, file ED21/585.
144 Eaglesham, *From School Board,* p. 38.

The arrangements were, to say the least of it, ingenious, and came under close scrutiny by the Cross Commission,[145] which spent much effort looking into the legality of rate payments for higher grade schools. About half the school consisted of Seventh Standard pupils, and the other half had progressed beyond that stage. In order to obtain Education Department grant, the Seventh Standard pupils had to devote at least 20 hours per week to subjects in the Code. However, since Seventh and ex-Seventh Standard[146] students were taught together for some classes, it was found necessary to inter-weave the two sets of requirements (from the Education Department and the Science and Art Department) by putting a liberal interpretation upon Reading and Writing. One commentator described the situation: 'Presumably visitors making awkward enquiries would find that although one half of the class [ex-Seventh] were occupied with "Theoretical Chemistry" and the other [Seventh] with "Writing", both were in fact copying down the same notes from the blackboard'.[147]

Visitors came from far and wide. Government ministers, deputations from other towns, even a professor from an American college, all were to be greeted by the school's headmaster, Mr. Cox. In choosing him, Birmingham's School Board had selected a good candidate. By 1901 he was to become the President of the Association of Headmasters of Higher Grade Schools and Schools of Science.[148] The school premises were far from ideal, however, and the heating on occasion plainly inadequate: the temperatures in four classrooms one autumn morning were recorded as 50, 47, 50 and 55 degrees Fahrenheit respectively.[149] Over time the problems mounted. One teacher suffered from a kidney complaint having caught a cold in his classroom. Cox himself was unwell with neuralgia and nervous exhaustion. And another teacher was 'extremely ill and overtaxed' and later died.[150] Cox set very high standards, recording in the Log Book that a teacher was one minute late,[151] and berated himself when he too was late one day.[152]

The formula was, however, a huge success. At one point, temporary entrance exams had to be introduced to weed out weaker candidates. Attendance figures were always very high; and only the lightest of discipline was needed.[153] This achievement was despite the very long hours of attendance. A second higher

---

145 *Royal Commission Appointed to Inquire into the Working of the Elementary Education Acts* (1886).

146 Those who had progressed beyond the Seventh Standard.

147 Eaglesham, *From School Board,* p. 38.

148 *The Times,* 16 Nov. 1901.

149 Birmingham Archives and Heritage, Log Book of the George Dixon Higher Grade School, 1884-1906, File MS/S/80/1, 14 Nov. 1893.

150 Ibid., 14 Feb. 1889.

151 Ibid., 7 March, 1892.

152 Ibid., 8 Feb. 1894.

153 M. Vlaeminke, *The English Higher Grade Schools: A Lost Opportunity* (2000), p. 54.

grade school based on the Bridge Street model was opened in Waverley Road in 1892,[154] and the school in Bridge Street itself had to be transferred to Oozells Street when the Science and Art Department threatened to withdraw its grant because of the unsuitability of the premises.[155]

An analysis of the social background of the parents in 1892/3 showed that, while 5% were professional / employers / managers; and 19% were semi-professional, merchants and traders; as many as 67% were skilled or semi-skilled workers, clerks and other white-collar occupations; and a creditable, though still too small, 9% unskilled working class.[156] This report showed clearly that schooling of this nature attracted children from all backgrounds, but not in the same proportions as were found in the population of Birmingham as a whole.

The significance of the new school in the overall structure of the country's educational system was best described by Austen Chamberlain many years later: 'It was quickly seen that the idea with which he [Dixon] was experimenting was a real attempt to fill the gap which existed between the old primary school then established and the higher education of this country'.[157]

What had Dixon achieved? His Board colleague, Crosskey, gave the best answer in evidence before the Cross Commission. He noted that the higher grade school was conducted on entirely different lines from secondary schools.[158] It was distinct from a technical school in that it did not teach a trade, but rather the principles which underlay a trade.[159] No other school provided such an education for those aged 12 to 14.[160] On the other hand, by highlighting the extraordinary confusion and overlap between different if not competing government departments, Dixon was gently adding fuel to the fire which would eventually see the complete (and very necessary) re-organisation of educational administration and, in the process, the abolition of the higher grade schools themselves. By the date of his death in 1898, the fire was almost alight, and burst into flames with the Education Act of 1902.

As a result of all these endeavours, Birmingham was proud. A contemporary writer recorded in 1885 that it provided 'a set of schools that cannot be equalled by any town in the kingdom, either for number, magnificence of architecture, educational appliance, high-class teachers, or (which is the most important)

---

154 Taylor, 'History of the Birmingham School Board', p. 203.

155 Birmingham Archives and Heritage, *Birmingham School Board Annual Report 1896*, File SB/B1/4/8, p. 14.

156 Vlaeminke, *English Higher Grade Schools,* p. 50.

157 *Birmingham Post,* 5 March 1934.

158 The vocational nature of higher grade schools contrasted greatly with the literary bias of the grammar school curriculum.

159 *Second Report of the Royal Commission Appointed to Inquire into the Working of the Elementary Education Acts, England and Wales* (1887), Q. 30,862/4/7.

160 *BDP,* 23 Feb. 1885.

means for the advancement of the scholars, to whom every inducement is held out for self-improvement, except in the matter of religion, which, as nearly as possible, is altogether banished from the curriculum'.[161]

Riding on the back of this communal self-confidence, Dixon was selected by the BLA in 1884 (with a characteristic show of reluctance on his part) as the third Birmingham Liberal candidate, to accompany Bright and Chamberlain to Westminster. The Third Reform Act and the associated re-distribution of seats were about to follow. Dixon's preference, however, remained with the educational work he loved: 'I would rather work in a narrow sphere, and do what little I attempt well, than extend my work over a larger area with very little satisfaction in any direction'.[162]

Early in the following year, Dixon was still sticking to the same line: 'my desire is to remain at the School Board, where it seems to me that my services will be more valuable than in Parliament'.[163] He was also careful to set out his political line that he would be taking in Parliament, should he be re-elected. Dixon welcomed Gladstone's continued leadership of the party, and looked forward to the introduction of measures 'advocated by the advanced section' of the Liberal party. He added that he had 'no other desire than that of advancing what may seem to me to be the highest interests of the people'.[164]

Locally, the Conservatives knew that they would be defeated by the Liberals. Lord Randolph Churchill, who stood unsuccessfully against John Bright, wrote to Lord Salisbury, holding out hopes – but only in the future: 'Bright and the old lot' (and there was little doubt that this grouping would have included Dixon) 'will gradually pass away and then we shall succeed to the inheritance'.[165] Dixon himself was determined that his return to the Commons would be on his terms. In July 1884 he stated publicly: 'Now you must remember I am getting to be an old man – [A Voice: "A grand old man," and laughter] – and if I go back to Parliament I shall have to claim one of the privileges of age – one that is always accorded to the members of the House of Commons above sixty years of age – and that is that, in consideration of their failing strength, they are only expected to do a minimum amount of work – they are not called upon to do, as I once did for you in the House, a maximum amount of work'.[166]

Bright and Dixon continued to maintain their good working relationship. In 1884, Bright visited Abraham Dixon at Cherkley Court, reporting in his diary: 'Walked to the top of Boxhill; the country and the view of unsurpassable beauty. Called on Mr Dixon. His house is large and almost palatial, his conservatory

161 W. Showell, *Dictionary of Birmingham* (Birmingham, 1885), p. 277.
162 *BDP*, 4 July 1884.
163 Ibid., 2 Feb. 1885.
164 Ibid., 28 Oct. 1885.
165 Quinault, 'Bright and Chamberlain', p. 628.
166 *BDP*, 4 July 1884.

very fine; Victoria Regia [a genus of water lilies] there. His brother is my friend George Dixon of Birmingham'.[167] A year later: 'My birthday – 74. How my life has passed on to almost old age! And how much have I had to be grateful for. To Birmingham to George Dixons'.[168] There was a further visit to Dixon's house a few weeks later.[169] These frequent visits to Birmingham, and visits to Dixon, were far from normal, as Bright normally went to his constituency only once a year, and, for the most part, when he did, stayed with Chamberlain. A final reference by Bright came in the spring of 1886 when: 'George Dixon called to discuss Irish question. His view agrees with mine and Chamberlain's'.[170]

By 1885, the law had changed, and the town of Birmingham was no longer a three-member constituency. It had instead seven separate single-member constituencies. The pressure was on Dixon to become a candidate. The *Birmingham Daily Post* published an editorial supporting Dixon, Bright and Chamberlain by universal consent. But Dixon wrote modestly in reply: 'Trusting … I shall not be asked to become a candidate by any of the new constituencies'.[171]

Yet Birmingham was by now used to Dixon's 'No!' becoming in due course 'Yes, but under protest'. And very shortly after Dixon was returned as the first representative for the new constituency of Edgbaston.

In terms of wealth, Edgbaston was second only to Kensington nationally, and for Dixon the annual migration between the two constituted something of a natural progression. However, whilst the journey from Kensington, with its grand new Museums, to Westminster took Dixon through some of the grandest parts of London, his walk from The Dales to the centre of Birmingham for many years served to remind him of the poverty and deprivation that pervaded much of urban Britain. It was a salutary contrast that kept him ever alert to the cause for which he was fighting.

Amidst all the debate about Dixon's possible return to Parliament, his beloved wife Mary died.[172] It is not entirely clear how ill Mary had been during the nine years from her husband's enforced early retirement from the Commons in 1876, until her death in March 1885. Writing many years later, Katie Rathbone described her mother as an invalid, being treated with homeopathic medicine, but 'in those days very little was known about growths, and – well – nothing was done'.[173] A final operation, to remove the growth, was performed by one of the finest surgeons in the land, Lawson Tait, a Birmingham

---

167 R.A.J. Walling (ed.), *The Diaries of John Bright, with a foreword by Philip Bright* (1930) p. 520: entry for 9 Nov. 1884, p. 520.

168 Ibid., p. 532: entry for 16 Nov. 1885.

169 Ibid., p. 533: entry for 7 Dec. 1885.

170 Ibid., p. 536: entry for 18 March 1886.

171 *BDP.*, 2 Feb. 1885.

172 *The Times,* 28 March 1885, reported the death as having occurred three days earlier.

173 Birmingham Archives and Heritage, File MS 2239, Bundle 26A, p. 1.

resident. Mary herself was glad that an operation had taken place. 'it was a relief to be rid of the great weight'.[174] But the surgeon could not save her, and she died two or three days later.[175]

The family's reaction was to 'set their teeth and go on'. The School Board sent its condolences and, from his brother Joshua's house in Devon, Dixon replied: 'The life of my dear wife would have failed in its highest mission if it had not created in all that were nearest to her a continually increasing desire that their lives also should be devoted to the well-being and the happiness of those around them. Hoping that my efforts in the public service may be more successful in the future than they have been in the past'.[176]

A few days later, Caroline Stansfeld died too.[177] It was a remarkable symmetry for Dixon and his brother-in-law. They were born in the same year and their wives died in the same year. Eventually they were both to die in the same year too. For the closing years of their lives, they arranged to share the same accommodation during the Parliamentary season, at Stoke Lodge, 41 Hyde Park Gate. They co-resided despite the very substantial difference of opinion which was to develop between them on a new but very fundamental issue of the day, Ireland. The issues changed, but political and family life perennially adapted to respond to new debates.

174 Ibid., Bundle 26A, p. 4.
175 Ibid., Bundle 47, p. 15.
176 *School Board Chronicle,* 33, 16 May 1885, p. 485.
177 Birmingham Archives and Heritage, File MS 2239, Bundle 47, p. 16.

CHAPTER SEVEN

The Zenith 1885-98

DIXON NEVER RETIRED. Whilst for health reasons his elder brother Abraham Dixon had left Birmingham in his fifties, the younger brother, now a widower, continued his own demanding lifestyle. In 1885 the family holidayed in Scotland, where by chance they met the Powell family in Gairloch, and Dixon's son Charles subsequently became engaged to Agnes, the youngest Powell daughter. Dixon's family always remained close and supportive. And they remained committed to life in Birmingham. The conurbation described by de Tocqueville in 1835 as full of 'faces brown with smoke' and resounding to the 'sound of hammers and the whistle of steam escaping from boilers',[1] had developed into a regional metropolis of great civic assurance. Among its amenities were the concerts of Birmingham's Triennial Music Festival, which ran from 1784 to 1912, and for which celebrated musicians like Mendelssohn, Sullivan, Dvorak and Elgar, wrote special compositions. In 1885 the highlight was the first performance of Gounod's *Mors et Vita [Death and Life]* commissioned by the Birmingham Festival several years previously.

Dixon pressed on with his work as Chairman of the School Board, whilst seeking to re-enter national politics. He was also actively re-arranging his own private financial affairs. Almost totally obscured from the outside world was the incorporation of the Dixon Investment Company ("DIC"). Quite

---

1 A. de Tocqueville, *Journeys to England and Ireland* (ed. J.P. Mayer) (1958), p. 94.

a lot of the detail is still obscure today, although a complete record of its statutory paperwork, including the Annual Returns, is available at the National Archives.[2] This was no small enterprise, the opening balance sheet totalling £100,000 upon registration on 27 May 1885.

The first object of the Company was 'to acquire certain of the lands, property, business and investments of George Dixon, of Birmingham, Esquire, and Abraham Dixon, of Cherkley Court, near Leatherhead, in the County of Surrey, Esquire, in the several Colonies of New South Wales, Victoria, South Australia, and New Zealand'.

The precise origins of these assets is uncertain. The younger, and first-named, brother had lived in Australia and New Zealand in the mid-1850s, while there is no record of Abraham ever having visited. Nor does the brief history of Rabone Bros. record Australasia as being a significant market for the Dixon brothers. Pretty clearly, therefore, the initiative came from George Dixon.

Looking at the situation in the twenty-first century, when investors are much more aware of the fiscal implications of their actions, it is appropriate to enquire whether the incorporation of DIC was driven by tax avoidance, for there were both death duty and income tax advantages in holding certain investments outside the United Kingdom.[3] There is no evidence, however, that this line of thought was being followed.

On the other hand, philanthropic motives did enter into the equation, and there is supporting evidence of this intention when Dixon wrote home whilst visiting New Zealand a few years later. Contemplating assistance to emigrants, he wrote that: 'A working man, if he chooses, can save £40 per annum and after 10 years with £400 can buy a property, especially if he takes a mortgage [from the Dixon Investment Company] and may thus work their [sic] way up into independence and even wealth'.[4] This approach was consistent with the thrust of Dixon's earlier support for Joseph Arch and the National Agricultural Labourers Union. Nonetheless, the identity of the borrowers and investments in 1885 does not indicate that this policy, if policy it was, was being pursued at the outset.

The overwhelming majority of the investments were in New Zealand rather than in Australia, and a scrutiny of borrowers from the Christchurch area, whose total balances (viz. £26,240) represented more than a quarter

---

2 The National Archives: Public Records Office, Statutory Records of Dixon Investment Company Ltd, 1885-1954: BT31/36585/21203.

3 The author is very grateful to John Avery Jones for his input into this topic.

4 Nelson Provincial Museum, NZ; Alexander Turnbull Library, Wellington, NZ; and Joseph Chamberlain Papers, Special Collections, University of Birmingham. Letter dated 16 Nov. 1888 from George Dixon to the family in England, written from Wanganui, whilst travelling through New Zealand, p. 33 of typescript version of collected letters. Subsequent references below annotated "GDNZ". The original manuscript letters are also in the Special Collections.

of the total, shows them to be a list of blue-chip risks.[5] They thus included a former Prime Minister of New Zealand, Sir John Hall, as well as the leading private boys' school, Christ's College, and the South Island's leading newspaper, the Press Newspaper Company. Curiously, an investigation of the records of these three investors today has failed to show any sign of a loan or advance from DIC.[6] None of the individual balances represented an especially large figure in the fortunes of any of the three, so they may have been short-term. Indeed, it is conceivable that the balances were treated as a bridging loan from the Company to finance a trading debt with the Rabone business.

One possible partial explanation stems from the fact that Dixon's cousin Waring Taylor, a prominent politician in Wellington, was adjudged bankrupt on 28 June 1884.[7] This development was followed by bitter quarrelling amongst the various creditors. Dixon was one of his principal overseas creditors, and his sister Mary was also clamouring for settlement. Given that a number of the borrowers were eminent local politicians, who had moved in the same circles as Waring before his downfall, it is possible that a scheme of arrangement was concluded whereby debts due by these individuals to Waring were acquired by DIC as part of a complex settlement process. At any rate, the Dixon Investment Company was incorporated shortly after Waring Taylor's downfall.

Evidence from the early years of the twentieth century shows that DIC developed into a mature financial entity whose capital had more than doubled to £220,000 in 1902, four years after George's death. The Company also had an effective loan application form, well suited to the needs of the day.[8]

In addition, the Company had an investment in Manawa Farm, Whareama, outside Wellington on North Island. It was valued in 1885 at the very precise figure of £21,557.42, having been acquired in settlement of a debt, and Dixon paid it a visit in 1888.

Dixon's financial re-organisation did not end there, for on 31 December 1885 the old firm of Rabone Bros & Co. was dissolved by mutual agreement, and replaced by the new firm of Rabone Bros and Co.

The most significant consequence of this change was that, at long last, Abraham Dixon was able to withdraw completely from the business, having been a sleeping partner for many years. His younger brother did not suffer ill-health to the same extent, although poor eyesight shadowed him all his life, compelling him to wear a green eyeshade on occasion.

---

5 The author wishes to thank Binney Lock, Jean Garner, Garth Cant and many others in Christchurch for their considerable assistance here.

6 The author wishes to thank Kate Foster, Jane Teal and Michael Vance respectively for their hospitality and considerable assistance in coming to this conclusion.

7 Patterson, 'Whatever Happened to Waring Taylor?', p. 117.

8 See Appendix 1.

Meantime, in 1885 Dixon was returned as the first MP for the new constituency of Edgbaston, which he was to represent until his death. He had been selected as prospective candidate less than three weeks after Mary's death, with one speaker mentioning the aspiration that one day Dixon might run the Education Department. That was never to be; but it shows the high opinions of his abilities. Indeed, Dixon's supporters honoured him: 'because of all men in the town he had borne – long might he continue to bear – without abuse, the grand old name of gentleman'.[9]

His election necessarily involved his resignation as President of the BLA, which he tendered in early December. Since this body was responsible for choosing Liberal candidates, to have continued in office would have conflicted with his position as a newly-elected MP.[10] Dixon himself perceived his resignation as being to some extent a relinquishment of power, for it was a period when the status of an MP relative to his constituency was under discussion. Dixon was quite clear as to his own position within the BLA. He agreed in 1884 that: 'It was perfectly true that they did intend to dictate to their representatives and to the Houses of Parliament, what were the measures that they required them to pass'.[11] And a year later, he stated that: 'We were getting every year more and more into the position of being represented in Parliament by delegates'[12]. But this trend had now reached its apogee.

The events of the coming months in Westminster, centred on the split in the Liberal party over Home Rule for Ireland, were to have a profound effect on the country, and nowhere more so than in Birmingham, which was shortly to become a stronghold of the breakaway party of Liberal Unionism, led by the intransigent Joseph Chamberlain. Even within families there were severe divisions, and the change in attitude of *The Dart and Midland Figaro* exemplified it totally. Having satirised both Chamberlain and Dixon, the *Dart* now warmed to the steady achievements of the constant George Dixon.

In early 1885, it proclaimed 'The school at Bridge Street is worth attention, and is one of the most satisfactory blossoms on the big Board School tree'.[13] Early autumn saw Dixon described as 'the amiable gentleman whom Mr Joseph Chamberlain shifts about as he wants him'.[14] A few weeks later, 'The Liberal party has several gentlemen in its ranks. Mr George Dixon is one of them. … If Birmingham Liberalism were synonymous with George Dixon, it would be better for all of us'.[15]

---

9 *BDP,* 17 Apr. 1885.
10 Ibid., 4 Dec. 1885.
11 Ibid., 11 March 1884.
12 Ibid., 4 Feb. 1885.
13 *The Dart and Midland Figaro,* 13 March 1885.
14 Ibid., 23 Oct. 1885.
15 Ibid., 27 Nov. 1885.

Yet there were fears that he might be too pliable. In the run-up to Christmas, poetry was used to describe the attributes of Birmingham's seven new MPs, and of Dixon it was written:

> *Edgbaston Georgie, MP long ago,*
> *Till he had to step out to accommodate Joe,*
> *Is now on good terms with the great Caucus King;*
> *So he marches next in this wonderful string;*
> *He had to sit out in the cold a long while,*
> *But now he goes back to the House with a smile;*
> *He'll vote always with Joe, on the true Caucus plan,*
> *And let bye-gones be bye-gones – this pliable man.*[16]

In summer 1886, Dixon was still described as a 'jelly-fish', knuckling under to his old rival, Chamberlain.[17] It was the time of another election campaign, and the publication was robustly on the side of the Gladstonian Liberals. Again, a cartoon appeared. Bearing the caption 'A Political Beauty Show', and all clad in dresses and sitting on a bench, Chamberlain was described as 'Uncertain temper, just divorced'; Bright was 'Aged, grumpy'; and Dixon 'Very easy natured. Do anything for a quiet life'.

In the meantime, the timing of the 1885 general election had clashed with that of the triennial School Board election, and there was anxiety in some quarters that the usual religious strife associated with the Board elections should not be added to Parliamentary issues.[18] Thus there was a repeat of the tactics adopted in the 1879 election,[19] whereby the Conservatives eventually offered to reduce the number of their candidates, if the issue of the introduction of Bible-teaching in place of Bible-reading could be referred to the BLA after the election. In that case, there would be no contest.[20]

On 18 December 1885, the BLA duly met in the Town Hall, Schnadhorst having been elected to succeed Dixon as President.[21] A petition in favour of Bible-teaching with no fewer than 22,767 signatures was sent to Dixon in his capacity of Chairman of the Board.[22] Interestingly, there were indications that he had some sympathy for the proposals,[23] which in broad outline involved the reciting of the Lord's Prayer daily, and also a daily Bible lesson, with historical, geographical and grammatical explanations. Dr. Dale,

---

16 Ibid., 11 Dec. 1885.
17 Ibid., 18 June 1886.
18 Richards, 'Religious Controversy and the School Boards, 1870-1902', p. 192.
19 See above, Chapter 6, p. 190.
20 Taylor, 'History of the Birmingham School Board', p. 69.
21 *BDP*, 19 Dec. 1885.
22 Ibid., 18 Dec. 1885.
23 Ibid., 19 Dec. 1885.

however, opposed the proposition vigorously, and the vote for change was soundly defeated.

Dixon was on this occasion on the losing side. Nonetheless, the impression had been created that he was not unsympathetic to the views of the Conservatives. That development was to be of great importance in the conduct of the next triennial election three years later,[24] and it was a sign of Dixon's perennial moderation on contentious issues.

On the national stage, meanwhile, Dixon was also going to face an entirely new problem. The Liberals' divisions over Irish Home Rule were to have unfortunate consequences – including negative ones for Dixon's continuing campaign to have School Boards established across the country.

The Irish situation had featured prominently in his early election campaigns. Throughout there was consistency: Ireland had been misruled by the British, and the British were in the best position to rectify the situation. At the same time, whilst there were divisions within the local Chamber of Commerce on the issue, Dixon was concerned that there be no undermining of the principles of Free Trade, to which he always remained faithful.

He spoke increasingly frequently on the subject of Ireland as the 1880s progressed and, although his sympathies overall were in line with the majority of those around him in Birmingham, he did not necessarily agree with all the detail. As ever, he remained his own man, and he found himself estranged in particular from the BLA. History has never claimed him as a major player in the Home Rule crisis but, like all MPs, he had to take a position.

Fortunately for him, the split in the party did not split the family, for Stansfeld remained a Gladstonian Liberal. Katie described the situation: they 'remained living in the same house, both in Parliament, and in complete amity – unusual rather – the Home Rule question made people very quarrelsome and divided families'.[25]

By 1886 Dixon's position was clear enough. He remained a Unionist for the time being. The 'real central question' was overpopulation in certain parts of the country. 'The British government would be much better able to deal with this question than an Irish parliament, owing to its possessing a power and wealth which an Irish parliament never could have'. To his mind, the solution was relatively straightforward. The Liberal government had been elected to reform English local government and, if that principle were extended to Ireland, this 'would give to her all that would be necessary in order to create there prosperity and contentment'. Ultimately 'he wished Ireland to have the same liberties and advantages, so far as legislation was concerned, as were

---

24 At the next School Board meeting in February, Dixon felt obliged to vote as the representative of the 2,000, even though he personally felt sorry for so doing: see *BDP*, 5 Feb. 1886. This was an interesting example of the discipline of the Birmingham Liberal Association in action.

25 Rathbone, *Miscellaneous*, File 47, p. 16.

given to every other part of Great Britain'. Then, rather patronisingly, Dixon added that he did not think that the Irish were ready for Home Rule, on the basis that the zeal of an Irish parliament would lead the country into debt, and relations between England and Ireland would deteriorate further.[26]

In the 1886 general election Dixon was returned unopposed, although the Liberals nationally suffered a heavy defeat at the hands of Lord Salisbury's Conservatives.

In the autumn, Dixon was visited by Henry Sidgwick, the founder of Newnham College, Cambridge, which his daughter Katie had attended from 1879 to 1882. Sidgwick recorded the visit in the following terms: 'spent three pleasant days with Mr George Dixon (MP) a thoroughly <u>nice</u> man. (This is not an adjective I often use, nor did I expect to apply it to a leading BRUMMAGEM politician, but it is the word for Dixon; he is not brilliant nor exactly impressive, and though he is able, it is not his ability that strikes one so much as a gentle thoroughness, sustained, alert, mildly humorous)'. These were astute observations. Sidgwick also contrasted Dixon's benevolence with the reputation of others locally. Without naming names, the main reference could only have been to Chamberlain.

Sidgwick asked Dixon why the Liberal Unionist phalanx in Birmingham appeared to be united. In reply, Dixon 'thought it was half an accident; the party was really divided here as elsewhere just below the top, but that Bright and Chamberlain and himself – no one of the three ordinarily in the habit of taking his opinions from either of the other two – happened to coincide on this question'. And Sidgwick accepted that, musing: 'they, I gathered, were the three recognized leaders. Bright being the old time-honoured political chief, Chamberlain the established 'boss' in the industrial action of the municipality, and Dixon the educational boss'.[27] Again, these were astute and accurate observations. Bright's reputation as a national politician lingered on, and Sidgwick would certainly not have contemplated deriding him as he had done Chamberlain.

The partisan *School Board Chronicle* spelt out the ramifications of the party split: the political revolution of 1886 meant that 'the hopeful struggle [for the establishment of School Boards nationwide] came to an end. … Bravely, now and again, he [Dixon] cast himself in front of the hosts of the party into which his political fortune had drifted him, and strove in vain to stem reaction on what had become his own side of the House'.[28] Chamberlain said much the same thing: in referring to the sacrifice involved in abandoning the Liberal party, and joining the Liberal Unionists, Dixon 'shared our view of the danger

---

26 *BDP,* 30 Apr. 1886.
27 A. Sidgwick and E.M. Sidgwick, *Henry Sidgwick: A Memoir* (1906), p. 456.
28 *School Board Chronicle,* Vol. 59, 29 January 1898, p. 120.

involved to our country'.[29] The local Birmingham response was that Dixon was safe enough in his Edgbaston constituency, 'as long as he votes with Lord Salisbury' [the Conservative leader].[30]

Dixon was by now in his late sixties, and *The Dart and Midland Figaro* for one was becoming restive about his impotence in national politics. After a series of articles on the Liberal Unionists, and a report of one of their meetings, it noted:

> … regret was the feeling with which we listened to the speech of Mr George Dixon. What a contrast to the days when he sarcastically declared that "Birmingham was Mr Chamberlain". He would repeat this now-a-days, but with different emphasis and meaning, and would in all earnestness limit the political thought and progress of Birmingham within the bounds of the Highbury platform. Mr Dixon shines as an educationist, and it is to be hoped he will henceforth direct his main attention to educational matters, otherwise he may one day find that an enemy has sown tares amongst his wheat, and that the alliance between the Chamberlainites and the Conservatives has marred and hampered the whole of Mr George Dixon's educational work in this town.[31]

Dixon did play a small part in the 1887 Round Table Conference which sought Liberal Reunion, but on this occasion he favoured the relatively firm attitude of Lord Hartington to that of Chamberlain. Dixon went out of his way to stress how very indulgent the party must be to the Conservative government, to ward off the prospect of Gladstone's return to power, with the risk of re-opening the Irish question. Hartington himself believed that 'Liberal Unionist Liberals would find Conservative legislation quite progressive and could itself influence its ally further in the same direction'.[32] This was indeed an approach that Dixon supported just two years later, in the context of local government reforms. By contrast Chamberlain, who was unable to attend, simply sent a telegram, indicating that he would consider reunion, provided that there was no talk of proposing the rejected Home Rule scheme again.

The split in the national Liberal party did not, however, affect party labels in the Birmingham School Board: Dixon remained a 'Liberal' there, even while being a 'Liberal Unionist' in the Commons. The question had no bearing on his relationship with, for example, his Vice-Chairman, MacCarthy, who remained

---

29 Ibid., p. 150.
30 *The Dart and Midland Figaro,* 6 May 1887.
31 Ibid., 1 June 1888.
32 M. Hurst, *Joseph Chamberlain and Liberal Reunion: The Round Table Conference of 1887* (Newton Abbot, 1970), p. 85.

a Gladstonian Liberal throughout.[33] Indeed, party labels were attached with little glue, the Conservative label being substituted for the Church label, and *vice versa*, periodically. To some, being a member of the School Board was not even 'politics'.[34]

There was now a broad re-awakening of interest in education as a topic: 'Educate, educate, educate, is the burthen of the lesson from Germany' was the phrase proclaimed by the *Spectator*,[35] amidst another host of Royal Commissions.[36] Dixon soon felt himself under pressure from his constituents. In Parliament he was to compare the 1870 situation, when Bright had said that 'to teach the children in elementary schools to read and write is enough', with the current situation: 'The working men of Birmingham are really in advance of the School Board; they are continually pressing it forward; their complaint is that it does not do enough; they watch the course of legislation on the subject; and they express in the strongest terms their dissatisfaction at delay'.[37] The clamour was for 'what is sometimes called secondary education', and 'evening continuation schools'.[38]

Dixon's exemplary influence was not going unnoticed in high quarters. In a deputation to see Lord Cranbrook, Lord President of the Council, the latter referred to Dixon's arrangements for financing the Bridge Street School. 'Mr Dixon had said that he had gone round the Elementary Education Act; but, though the way in which he had done so was much to his credit, he [Cranbrook] was afraid he must accuse him, though without offence, of having used corrupt influences in order to achieve what he had done. He had paid out of his own pocket money which should have been paid under other circumstances out of the rates, or by the Government. It was very much to his honour that he had done so much to show that he was thoroughly in earnest in this matter.'[39]

Now in the second half of his seventh decade, Dixon was doing two very significant jobs at the same time, and in locations more than a hundred miles apart. Eventually the Birmingham Board meetings were re-scheduled for Saturday afternoons, to allow him to devote as much time as possible to Westminster.[40] Still he grappled with the detail with a very occasional flash of

---

33 Taylor, 'History of the Birmingham School Board', p. 98.

34 For example MacCarthy, discussing Dixon's workload, said 'Very few men in the country could do for education what he could, while there were thousands who could do the work of politics': see *School Board Chronicle*, Vol. 40, 14 July 1888, p. 32.

35 *Spectator,* 26 June 1886, quoted in W.H.G. Armytage, *The German Influence on English Education* (1969), p. 66. It was to be re-cycled by New Labour in the late 1990s in noun form, 'Education, education, education'.

36 The Samuelson Commission on Technical Education, the Cross Commission on Elementary Education and the Bryce Commission on Secondary Education were all active in the 1880s and 1890s.

37 *Hansard*, Vol. 339, Col. 405, 1 Aug. 1889.

38 Ibid..

39 *BDP,* 22 March 1887.

40 *School Board Chronicle,* Vol. 47, 30 Jan. 1892, p. 113.

humour: there were never enough schools for all the children – perhaps measures should be taken to stop children being born, he quipped on one occasion.[41] There was too the continuing problem of the grinding poverty of the era. The Government urged School Boards generally to exercise extreme caution in enforcing compulsory attendance, against the backdrop of children turning up at school who had been unfed for more than twenty-four hours at a time.[42]

Birmingham stood out for tackling related issues. In 1888 a partial solution was eventually found for the humiliating problem of requiring needy parents to approach the Board of Guardians. As an experiment, poor people could apply at the School Board offices, for payment of fees to Denominational schools, as well as for the remission of fees to Board schools. In the case of the payment of fees, Board officials would act as agents for the Board of Guardians – a fine distinction, but it overcame the perceived Clause 25 complication.[43] In any event, legislation enabling the eventual provision of free education was just over the horizon, in the shape of the Elementary Education Act of 1891, although there were still just under 800,000 paying fees in 1895.[44]

At the same time, Birmingham was significantly more munificent in providing possibilities for free education than were other places. In the mid-1880s no less than 33% of its children received free education, whilst the national figure was 4.43%.[45] There was also one school, Staniforth Street Free Order School, near the heart of the town, where all pupils attended free of charge. It was the only such school that had ever been established.[46]

What Birmingham was doing, however, went very much against the grain of central government policy. Some years later, R.L. Morant, wrote:

'[The] cardinal principle, recognized both by School Boards and by the Education Department (as it is still to this date by the Science and Art Department) [is] that parents should be made to pay as much as possible towards the school expenditure. So much so that the statutory limit of 9d. as a maximum fee was often evaded at least in the higher portion of these schools by an arrangement of lower fees in the lower school so as to bring the <u>average</u> fee of the school within statutory requirements (e.g. Sheffield)'.[47]

---

41 *BDP,* 12 Oct. 1886.
42 *Hansard*, Vol. 317, Col. 1154, 18 July 1887.
43 See Birmingham Archives and Heritage, *Birmingham School Board Annual Report 1888*, File SB/B1/4/8, p. 19; and above, Chapter 5, p. 173.
44 Sutherland, *Policy-Making,* p. 328.
45 Hurt, *Elementary Schooling,* p. 158.
46 *School Board Chronicle,* Vol. 37, 23 Apr. 1887, p. 418. Birmingham's free schooling also got a special mention in the Commons: *Hansard*, Vol. 314, Col. 1261, 9 May 1887.
47 National Archives, file ED24/38, 'Higher Grade Schools in England, with their Origin, Growth, and Present Condition', p. 6. This paper was signed by R.L Morant in 1897, and revised in 1901. 'Elementary schools' were defined as those which charged no more than nine pennies per week.

Yet whilst such provision was expensive, all this was being achieved cost-effectively. Dixon made comparisons with the London School Board, where expenditure was double per child, and double per head of the population.[48] There was also the interesting complication that Birmingham was finding that some of its Board schools, although overcrowded, were attracting children from better-off homes. Such children, with family support, were more likely to pass their exams,[49] with consequent benefits in terms of grants received. Whilst this might have been attractive from a financial point of view, and from the point of view of breaking down class barriers, this was not the intention of the 1870 Act, as understood.

Just how wealthy were certain parts of Birmingham was evidenced by the size of the testimonial given to Schnadhorst upon his retirement as the BLA president in 1886 – a staggering 10,000 guineas (£10,500). Undoubtedly Schnadhorst had played a key role in organising the highly debatable voting system introduced by Disraeli in the Second Reform Act.[50] As a result, all Liberal supporters were told how to allocate their two votes between the three Birmingham candidates. Dixon himself had deplored this system from the outset, but he was a member of the party that benefited, although quite possibly he would have been returned to Parliament in 1868 even without the system. At any rate, it was he who chaired the committee to present the testimonial. How much of this figure he himself contributed is not known.

Dixon's speech at this event may have been appreciated by his immediate audience. However, it would surely not have found favour in many other quarters, describing as it did the Caucus as 'one of the simplest and most beautiful and, at the same time, one of the most effective engines of political warfare that had ever been invented. The real difficulty in working the Liberal associations consisted in the difficulty of combining in one common object all who were nominated by the different associations. Though it might be an easy thing for Conservatives, who were of one mind, or who had no mind at all [laughter], it was no easy matter to reconcile the opinions and to lead Liberals, who would think for themselves'.[51]

Now secure as both MP for Edgbaston and Chairman of the School Board, Dixon began to plan for a second journey to New Zealand. Aged 68 by the time he sailed in the summer of 1888, he needed a break from political turbulence.

---

48 *School Board Chronicle,* Vol. 37, 12 March 1887, p. 265. London was however rather more adventurous in social work, and Birmingham followed its lead, for example, in the education of feeble-minded children: see Birmingham Archives and Heritage, *Birmingham School Board Annual Report 1894,* File SB/B1/4/8, p. 50.
49 Birmingham Archives and Heritage, *Birmingham School Board Annual Report 1887,* File SB/B1/4/8, p. 20.
50 The system only operated in the period between the Second and Third Reform Acts of 1867 and 1884, the latter introducing universal single member constituencies.
51 *The Times,* 10 March 1887.

He also wanted to meet his Taylor relatives once again. He could afford to take time away from Parliament, which did not meet from early August for almost six months. And he wanted to see at first hand the management of the Dixon Investment Company. Unfortunately for his colleague Mundella, who was a director of the New Zealand Loan and Mercantile Agency, it had been found that various debenture issues were not adequately secured.[52] In such a context, Dixon did not want his own company to face a similar risk.

He still remained concerned about working-class conditions within Britain. In December 1887 Dixon accordingly chaired a meeting on state-directed colonisation. He identified the major problem as unemployment, and he advocated both state-directed colonisation, and legislation to facilitate placing the unemployed on the land in England 'or, at any rate of keeping those who work in the county districts there rather than leading them into the towns'. How that was going to be done, he did not elucidate.[53]

With his son James, Dixon sailed aboard the *Doric*, operated by Shaw Savill & Albion. Their contemporary literature extolled the advantages of emigration to New Zealand. One pamphlet stressed one reason 'above all other', which was that it was 'a land where merit is the sole passport to success'. It had three great advantages over Great Britain: [1] work for all willing and able to work; [2] a form of government which secured all the electoral and elective advantages that a democracy can reasonably expect (except those of electing a governor), with no hereditary aristocracy and no irritating remnants of feudal servitude; and [3] meat, fish and vegetables of all kinds.[54] No wonder Dixon liked New Zealand so much, suggesting 'that we should all go out and live there', recollected his daughter Katie.[55]

The New Zealand newspapers gave his visit – a rare one by a British MP – extensive coverage, especially his visits to inspect schools. As always, Dixon's attention to small details was noted. Thus at the East Christchurch main school: 'He paid particular attention to the structural arrangements, and was not favourably impressed by the fact that many of the rooms are lighted from the right, or from some other direction than the proper one, viz. the left-hand side of the children'.[56] (As most children are right-handed, light coming from that direction overshadows what they have just written).

Amongst the properties that he visited was Terrace Station, Hororata, the home of the former Prime Minister, Sir John Hall. Unfortunately, however, Sir John, famous most especially for the introduction of votes for women in

---

52 Armytage, *Mundella*, p. 301.
53 *BDP*, 5 Dec. 1887.
54 Alexander Turnbull Library, Wellington, Shaw Savill pamphlets Vol. 5A: R. Laishley, *Emigration* (9 March 1891).
55 Rathbone, *The Dales*, p. 100.
56 *Lyttelton Times*, 30 Nov. 1888.

1893, was himself away in Britain at the time.[57] *The Dictionary of New Zealand Biography* entry for the Yorkshire-born Hall[58] could in many respects also have been written about Dixon, with only minor amendments: 'His diverse career reflects the nature of a new and regionalised society, largely dependent on the political talent of the small, leisured elite. ... His speeches were cool and methodical, impressing by their mastery of facts and figures. ... He had his limitations: he was often successful in convincing, but rarely able to arouse'. The entry also pointed out that Hall went into politics as a matter of both inclination and duty. What it did not add was that he had a deep loathing of Chamberlain, a point reflected strongly in Hall's diaries.[59]

Dixon wrote home describing in great detail his experiences of this trip, his letters being the only extensive items of correspondence which survived the German bomb of 1941.

He had much to say about the various Taylor cousins, then living in the North Island. John, aged 76, lived alone on a run to which the journey was too rough for Dixon, so he paid John's expenses to come to see him instead.[60] There was a brief passing reference to Frederick 'the one who mis-managed Manawa', which might explain why that property had landed up in the opening balance sheet of DIC upon its incorporation three years earlier. There was passing reference to Dixon meeting with Waring,[61] who looked 'thin and wan', although he lived to 1903. The bankrupted Waring Taylor[62] had been sentenced to five years' penal servitude in 1885 for fraudulently plundering funds which he had been entrusted to invest.[63] The *New Zealand Times* had then pronounced that Taylor 'holds the undisputed championship amongst New Zealand defaulters and scoundrels'.[64] The Dixons had evidently not completely severed all ties with their black sheep.

Amongst this correspondence was a revelation of the extent to which Dixon had faith in the state's power to deal with problems which individuals on their own were seemingly incapable of resolving. He was appalled at the scale of the loss of sheep, whenever there was a drought. 'It is the most painful death known, not mere starvations, but death from thirst, Government ought to interfere'.[65] It was a typical example of Dixon's respect for interventionism, a philosophy espoused two decades earlier when he had called for the introduction of compulsory and free education.

---

57 J. Garner, *By His Own Merits: Sir John Hall, Pioneer, Pastoralist and Premier* (Hororata, 1995), p. 224.
58 *Dictionary of New Zealand Biography: Vol. 1, 1769-1869* (Wellington, 1990).
59 Hororata Station, South Island, New Zealand.
60 GDNZ, p. 21.
61 Ibid., p. 23. Letter written from Palmerston, 16 Oct. 1888.
62 See above, Chapter 7, p. 205.
63 The author is very grateful to Susan Geason for this information.
64 Patterson, 'Whatever Happened to Waring Taylor?', p. 118.
65 GDNZ, p. 38.

Dixon was captivated by what New Zealand had to offer to the many back at home, who lived in industrial squalor. Christchurch made a special mark: 'We are charmed with Christchurch, and never saw as much evidence of well-to-do-ness, all so new and clean, and good and solid brick and beautiful stone, and very fair architecture. Lovely trees everywhere, all planted by the Colonists, many of them English trees – planes, elms, etc. The Gardens are beautifully kept and the lawns as green and closely mown as at home, and the public gardens and park most charming. The river is quite unique, lovely weeping willows on both banks for many miles, and its windings are perpetual, and the water perfectly clear'.[66]

His journeyings were also reported in the Birmingham press, for an English émigré living in Masterton wrote about Dixon's visit to what by default had become a DIC asset: the Manawa station. But the property was a little disappointing. The writer's letter thus recorded: 'I gathered from him that he is interested in the state emigration movement that is being talked of on your side of the world; but he will hardly be able to experiment on his own land with emigrants. A hundred acres of the Manawa hills would not keep a colonist in bread, meat and clothing'. Yet he seemed to be enjoying himself: 'Mr Dixon looks hearty for a man of his years. The only apparent infirmity is a slight deafness; but then what a splendid thing it is for a politician to possess this defect'.[67]

Meantime, back in Birmingham the triennial School Board election was taking place. As already noted,[68] Dixon played no part in it whatsoever, yet [with the solitary exception of the usual single Catholic candidate, for whom local Catholic voters plumped all their fifteen votes], he headed the polls, supported by both sides, and shown in official records with no party label at all.[69]

Dixon himself recalled that he had spoken in July 1888, and 'he thought the result of that would be that, when he returned, he would not even have been nominated'.[70] Yet either he was suffering from a loss of memory, or there was an element of false modesty here. The Minutes of Dixon's last Board meeting, before he left, recorded a Resolution wishing him a successful voyage, and hoped that he 'be restored to the Board again in full health and vigour'.[71]

Dixon's stance on the religious issue was well remembered,[72] so that the Birmingham Clerical and Lay Council, speculating that he was sympathetic to

---

66 Ibid., p. 39.
67 *BDP,* 11 Dec. 1888.
68 See above, Chapter 1, p. 16.
69 Taylor, 'History of the Birmingham School Board', p. 71. On this occasion, the two major parties bore 'Secular' and 'Scripture' labels, reflecting the usual strong religious undercurrents.
70 *School Board Chronicle,* Vol. 41, 16 March, 1889, p. 278.
71 Birmingham Archives and Heritage, School Board Minutes, File SB/B1/1/7: 5 July, 1888.
72 See above, Chapter 7, p. 207.

their views, initially nominated him.[73] The BLA then convened, and resolved (despite being far from supportive in matters relating to national politics) that Dixon's name could not possibly be omitted, because of his devoted services in the past.[74] But the BLA took the precaution of nominating nine candidates rather than the usual eight, to cover the uncertainty.[75]

No label to denote Dixon's grouping was attached to his name on the ballot papers. There was simply a blank in a year distinctive for the total absence of party political names across the board. Instead, the labels were simply 'Roman Catholic', 'Scripture', 'Secular', 'Independent', and 'Socialist'. By 1891, the candidates were 'Roman Catholic', 'Liberal', 'Denominational', and 'Independent'. Dixon by then carried the 'Liberal' banner. Hence there is no suggestion in the School Board world that the divisions in the national party[76] were mirrored at a local level.

The results declared, the Board then elected Dixon Chairman once again, *in absentia*, and awaited his return.[77] He re-took his seat on 7 March 1889. After thanking the town for its support, he simply resumed as if nothing had happened. Indeed, he immediately reported on his findings in New Zealand, praising amongst other things the good results of mixing the sexes in schools.[78] With some justification, the following three-year period 1889-92 could well be considered the second zenith of Dixon's career, even though he was shortly to reach his seventieth birthday – the first having been his role in building pressure for educational reform in 1870.[79] It was a mixture of 'business as usual', and a number of episodes which showed that there were problems ahead.

Not long after he had returned from New Zealand, John Bright died, leaving Dixon as the senior representative for Birmingham in Parliament. Bright had had an enormous popular following in Birmingham, and so had Dixon, but they were very different men. The *Daily News* summarised the position: 'After the death of John Bright, Mr Dixon was perhaps the man most universally respected in Birmingham. He had none of Mr Chamberlain's showy qualifications. But he had "character", and in England character always counts'.[80]

---

73 *BDP,* 25 Sept. 1888.
74 Ibid., 18 Oct. 1888.
75 Taylor, 'History of the Birmingham School Board', p. 70.
76 A cartoon appeared in *The Dart and Midland Figaro* on 9 Nov. 1888 of Gladstone, who was at the time paying a visit to Birmingham, trying to fell the tree of Birmingham Unionism, one of whose branches was the Dixon branch.
77 Birmingham Archives and Heritage, School Board Minutes, File SB/B1/1/7, p. 135.
78 *School Board Chronicle,* Vol. 41, 16 March, 1889, p. 278.
79 See above, Chapter 3, p. 106.
80 As quoted by the *BDP,* 25 Jan. 1898.

Dixon continued to support the cause of continuing British rule in Ireland, and in particular he sought to refute the argument that past English governments had ignored the wishes of the Irish people. That was a nonsense he suggested, citing the examples of the disestablishment of the Anglican church, and the reform of the land laws. He went on to point to rising prosperity, saying that, for example, in 1851 284,000 families had lived in mud huts without windows, whilst by 1881 the figure had been reduced to 41,000.[81] That statistic may have been true; but just how many English families by then were living in mud huts without windows?

In his final decade in Parliament, Dixon's voting pattern became increasingly independent. His heart was with the welfare of the working classes, and more particularly he wanted to reduce the burden of indirect taxation imposed on them. It was 'a gratifying statement' that in 1842 they had paid 27/4d per head, whilst by 1882, the comparative figure was just 25/0d, for example. Moreover, in 1889 he supported the Conservatives on many issues because they had gone twice as far as the Liberal leaders had formerly proposed to go on local government reform.[82] On the other hand, Dixon opposed two education Bills proposed by Lord Salisbury's government, on the grounds that they were taking things in the wrong direction.[83]

Almost a year later, in a speech in support of Liberal Unionist leaders, Dixon explained in more detail why there were still differences of opinion. 'They might not all of them agree with everything that Mr Chamberlain had said and done; but then it was to be expected that amongst advanced Liberals, who thought their own thoughts and who arrived at their own judgements, that they should agree preferably with all their fellow workers'.[84]

It was an independence that Dixon could well afford. After the first general election when he was returned for the new constituency of Edgbaston, his seat was never to be contested again until after his death. At a local level, a measure of his considerable popularity was his lead in the 1891 School Board election, when he headed the polls by a substantial margin: 47,431 votes, to the next candidate, Miss Dale, who secured 40,957 votes, pushing the normally victorious Roman Catholic candidate into fourth place.

The conduct of the election was not however without its problems. As Dixon had foreseen in 1867,[85] the complexity of the electoral system of the period caused considerable difficulty in practice. Thus the guidance to Liberal supporters whose surnames began with the letters A to G was to cast five votes for each of three candidates, and those with letters H to Z was to cast three

---

81 *BDP*, 1 July 1889.
82 Ibid..
83 *Daily Argus*, paper clipping Jan. 1898.
84 *BDP*, 20 May 1890.
85 See above, Chapter Three, p. 73.

votes for each of five candidates. One of the problems subsequently disputed was as to whether a ballot paper marked not with the number 3, as intended, but with three crosses was equally valid.[86]

In the field of education, it was only in 1889 that Birmingham truly got to grips with the attendance issue. Until then, the local magistrates, despite entreaties from the Board, took a lax view.[87] But in that year prosecutions were placed before a stipendiary magistrate, who adopted a more robust approach.[88] The Board still remained concerned that: 'only the very lowest and most neglected are now out of school, and these are precisely the cases that require the application of compulsion most and cause the greatest amount of trouble'.[89] It was taking time to build new schools across the country. There was also the urgent problem of there being up to 100,000 children, as one MP estimated, who were simply unable to attend 'owing to their extreme wretchedness'. Universal free schooling was in the offing but, in a Parliamentary answer, the Conservative Hart Dyke[90] made specific reference to the Birmingham School Board and its pioneering work in introducing free orders: a very significantly higher percentage of Birmingham children received free education than the national average.[91]

Standards were rising overall, even if not as rapidly as in some other towns, since Birmingham had endemic problems of poverty with which to contend. In 1889, the level at which exemption from attendance applied was raised from the Fifth to the Sixth Standard. That prevented the majority of children from leaving school before they reached the age of 12.[92] Teaching standards were also set to rise, with a continuing dialogue between the Board and Mason's College concerning training colleges.[93] And to celebrate a local triumph, all Board School pupils were given a day off when one of their former colleagues won fifth place in the mathematics tripos at St. Catherine's College, Cambridge.[94]

Dixon consistently still opposed state support for voluntary schools, on the grounds of the quality of their product. 'Advanced educationists' (and he numbered himself amongst them) 'were of the opinion that the voluntary

86 National Archives, file ED/9/22.
87 Dixon led a deputation to see the magistrates to remonstrate about the small size of penalties as early as 1877: see Birmingham Archives and Heritage, School Board Minutes, File SB/B1/1/3, p. 295.
88 Smith, *Conflict and Compromise*, p. 211.
89 Birmingham Archives and Heritage, *Birmingham School Board Annual Report 1890*, File SB/B1/4/8, p. 24.
90 For Sir William Hart Dyke (1837-1931), and Vice-President of the Committee of the Council on Education (1887-92), see *ODNB-online*.
91 *Hansard*, Vol. 314, Col. 1261, 9 May 1887. See also above Chapter 7, p. 216.
92 Birmingham Archives and Heritage, *Birmingham School Board Annual Report 1889*, File SB/B1/4/8, p. 20.
93 Ibid., p. 30.
94 *School Board Chronicle*, Vol. 42, 10 Aug. 1889, p. 126: this student had progressed via a Foundation Scholarship at King Edward's School, to Mason's College, followed by success at London University exams and then onto Cambridge University.

schools could not give a secular education of equal efficiency to that which was given in the Board schools', simply because they lacked the financial resources to compete. He thus hoped that the time would eventually come 'when the inferior voluntary schools would be superseded by the superior Board schools'.⁹⁵ However, there was too much antipathy, especially in the countryside, to the role of School Boards, for Dixon's hopes to be realised.

There were also dangers inherent in the proposition that Town Councils should take over technical education. Dixon objected to this proposal, on the grounds that they knew nothing about the matter and would be competing with many other committees for expenditure.⁹⁶ If Town Councils took over elementary education too, it would put at risk the principle of financial ring-fencing, established in the 1870 Act through the medium of the precept.

In due course, a Technical School did open under the auspices of the City Council, adding further to the complex web of educational institutions. It was, however, another rung in Dixon's vision of an educational ladder, and to that extent he rejoiced: 'It was merely a question of time, but some of them, he hoped, would live to see the most complete and perfect development of education, not for any particular class in Birmingham, but for every class'.⁹⁷

In April 1890, Dixon delivered an important speech on 'socialism'. He proclaimed himself to be a socialist 'to the extent that he desired to substitute the action of the state for that of the individual whenever there was reasonable ground for believing that the well-being of the community would be thereby promoted'. After all, when referring to the 1870 Education Act, the Social Darwinist Herbert Spencer had claimed that Parliament was working to secure the survival of the un-fittest. Dixon disagreed. So far as compulsory education was concerned, the whole nation had adopted socialistic principles twenty years previously – and 'the result of this action had been altogether satisfactory'. He added further examples of beneficial socialism: the Post Office, the Factory Acts, the public provision of gas, water, sewage disposal, free libraries, baths, parks, cemeteries, and even work-houses.

However, there were limits to how far socialism could go. Dixon opposed any form of confiscation, or anything which crushed out individual freedom and energy. As for those whom he called the 'extreme socialists', he heartily differed. These were those who would become the sole owners of land and capital, organising and directing all productive operations, thus saving rent and interest. They would then distribute the proceeds of labour amongst workers in proportion to the value of that labour. But who was to decide that? Dixon objected to the Fabians' approach too, for their desire to levy excessive taxation on the rich amounted, in his opinion, to confiscation. In summary, such out-

95 *Hansard*, Vol. 15, Col. 965, 31 July 1893.
96 Ibid., Vol. 340, Col. 521, 26 Aug. 1889.
97 *School Board Chronicle*, Vol. 44, 16 Aug. 1890, p. 155.

and-out socialists 'committed the fault of diverting the attention of others from the real source of the evils that still remained, and fixed it upon an imaginary, illusory, merely academical [sic] plan, which he believed would be a failure'.[98]

This was Dixon's philosophy in the closing years of his life. It was aptly described in the following terms: 'In the great provincial cities, where municipalisation became increasingly the vogue, it had not been identified in the minds of its promoters with any collectivist principles. They were simply empirical Englishmen facing public needs, and trying to meet each of them specifically in what appeared the most practical way'.[99] Dixon was far from being a collectivist, although he was not afraid of being associated with 'socialism', if that helped his case.

The brightest spot of the new decade for Dixon was the final introduction of free schooling nationwide in 1891. At long last, Dixon could feel that the two most important goals of his long campaigns had been achieved.[100] It was Lord Salisbury's Conservative government which introduced the measure, and when the day came, there was very little opposition indeed.[101] There was no doubt that a huge burden was thereby lifted from many parents across the country, for as long ago as 1879 there had been stories of people being driven to suicide, unable to afford the fees.[102]

The success of the eventual change was a tribute to long and sustained pressure from the advocates of free and universal elementary schooling. Dixon strongly endorsed the Government's approach, although with reservations, and for some time was able to bask in reflected glory. Thus the *School Board Chronicle* spoke of free education: 'Mr Chamberlain once said that it was a Birmingham question. No doubt it was, to the extent that it was first proposed by Mr George Dixon, and from Birmingham it had spread throughout the country'.[103] In fact, the concept of free education had been in circulation in many quarters long before Dixon entered politics. Nonetheless, he had been a steady and also a practical advocate in the cause.

His overall success was being feted across the world. A year before, *Harper's New Monthly Magazine* observed that: 'the opportunities for education in Birmingham are exceptional. They are not equalled by those of any other city

---

98 *BDP,* 2 Apr. 1891.

99 Ensor, *England,* p. 128.

100 'Free and compulsory education' was the most significant feature of his platform, the NEL having had a six-point programme: see above, Chapter 3, p. 90.

101 The Second Reading was carried by 318 votes to 10: see *Hansard,* Vol. 354, Col. 1359, 24 June 1891. Technically, the Bill was 'to make further provision for assisting Education in Public Elementary Schools in England and Wales': see Sutherland, *Policy-Making,* p. 300. It was only in 1918 that Fisher's Act formally abolished fees altogether: see E. Midwinter, *Nineteenth-Century Education* (1970), p. 44. See also above, Chapter 7, p. 212, with regard to the pace at which the 1891 legislation became effective.

102 Morton, *Education and the State,* p. 30.

103 *School Board Chronicle,* Vol. 43, 17 May 1890, p. 507.

in the kingdom'.[104] The article itself was entitled 'The Best-Governed City in the World'. From France came the tribute: *'Birmingham est un exemple, unique en Angleterre, d'ensemble bien organisé'*.[105] In Parliament, the Conservative MP Lord George Hamilton, later to become the Chairman of the London School Board, said of Dixon that 'his views carried weight, the hon. Gentleman being Chairman of a School Board which, from an administrative point of view, was the ablest and most economical in the Kingdom'.[106] From the Bishop of Coventry, later to be the leader of the Church party in the Board, came the observation 'His busy mind had been constantly exercised in devising new improvements in educational methods for the country at large'.[107]

This praise was all tempered by the fact that the new funding of free education offended one of Dixon's key principles: it was to be financed by central government money distributed across the country, although without control over its application. But, sensibly, Dixon did not obstruct the change, explaining that: 'Unquestionably, I prefer public control to private management, and I have always done so; but I separate the two questions, and am content to let the question of public control wait until a later period'.[108]

Chamberlain, by contrast, had come to the conclusion that there were no grounds for popular control of voluntary schools, although popular representation would be sensible.[109] Now working alongside the Conservatives, he had to face the issue of widespread antipathy to the School Board movement, in the countryside especially. More than that, he had changed his mind on the future of the voluntary sector: 'To destroy the denominational schools is now an impossibility. I was one of those who believed that they would gradually die out, that the Board schools would necessarily take their places. I was mistaken. The costs would be immense'.[110]

Dixon's stance on costs was somewhat unconvincing overall. He called for free education for children aged under five, and over fourteen but, untypically, he failed to do his homework: 'Well, I am not the Chancellor of the Exchequer, and cannot divine the means by which that difficulty may be overcome; but so important is it that it is worth almost any sacrifice to make the measure a complete measure, instead of an incomplete one'.[111] It was all very well his saying things such as 'the best education … was the truest economy',[112] or,

---

104 J. Ralph, 'The Best-Governed City in the World', *Harper's New Monthly Magazine,* 81 (New York, 1890), p. 101.
105 M. Leclerc, *L'education des classes moyennes et dirigeantes en Angleterre* (Paris, 1894), p. 128.
106 *Hansard,* Vol. 15, Col. 969, 31 July 1893.
107 *School Board Chronicle,* Vol. 46, 14 Nov. 1891, p. 584.
108 *Hansard,* Vol. 354, Col. 1255, 23 June 1891.
109 Ibid., Vol. 353, Col. 1878, 8 June 1891.
110 *BDP,* 25 Apr. 1891. He had earlier made very similar comments, as reported in the *School Board Chronicle,* Vol. 39, 2 June 1888, p. 582.
111 *Hansard ,* Vol. 354, Col. 1254, 23 June 1891.
112 Ibid., Vol. 15, Col. 967, 31 July 1893.

that educational expenditure was simply taking 'money out of one pocket, and put[ting] more into the other'.[113] Yet such words did not indicate how funding was to be supplied.

One blessing of free education was the tendency for attendances to rise,[114] and so long as the grant system was calculated by reference to these figures, grants to individual schools rose too. Another consequence was a rapid increase in attendances at evening classes, to the point where the Birmingham School Board needed to establish a separate Evening School Committee.[115] There was 'a rush of scholars altogether beyond the most sanguine anticipations. Hundreds of young people remained in the streets, unable to get into the various School rooms'.[116]

Against this backdrop, it was not unexpected to find Dixon taking a pro-Conservative stance at the time of the 1892 election, when he was again returned unopposed.[117] In a speech, which once more featured sentences of near record-breaking length, he applauded the Conservatives in the recent past for passing more liberal measures than any Liberal government that he had known. At the same time, he claimed that he had not changed his basic principles since he entered Parliament twenty-five years previously. He thought that he was entitled to call himself now 'an advanced Liberal of the old Birmingham type'.[118]

Again, in the triennial School Board elections in 1891, Dixon's stature was reflected in the results. He led the poll by a very large margin, beating even the Catholic candidate, for the first time since 1873.[119] He moderated his by now customary hints that he did not relish the workload of two jobs, on this occasion merely suggesting that he could do his duties as an MP just as effectively without being chairman of the Board,[120] a reversal of an earlier stance.

In 1892, the Board ventured into new territory. It bought land in an area ostensibly tenanted by middle-class families, and Dixon observed that 'the erection of a school there would be interesting as showing the extent to which such families availed themselves of the provisions of the Education Act'.[121] This test would be intriguing, for the assumption ever since 1870 had been that no respectable middle-class Englishman would ever send his child to a

---

113 Ibid., Vol. 40, Col. 642, 5 May 1896.

114 Ibid., Vol. 354, Col. 1256, 23 June 1891.

115 Taylor, 'History of the Birmingham School Board', p. 219.

116 Birmingham Archives and Heritage, *Birmingham School Board Annual Report 1891*, File SB/B1/4/8, p. 32.

117 I. Cawood, 'The 1892 General Election and the Eclipse of the Liberal Unionists', *Parliamentary History*, 29 (2010), p. 346.

118 *Birmingham Faces and Places: An Illustrated Local Magazine* (Birmingham, 1893), Vol. 5, p. 79.

119 Taylor, 'History of the Birmingham School Board', p. 73. As always, these figures must be considered against the backdrop of the 'vote as you are told' system.

120 *School Board Chronicle*, Vol. 46, 14 Nov. 1891, p. 584.

121 *BDP*, 4 July 1892.

public elementary school if he could afford to do otherwise.[122] In 1893, Dixon drew attention in Parliament to the serious inadequacies of a small minority of voluntary schools: 'It was the very best thing for the voluntary system that these inferior, imperfect, inefficient and bad school buildings should either be improved up to the level of the day, or that they should be shut up'.[123]

Dixon was, however, beginning to lose some of his astuteness. A new problem was looming. Once school provision had mushroomed, the rate of new building began to decline. The consequence was a decrease in the number of vacancies for head teachers, 'and the hope of attaining to that position is much diminished'.[124] Staff issues were coming to the fore.

Thus heading the School Board polls in 1894 with 146,009 votes was a former headmaster of a Board school by the name of Ansell. Dixon came fourth, like a 'bolt from the blue',[125] capturing no more than 20,228 votes.[126] Discontent had been simmering for a while, the main reported issue being the size of the salaries paid to assistant teachers.[127] Over the next couple of years, this discontent had broadened into complaints about excessive inspection, and 'educational fads, to which the Board was prone'. Deputations to the Board proved useless, and the new Birmingham Teachers' Association became involved.[128] It was difficult for Dixon, now in his mid-seventies and much in London, to keep grasp of administrative details. There were suggestions that he was losing touch. He made a public statement concerning Inspectors being drawn from the ranks of the Head Masters, when upon closer inspection this proved not to be the case.[129] In fact, Dixon had offered the next vacant seat on the Board to Ansell, if he would refrain from contesting the election. But this idea was rejected.

Board Minutes around this time reveal that on several occasions Dixon sent apologies for absence,[130] whilst a speaker at a meeting of the BLA in April reported that it was commonly rumoured that he wanted to retire from Parliament.[131] Even the family had become involved, with Katie proposing a Christmas toast to her father:

---

122 E.J.R. Eaglesham, *The Foundations of Twentieth-Century Education in England* (1967), p. 9.
123 *Hansard*, Vol. 40, Col. 964, 31 July 1893.
124 Birmingham Archives and Heritage, *Birmingham School Board Annual Report 1891*, File SB/B1/4/8, p. 37.
125 Taylor, 'History of the Birmingham School Board', p. 74.
126 Ibid., p. 75.
127 *School Board Chronicle*, Vol. 48, 31 Dec. 1892, p. 767.
128 Taylor, 'History of the Birmingham School Board', p. 74.
129 Birmingham Archives and Heritage, *Birmingham School Board Annual Report 1895*, File SB/B1/4/8, p. 127.
130 Birmingham Archives and Heritage, File SB/B1/1/11, pp. 355, 460, and others.
131 *BDP*, 6 April 1894.

So fill up your glasses with wassail so sweet,
And drink to his health, as you stand on your feet,
And let us remind him he needs a good rest,
And should kick himself free when by politics opprest.
Let us beg him to take our advice as well meant
And to cut the old Houses of Parl-i-ament.[132]

He should have stood down whilst he was still ahead.

When the Board met again after the election, Dixon was not impressed with Ansell. The latter wanted to serve on only two committees, whilst Dixon pointed out that it was the custom to serve on three or sometimes four, so that Ansell would be doing less than anyone else.[133] Dixon tackled the issue in typical fashion. He formed a special sub-committee of two persons, Ansell and himself, to review the uniformity of pupils' handwriting styles.[134]

'To the last hour in which he retained the position of Chairman of the Birmingham School Board his lively concern for the minutest detail of administrative efficiency was the cause of admiring wonderment on the part of his attached colleagues. The simplicity and the transparent honesty of all that George Dixon said and did reconciled his fellows even to the most obstinate opposition on his part. If the brilliance of genius was denied him, in his solid excellencies, of greater practical worth, he had ample compensation'.[135]

The salary issue was addressed by increased scales, effective from April 1895,[136] but no attempt was made to address a criticism implicit in the teachers' complaints. The work of the Board had grown phenomenally since its foundation, and its management style of operating through committees had not changed accordingly. There was also a certain inflexibility of mind, for the financial crisis of the voluntary schools was coming to a head. Dixon was still pressing for School Boards everywhere, and 'how long it would take he could not say, but a hundred years was not long in the history of a nation'.[137] There were 2,470 Boards, but of these 2,293 were parish Boards, invariably of very small size, and with a reputation that in no way matched Birmingham's.[138] All

---

132 Birmingham Archives and Heritage, File MS 2239, Bundle 37.
133 *BDP*, 3 Dec. 1894.
134 Birmingham Archives and Heritage, *Birmingham School Board Annual Report 1895*, File SB/B1/4/8, p. 42.
135 *Daily Argus*, paper clipping, Jan. 1898: obituary of George Dixon.
136 Birmingham Archives and Heritage, *Birmingham School Board Annual Report 1895*, File SB/B1/4/8, p. 39.
137 *BDP*, 31 Oct. 1895.
138 N. Daglish, *Education Policy-Making in England and Wales: The Crucible Years, 1895-1991* (1996), p. 5.

around him there was change, with notably the arrival of the Conservative Sir John Gorst[139] as Vice-President of the Committee of Council on Education, and Sir Robert Morant, his private secretary.[140] Above all else, the Bryce Commission on Secondary Education was in the process of reporting, and administrative change was an inevitable outcome.

The writing was particularly on the wall for the type of Higher Grade School whose development Dixon had pioneered. In his 1897 paper,[141] Morant highlighted Birmingham (and Hull) as being especially problematic, saying 'It is this type of school which has caused the greatest difficulty, regarding the question of legality…'.[142] He continued: 'it cannot be doubted that this policy of letting School Boards supply a sort of Pretence-Secondary School has headed off the natural local pressure in the big towns for the development of true Secondary Schools, and has considerably postponed the establishment of Local Authorities for Secondary Education, besides making such establishments now an infinitely more thorny question than it otherwise needs have been'.[143]

For good measure, Morant compared the ratio of staff who were graduates in towns with Higher Grade Board Schools, and those with Secondary Schools, and found that the latter had a much more favourable ratio than the former. The staff:pupil ratio was better too.[144] Finally, he accused the towns with Higher Grade Board Schools of perpetuating class distinctions, on the basis that they were intended primarily for 'working men'.[145]

In late October 1895, Dixon presided over a conference in London, whose objects were 'to consider what steps shall be taken to resist the proposals now before the country for reopening the educational settlement of 1870, and for arresting the growth of a national system of education by giving largely increased grants, either from the Treasury or rates, to denominational schools'.[146] In early November, Dixon chaired the inaugural meeting of the Birmingham & Midland Education League,[147] after some earlier jocular suggestions that the name 'National Education League' be revived.[148] Ominously, the meeting was not well attended.[149] And a newly-formed National Education Association was established, with Dixon elected as its first Chairman.[150]

---

139 For Sir John Gorst (1835-1916), see *ODNB-online.*
140 For Sir Robert Morant (1863-1920), see *ODNB-online.*
141 See above, Chapter 7, p. 216.
142 National Archives, file ED24/38, 'Higher Grade Schools in England, with their Origin, Growth, and Present Condition', p. 15.
143 Ibid., p. 16.
144 Ibid., p. 17.
145 Ibid., p. 25.
146 *BDP,* 16 Oct. 1895.
147 Ibid., 4 Nov. 1895.
148 *The Times,* 19 Oct. 1895.
149 *BDP,* 6 Nov. 1895.
150 *The Times,* 14 Nov. 1895.

It was not as if Dixon had not served notice to Chamberlain of his actions: 'as an old educationist I think it right to inform you that I could not support any Government that proposed to make it incumbent on, or to permit, local authorities to support out of the rates voluntary schools which were not entirely under their management and control. And if such legislation were suggested to Parliament, I should feel it to be my duty, both in the House and in the country, to exercise all the influence I possess to oppose it at every stage. Hoping that you will do all you can to prevent the apprehended danger'.[151] It was to no avail.

Shortly before heading off to the south of France to recuperate from an illness, Dixon visited the Duke of Devonshire, the President of the Council of Education. Amongst other things, Dixon objected to the proposal that some superior authority be given power to revise the School Board precept, the alleged reason being 'to prevent what is harmful in the competition between voluntary and Board schools'. That rivalry could 'only mean that the standard of educational efficiency is to be lowered to suit the exigencies of schools on a lower level'.[152] He was bidding for quality in the elementary sector.

Correspondence in *The Times* included a very robust letter from an anonymous Liberal Unionist Churchman, who fairly stressed that times had changed and that the Church of England was prospering, whilst the Nonconformists were waning. The author noted that Ansell had trounced Dixon in the recent Board elections. Then, sticking the dagger in further, the writer suggested that the only reason why Dixon had not been opposed in Parliamentary elections was the existence of the compact between the Conservatives and Liberal Unionists, whereby both parties agreed that in certain constituencies they would not propose competing candidates.[153]

By now, Dixon was described as an 'old man fallen upon evil days'.[154] His stance of varying between support of some Conservative policies and opposition to others was mocked. P.A. Muntz, MP, and a cousin of the Birmingham Muntz family, said of Dixon's opposition to the government's proposal for financial help to the voluntary sector, that he 'appeared to have gone mad over it, and was in his second childhood, and did not realize how much they were indebted to the voluntary schools, and how much money they had saved the ratepayers'.[155] A member of the Lloyd family, G.B. Lloyd, stuck his oar in too: 'The argument against a monopoly of elementary education in the hands of School Boards seems to be much the same as against a monopoly of religious worship in the hands of a National Church'.[156] This argument might

---

151 University of Birmingham, Chamberlain Papers, Special Collections, file JC5/27/10.
152 *The Times,* 16 Dec. 1895. See also University of Birmingham, Chamberlain Papers, Special Collections, file JC5/27/11: Dixon to Chamberlain, 27 Dec. 1895.
153 *The Times,* 19 Dec. 1895.
154 *Hansard,* Vol. 40, Col. 644, 5 May 1896.
155 *BDP,* 29 Nov. 1895.
156 Rimmington, *The Rise and Fall of Elected School Boards,* p. 47.

have resonated with Dixon, for scarcely a quarter of a century previously, he had opposed any arrangements that strengthened the hand of the Anglican Church.

The arguments ranged widely. The very future of the School Boards was in doubt, due to the lack of limits over their expenditure[157] – the precept generally being inviolate. It was all very well for Dixon to counter criticisms by saying that the electors could have their say every three years. That degree of control seemed too remote. Central government believed it was reasonable that County and County Borough Councils should have a controlling say over educational costs, for there might well be other more pressing matters to consider.[158] It was all very well for Dixon to counter that education should be left in the hands of the experts, but the vast majority of School Boards were not run by people of the calibre of the Birmingham School Board. Much of the country's population was too dispersed and too poor to be able to afford the luxury of a Bridge Street Seventh Grade Technical School. It was all very well for Dixon to trumpet Birmingham's successes. But, it was argued, he should have spent even more time with the likes of Joseph Arch and recalled the problems of the overwhelmingly Conservative-dominated English countryside.

Nonetheless, Dixon was not alone. On 18 April 1896, the Birmingham School Board met and expressed its strong objections to the government's proposals. These were fourfold: the School Board's budget would be controlled by another authority, which had been elected for entirely different purposes; the School Board itself would be under the control of the County Council, the majority of whose members knew little about education; the legislation would permit the dissolution of School Boards, and the transfer of management to local managers far removed from popular control; and there was provision for changes to the management of Higher Grade Schools (which included the very Bridge Street Seventh Grade School whose foundation Dixon had personally helped finance), whose development might be permanently arrested.[159]

Once again, and for the final time, this issue put Dixon into conflict with Chamberlain, who was by now Colonial Secretary. As one historian observed: 'Perilous constituency situations were soon being reported from various directions, and open hostility from a large number of the Midland radicals who had followed Mr Chamberlain into Liberal-Unionism but were now looking to Mr George Dixon, MP, Chamberlain's not wholly approving senior, to bring him to heel'.[160]

Back from the south of France, Dixon once more chaired a School Board meeting on 25 April 1896. It was a Saturday. There was a discussion about

---

157 Ibid., p. 44.
158 *Hansard*, Vol. 40, Col. 710, 6 May, 1896.
159 Birmingham Archives and Heritage, School Board Minutes, File SB/B1/1/13, p. 322.
160 S. Maccoby, *English Radicalism, 1886-1914* (1953), Vol. 2, p. 228.

a conference of School Boards to consider the Education Bill.[161] Ansell unsuccessfully moved an amendment seeking a reduction in expenditure.[162] Then came a shock. No doubt mindful of the painful lesson of the early months of 1876, when he had pondered aloud for far too long the implications of his wife's serious illness, at the conclusion of the meeting the following terse letter was read to the Board:[163]

Dear Mr Davis,
I regret to have to inform you that the time has come when I feel it to be my duty to resign my position as Chairman of the Birmingham School Board.
I remain,
Yours sincerely,
George Dixon.

Dixon wished to concentrate his failing energies on fighting the forthcoming battle in Parliament. After the surprised Board had made the responses appropriate to the circumstances, he left.

The stage was now set for a second period of confrontation between Dixon and Chamberlain. But this time around both had mellowed, with Dixon aged nearly 76 and Chamberlain 60. In a speech in Birmingham Town Hall on 1 May 1896, Chamberlain recounted the early days of the NEL, and he admitted that he then

'went beyond him. I did not altogether agree with him. I was in favour of the extinction of the voluntary Schools. In 1870 it is known to all I thought that we were then on the eve of a National System which might very properly absorb the whole education of the country, and that it was undesirable that the two systems should go on together, and therefore – I was always a little more extreme than Mr Dixon – undoubtedly at that time I went beyond him in regard to the voluntary Schools'. Then, 'Well, gentlemen, I have changed my mind'.[164]

He had in fact changed his mind several years previously, and he was now acutely conscious that with four out of seven children being taught by the voluntary Sector and purportedly excessive competition from School Board schools, the cost to the rates would be totally unaffordable unless help were provided immediately.[165]

---

161 Birmingham Archives and Heritage, School Board Minutes, File SB/B1/1/13, p. 326.
162 Ibid., p. 331.
163 Ibid., p. 338.
164 National Archives, file ED24/28.
165 Ibid..

The debate in Parliament was lively. Dixon's speech as reported in *Hansard*[166] occupies 7.5 columns, although that was short by comparison with others. *['Cheers'], ['Opposition Cheers'],* and *['Loud Opposition Cheers']* punctuated the script. He hit the nail on the head: 'he knew that the religious difficulty had been one of the greatest magnitude and had seriously impeded the proper and full development of the secular education of the people. *[Cheers]*'.[167] And then he proceeded to explain his views on a variety of matters.

At the end of the proceedings, however, he was compelled to agree with Charles Dilke that he intended to abstain from voting – such was the range of issues of which he approved and disapproved.

In fact, this particular Bill was eventually to be withdrawn, partly because of objections from the county councils, partly because of disagreements within the government, and partly because of the determination of the opposition.[168] From Dixon's personal point of view, however, it was something of a hollow victory. Over the next few years, most especially after the 1899 Cockerton judgment, which successfully challenged the existing School Board funding of anything but elementary education, much was to change and in particular, financial help was ultimately to be provided to the beleaguered voluntary sector.

In January 1897, Dixon met with an accident in London. It was sufficiently serious to be reported in the press.[169] In his final appearance in Parliament a few weeks later, he showed that he was still very much his own master: 44 Liberal Unionists voted with the Government, and he alone voted with the opposition Liberals.[170] The issue was the financial plight of the voluntary schools, and the suggestion was that the School Boards should not receive the same assistance. He ended his Parliamentary career with the emphatic words: 'The grant, if made, should be made to all schools'.[171]

His elder sister Mary died in August, which 'greatly affected him'.[172] His own health was slipping away and, whilst he had resigned as Chairman of the Birmingham School Board, he was still an ordinary member. His failure to attend meetings should in theory have led to his eventual disqualification, but he was exempted from any penalty in view of his past services.[173]

Whilst Dixon was on the road to recovery in the closing months of 1897, he suffered a relapse in late December.[174] Those around him were seeking to

166 *Hansard*, Vol. 40, Cols. 637-44, 5 May 1896.
167 Ibid., Col. 638.
168 Eaglesham, *From School Board*, p. 106.
169 *Daily News*, 11 Jan. 1897.
170 Ibid., 4 Feb. 1897.
171 *Hansard*, Vol. 45, Col. 996, 1 Feb. 1897.
172 *Daily News*, 31 Aug. 1897.
173 Birmingham Archives and Heritage, School Board Minutes, File SB/B1/1/15, p. 110.
174 *The Times*, 25 Jan. 1898.

confer some form of public recognition upon him before he died, but this task was not easy. Family oral tradition has it that he was offered a national honour, that he had discussed the matter with his close family, but that he had no wish for the public attention that it would entail. So the offer was declined. Dixon 'protested that he wanted recognition only from those with whom he had worked so long'.[175] On 4 January 1898 the city council conferred on him the honorary freedom of the city. A copy of the council resolution was presented to him at home a few days later.[176]

He died on 24 January 1898. Joseph Chamberlain was among the most notable to pay tribute to Dixon and to his reputation as a mild-mannered, courteous English gentleman. At the funeral at St Augustine's Church in Edgbaston, Austen and Neville Chamberlain represented their father, who was unable to attend because of another commitment. It was the end of an era. Within months, both Stansfeld and Gladstone were dead too.

Dixon was at least spared what would have been the ignominy of the Conservatives' 1902 Education Act, by which the School Boards were abolished. The new Liberal leader Asquith[177] described these bodies as 'the best, the most fruitful and the most beneficial educational agencies that at present exist in this country'.[178] Dixon would most certainly have agreed.

---

175 *ODNB.*
176 *The Times,* 25 Jan. 1898.
177 For H.H. Asquith, 1ˢᵗ Earl of Oxford (1852-1928), see *ODNB-online.*
178 Eaglesham, *The Foundations,* p. 44.

CHAPTER EIGHT

Conclusion

FOR A MAN of his stature, Dixon has left few footprints in the sands of history. Despite his every effort to remain in Parliament until at least one of the two major objectives of the NEL (viz. compulsory and free elementary education) had reached the Statute Book, there is no Dixon's Act. The 1870 Act is known as Forster's. Then, in 1876 there followed Sandon's Act. The fact that Chamberlain had just become one of Birmingham's three MPs when Sandon's Bill received Royal Assent is irrelevant in this context. In 1876 the Conservatives were in power, and it was unthinkable that legislation of such substance should have been passed in the name of a member of the opposition party. In 1880, Mundella's Act was named when Dixon had been out of Parliament for four years. So this more effective Act which legislated for compulsion was passed in the name of Mundella, whom Forster had in 1870 named as Dixon's junior partner in stimulating educational zeal in the country.[1] After this spate of legislation, no specific named Act is associated with free education from 1891.

Furthermore, in an era of considerable personal glorification, where statues were constructed in honour of many leading men, and a few women, of the day, a statue in honour of George Dixon was conspicuous by its absence. He was opposed to the concept. Indeed, some years before his death, when he was appointed honorary treasurer of the fund in honour of his friend, J.S. Wright,

---

1 See above, Chapter 3, p. 106.

Dixon argued that the money it received should be used for scholarships, but to no avail.[2]

After his death, Dixon was buried in what was once a quiet corner of Witton Cemetery, sharing a gravestone with his wife Mary.[3] That of his elder sister Mary is close by. There are no other gravestones in the immediate vicinity, the family having purchased more than one plot for potential future use. It was an option that nobody subsequently has ever seen fit to exercise. Not far away rumble overhead heavy lorries and other traffic on the M6 motorway, in the process of traversing Spaghetti Junction nearby, and a reminder of the trade in goods which once gave Dixon his wealth and ultimately influence.[4]

So his tangible legacy today consists essentially of just one school bearing his name.[5] During the First World War, there was published a school song.[6] Its words were as follows:

> Let other schools boast of their fame
> Their age or the names carv'd in stone
> As founders great lords they may claim
> Or chant in a jubilant tone
> Of the part they contribute to History's page,
> And the glory they hold as their heritage.
>
> [Refrain] We'll sing of the Green and the Red,
> As we march with steady tread,
> Our banner 'STRENUE AGAS' [School motto: Act with Vigour] we fling
> While 'Hail to our Founder' we sing.
>
> If to sing our own praise we were met,
> Fitting modesty would be the rule.
> But to honour George Dixon we set
> All the heart and the voice of the school,
> Our founder a Birmingham citizen he,
> No mean city this and no unknown school we.
> [Refrain]
>
> All hail to the brave pioneers,
> Who in Bridge Street our journey began!
> Then in Oozells Street gloom toil'd for nine long years,

---

2 *BDP*, 14 May 1880.

3 See photograph.

4 See photograph.

5 George Dixon Academy.

6 British Library Gladstone correspondence files, E1766 W/5. Dated July 1915, price three pennies under the auspices of the George Dixon School, Birmingham. 'Song of the Green and the Red', these being the school colours. Words by W.J. Stokes, music by W.J.R. Gibbs, and published in London.

Till, arrived at the stature of man,
The first city school to maturity grown,
Rejoices at length, 'neath a roof of its own.
[Refrain]

Then 'Hail to our Founder' we cry,
As we struggle PER ARDUA AD ALTA [Through Hard Work to the
  Heights]
No primrose path ever can end high,
So our steps shall not slacken or falter,
But onward we press as G.D. did of yore,
And hand on to others the colours they bore.
[Refrain]

The words do not harmonise easily with the melody but, as a classic product of its era, it neatly captured the temperament of the school's founder.

Very recently, a blue plaque has been erected on the wall of the school,[7] commemorating Sir Michael Balcon, one of the pioneers of the British film industry, who was a pupil in Edwardian times. One of his more notable films was the 'Blue Lamp', whose leading character was one George Dixon. From this success there emerged the popular television crime series, Dixon of Dock Green. The portrayal of PC George Dixon by the actor Jack Warner is interesting in so far as he, very like the forerunner the real Dixon, adopted a simple, upright and straightforward approach to life.

A century or so earlier, in the months immediately preceding Forster's 1870 Education Bill, one of the anxieties of the original George Dixon had been focused upon the substantial increase in crime committed by young persons.[8] His quest to address this issue was a powerful driving force behind his campaigning with the NEL.

Dixon was also one of the early trustees of Mason's College,[9] which was later incorporated into Birmingham University, founded two years after his death. And the next generation of Dixons continued his legacy by extending their concerns into what became known as tertiary education. His son Charles Dixon was, for many years between the two World Wars, honorary treasurer of the Council of Management of Bedford College. His daughter-in-law Agnes (née Powell) and her sister Eleanor set up the Powell Library Fund at Birmingham University. Agnes's eldest sister Christiana was a celebrated Edwardian artist, whose works were to be split between Bedford College and Newnham College, Cambridge. Christiana married Wilmot (later Sir Wilmot) Herringham, who

---

7 See photograph.
8 See above, Chapter 3, p. 96.
9 See above, Chapter 6, p. 193.

was for a short period Vice-Chancellor of London University, and for many years Chairman of Council at Bedford College. Hence by indirect means, Dixon's concern for education at all levels was expressed among the following generations of his family.

There was one recurring theme behind Dixon's achievements: innovation. His activities were certainly not confined to the field of education. Five times he was to be seen setting in motion the formation of new organisations:

One was the creation of the original Birmingham Liberal Association,[10] which in a subsequent incarnation was to provide the vital organisational structure for the return of the town's MPs, town councillors, and members of the School Board.[11]

A second element of radicalism was the foundation of the Birmingham Education Society.[12] At a critical time, this body not only provided invaluable statistics to support the case for substantial government action, but it also furnished funding for the education of a large number of children from poor families.

Dixon's third achievement was the subsequent foundation of the National Education League.[13] Its membership comprised a rather more narrow grouping of supporters than those in the BES. They were the enthusiasts who were dedicated to campaigning.

Fourthly, Dixon was instrumental in the foundation of Edgbaston High School for Girls,[14] a reminder that he was concerned not only for the education of boys. The daughters of many of his colleagues also benefited by this act.

And, fifthly, Dixon provided the impetus for the opening of Birmingham's Bridge Street Seventh Grade School.[15] At the time, Dixon was pushing the definition of what constituted 'elementary education' as defined in the 1870 Act. So, in effect, this new school paved the way for the state's later involvement in secondary education.

Dixon was also at the forefront of other movements well outside the field of education. He took a leading part in the campaign to challenge the size of the Civil List, but wisely did not pursue the matter to the bitter end, as did Charles Dilke.[16] The manner in which Dixon disassociated himself will always remain in doubt, but it indicated his judgment of priorities. For a number of years Dixon also played a rather surprising role in presiding over the newly-formed National Agricultural Labourers' Union.[17] And finally he and others

---

10 See above, Chapter 2, p. 54.
11 See above, Chapter 2, p. 59.
12 See above, Chapter 2, p. 60.
13 See above, Chapter 3, p. 89.
14 See above, Chapter 6, p. 177.
15 See above, Chapter 6, p. 196.
16 See above, Chapter 5, p. 150.
17 See above, Chapter 5, p. 154.

in the family loaned a considerable amount of money to purchasers of land in Australasia.[18]

There is no doubt that the NEL played a significant part in the pioneering introduction of elementary education legislation in 1870. There had been attempts to legislate before, without success. But it so happened that in 1869 the time was propitious to try once again. Dixon was in the right place at the right time, and he rode the crest of the wave.

It was always envisaged that the campaign would be long and arduous. Right at the very outset it was agreed that funding would be by annual instalments over a ten-year period.[19] It transpired that the NEL endured for two years short of ten.

The NEL's campaign was neither a success nor a failure. Its objectives were far too complex to be judged in such absolute terms. Nonetheless, its initial campaign had set the country on the right course. Its conduct in later years was controversial and that fact has tended to obscure its achievement. But achievement it was, with Dixon – and Birmingham – at the heart of the campaign for compulsory and free education.

When considering the range of issues with which he was concerned, it can be seen that Dixon was in many ways a man well ahead of his time. He was often far-sighted enough to see certain problems emerging on the horizon. There was a twentieth-century agenda in many issues that were debated in the Birmingham Chamber of Commerce. The Limited Partnerships Act of 1907, for example, addressed the problems with which Dixon had been concerned nearly half a century previously. His call for the railways to be nationalised was only answered in 1948, but by then the concerns were completely different. No longer was it a lack of competition in getting goods to market, but an overwhelming lack of resources with which to re-build after the Second World War.

Dixon's modernity was reflected in his personal lifestyle. An electric generator, with its noisy, flapping belt and exciting rumble was positioned in an outhouse. His house, The Dales, was furnished in the new 'Arts and Crafts' style of William Morris, whilst a drawing-room at their rented accommodation in Queen's Gate was decorated and furnished by Agnes and Rhoda Garrett, which was the first job undertaken by Britain's first lady decorators.

In matters of health, the Dixons patronised the inappropriately-named dentist Dr Coffin,[20] while for more general medical services they consulted amongst others Dr Elizabeth Garrett.[21] On one occasion, Katie attended a gymnasium in Bayswater, where it was noted that she was not holding herself straight. A consultation was organised with the eminent lady doctor, at which Katie was accompanied by her father: 'I remember standing stripped with

---

18 See above, Chapter 7, p. 204.
19 See above, Chapter 3, p. 92.
20 Birmingham Archives and Heritage, File MS 2239, Bundle 2, p. 47.
21 Ibid., Bundle 46.

my back to her and my father, who must have been terribly embarrassed'. It was the sight of female legs about which he was 'always nervous'.[22] As that anecdote indicated, the Dixons took care of their health and consulted the best authorities. Yet not even the finest surgeon in the land, Lawson Tait,[23] could finally save the life of Mary Dixon in March 1885. She died two or three days after the very serious operation that was involved.

For all his very considerable wealth, George Dixon himself had few very personal belongings: a gold pencil case, a watch, a little tortoiseshell knife, and a gold watch chain. He used a large silk handkerchief, smelling of lavender, and, when using it for blowing his nose, would give 'a little flick crossways'.[24]

There was a curious contrast in Dixon's attitude to public expenditure on education, on the one hand, and private expenditure on the other. Just how much the provisions of the 1870 Act would cost the public purse was always of considerable concern to taxpayers, yet at key moments, he was relaxed on the subject. Katie Rathbone described this as being 'lavish where he thought money should be spent'.[25]

At the same time, he taught his children to be very careful about control of their expenditure. 'He spent hours and hours on his accounts, he thought in thousands [pounds sterling], but was right to a ha'penny'.[26]

In part, this pattern may have been attributable to his wife Mary's Unitarian upbringing, for she was much more austere in her lifestyle: 'When we went away with my mother', recalled their daughter, 'she reverted to her old standards, went into lodgings, had meat tea, no late dinner, lemonade instead of wine, and occasionally a pony carriage for an afternoon drive'.[27]

It is from a financial perspective that an insight is provided into the Dixon family's attitude towards equality between the sexes. It was not until the 1882 Married Women's Property Act that the substantial legal inequalities between men and women came to be reduced. Mary Dixon was reluctant to be lavish herself, because she 'didn't like spending so much of Puddy's[28] [George Dixon's] money'.[29] The use of nicknames abounded within the family. Dixon was variously Puddy, Ganterparder, or Puppy, whilst Mary was Muddy, Muffice, Mummy or Marion. The liberal use of such terms suggests a very relaxed family environment. Apparently, Mary Dixon managed well enough, because 'Puddy is very kind, and gives me as much as I want'. This comment marked their daughter Katie's first intimation as a youngster of any difference

22 Ibid., Bundle 2, p. 2.
23 Ibid., Bundle 47, p. 15.
24 Ibid., p. 19.
25 Rathbone, *The Dales,* p. 9.
26 Ibid..
27 Ibid..
28 Birmingham Archives and Heritage, File MS 2239, Bundle 2, p. 18.
29 Rathbone, *The Dales,* p. 9.

between the sexes: 'we were brought up, brothers and sisters together, all equal. ... we fought it out fair and equal, the stronger got the best of it, but then sometimes the sister was the stronger'.

The scale of Dixon's commitment to business and public affairs meant that his own family life was curtailed. As Katie much later wrote:

> He said once… there was only one thing he really cared about, and that was to see his children happy. And he had simply spent all his time and himself on his public work … we really didn't see much of him.[30]

Others remembered his commitment to children as individuals, Chamberlain's son Austen recalling him in 1934 'as a genial figure at a children's party'.[31]

The family were also very musical. Dixon's wife Mary had a 'beautiful' voice, according to Katie,[32] and the family loved it. The enthusiasm passed on to their son Charles, who frequently played the organ. Dixon himself became Chairman of the General Committee of the renowned Birmingham Triennial Musical Festival within weeks of first entering Parliament,[33] and was also a patron of the Birmingham Schools' Choral Union.[34] Music recitals were regularly held at the Dixon family home, even after Mary's death. One such event was scheduled for early February 1898, but was cancelled when he died in late January that year.

Dixon's modernity was reflected in his political affiliations. In his later years, he described himself as an advanced Radical. Thus, when analysing the formation of the Liberal Party, the historian John Vincent numbered Dixon among the Radicals, as opposed to placing him with other groupings, such as the great capitalists (of whom Mundella was deemed to be one), or the Anglican Liberals.[35] Vincent characterised Dixon and his allies as notably determined campaigners:

> The Radicals were not only involved in controversial social commitments, but they developed an equally distinctive way of carrying out their good causes. This generally took the form of lifelong commitment to a particular question, with a shadowy National Society providing outside backing, and a war of attrition carried on in Parliament in question time and in motions on the adjournment.

---

30 Birmingham Archives and Heritage, File MS 2239, Bundle 47, p. 20.
31 *Birmingham Post,* 5 March 1934.
32 Rathbone, *The Dales,* p. 7.
33 *BDP,* 19 Aug. 1867.
34 Ibid., 24 Oct. 1867.
35 Vincent, *Formation of the Liberal Party,* p. 38.

Examples cited by Vincent were Rathbone on Bankruptcy, Stansfeld on Contagious Diseases – and George Dixon and the campaign for National Education.

In Birmingham more specifically, Dixon was of the mould of the Chamberlainite Radicals, insofar as he sought 'co-operation among individuals across lines of occupation, social class and religious denomination'.[36] His success in that aim owed much to his warm personality, sincerity, and lack of self-promotion. However, Dixon was never seen as a leading light amongst the 'Civic Gospellers', no doubt because his ecumenical Anglicanism did not inspire him with the feeling of being a member of a persecuted minority[37] – here differing from the attitude of many in this grouping. He was in very close contact with them, however, and their mantra of business success, namely that the Eleventh Commandment was 'Thou Shalt Keep a Balance Sheet', could very well have been his own.

Yet, as was evident on so many occasions, the personal relationship between Dixon and Chamberlain, the Civic Gospeller par excellence, was not always easy. Entrepreneurs both, like magnets they sometimes repelled. If their essential difference was to be defined, Dixon was guided by the power of principle: the principle throughout being that the children of England needed to be better educated. Chamberlain by contrast was guided by the principle of power, exemplified in his quest for a seat in Parliament in 1876,[38] and a moving target of big causes for which he campaigned – being unafraid to split parties in the process.

George Dixon was thus a still centre amidst the striking personalities among Birmingham's nineteenth-century politicians. John Bright had national fame but, retaining his house in Rochdale as he did and typically visiting Birmingham only once a year, he was always remote from the town's political scene. There was little meeting of minds between himself and Dixon on Dixon's key issue of educational reform. Hence their relationship remained, for the most part, distant.

Putting together the details of Dixon's entire network of political contacts remains a difficult task. A major blow was the destruction of all the family papers at the premises of Rabone, Petersen and Company Ltd. by a German bomb in 1941. The sole remaining correspondence of any length is the sequence of letters to family members which he sent on his voyage to Australasia in 1888, describing his experiences there.[39] These communications perpetuated his travelogue of 1844, when he reported from Scotland and the

---

36 Denys P. Leighton, 'Municipal Progress, Democracy and Radical Identity in Birmingham, 1838-86', *Midland History,* 205 (2000), p. 117.

37 Ibid., p. 118.

38 See above, Chapter 5, p. 170.

39 See above, Chapter 7, p.215.

Iberian peninsula.[40] They give the flavour of a kindly and observant man, with strong family links.

From Dixon's reported speeches in Parliament and elsewhere, no impression is gained of great profundity. His mastery of detail, however, was absolute.

Further clues to his outlook on life come from his library of books, which the family preserved carefully. The author of this study had the chance, as a young man, to list its contents. Whilst the library appeared impressive, further scrutiny revealed that Dixon had in fact read very few of its books, for many pages remained uncut. When he did read, Dixon, like Gladstone, was in the habit of making notes in the margins. Thus it was instructive to find copious annotations in the chapters on commodities and the labour process in Dixon's copy of *Capital: A Critical Analysis of Capitalist Production,* translated from the third German edition of the work by Karl Marx, then relatively unknown in the UK, and published in 1887. Sadly, however, the contents of Dixon's library were subsequently dispersed, and when the author came to start researching this book, the volumes were nowhere to be found.

Dixon also learned much from direct observations. He travelled widely around the world: to Canada, at a date unknown but quite probably around 1850, and twice to Australasia, in the mid-1850s and again in 1888-9. Those visits were essentially of a business nature. But Dixon also travelled extensively to the continent of Europe on holiday, where he and other members of the family enjoyed mountaineering. He was also a life-long enthusiast for riding horses, and gardening.

His active lifestyle included his daily walk to work – always dressed in a black coat, top hat and carrying an umbrella. The family made fun of him in his later years, speaking of him in the manner of 'Onward Christian Soldiers':[41]

> Look at Mr Puddie
> Walking as to war
> With his umberella
> Going on before.

This image was the style of the well-travelled provincial Englishman – not that of someone who enjoyed something more cosmopolitan. It was not as if he could not have afforded more, for he died worth £184,766.5s.11d.,[42] with his investments dominated by holdings in railway companies. But Dixon and his personal style eminently matched each other. He was a respectable and self-confident entrepreneur and had no hesitation in appearing as such.

---

40 See above, Chapter 1, p. 25.
41 Rathbone, *The Dales,* p. 121.
42 Probate Office records.

* * * * *

It is interesting to compare Dixon's personal standing as a merchant with other similar contemporaries, a comparison facilitated by Malchow's research:[43]

George Dixon rose from relatively modest circumstances to become a leading businessman. But like many successful contemporaries, he did not literally come from 'rags' to 'riches'. Dixon's father was certainly not a merchant, but he did have sufficient resources to enable his son to attend Leeds Grammar School.[44]

Dixon's rise was thus within the middling sort, to reach the outer ranks of the plutocracy. As an urban businessman, however, he steered clear of the landed gentry. Indeed he was regularly critical of rural landowners, as shown by his support for Joseph Arch and the agricultural labourers in the 1870s.

Family oral history – which may well be a case of retrospective wishful thinking – has it that George was offered a peerage; that he consulted his family on the matter; and that they preferred that he decline, on the basis that they did not want the attendant publicity. Nonetheless, in his dying weeks he did accept the Freedom of the City of Birmingham, as it had then become.[45] However, such recognition arose not because of his mercantile past, but because of his contribution to educational reform and administration. This record matches that of the businessmen sampled by Malchow, of whom more than a quarter were offered some sort of honour.[46] Indeed, it must be emphasised that Malchow's survey of 86 'gentlemen capitalists' comprises only merchants who partook in political activities. Their collective rise brought them high, but not to the very top of the social ladder. Thus the novelist Anthony Trollope, who specialised in dissecting the political and social elite, observed in 1858 that '… Merchants as such are not the first men among us; though it perhaps be open, barely open, to a merchant to become one of them'.[47]

Accordingly, Malchow noted that only a relatively small minority (around 10% of the merchants he studied) attempted to establish a large, viable landed estate.[48] George Dixon was not amongst that 10%, although as a significant shareholder in the Dixon Investment Company he did gain possession of a large farm in New Zealand, as a result of a financial default by a borrower.[49]

As for the politics of these successful merchants, a mere 15% of the 86 surveyed by Malchow supported the Conservative Party before the split in the Liberal Party in 1886 – and those 15% were often Church supporters.[50]

---

43 See above, Chapter 2, p. 36.
44 See above, Chapter 1, p. 18.
45 See above, Chapter 8, p. 231.
46 Malchow, *Gentlemen Capitalists*, p. 98.
47 Anthony Trollope, *Doctor Thorne*, (1858), pps. 11-12.
48 Malchow, *Gentlemen Capitalists*, p.368.
49 See above, Chapter 7, p. 216.
50 Malchow, *Gentlemen Capitalists*, p.135.

Here, George Dixon was very much like the majority of merchants who were Gladstonian Liberals until the break over Home Rule. Subsequently Dixon was in the forefront of those who became Liberal Unionists, following the lead of Joseph Chamberlain.

The most consistent feature noted amongst all these merchants was one of family solidarity – they supported each other's causes most especially.[51] Dixon exemplified that, remaining on close terms with many relatives. In particular he had a good working relationship with his brother-in-law, Sir James Stansfeld. They both shared lodgings perfectly amicably as widowers from the late 1880s onwards, even though they were by then members of different political parties, as Stansfeld remained loyal to Gladstone and the Liberals. Additionally, Abraham Dixon had married into the Quaker Rathbone family, the eminent Liverpool merchants, which provided the basis for a degree of co-operation between George Dixon, on the one hand, and William Rathbone over mutual points of interest.

In many ways, then, Dixon was very typical of his type of successful businessman. There was, however, one important exception. Malchow observed that 'after 1860 many [Birmingham businessmen] sought rural retreats close enough to the city to be able to continue to play an active part in business but distant as possible from the encroaching lower-middle and middle-class suburbanites'.[52] Abraham Dixon's move to the aristocratic surroundings of Cherkley Court in Surrey was an extreme example, since he retired early from business. But his brother George decidedly bucked this trend. He resolutely stayed put at The Dales, in the heart of fashionable Edgbaston, and within walking distance of his offices in the centre of Birmingham. He made his career with the old-established firm of Rabone Bros. and never quit either the firm or its urban base.

* * * * *

Ultimately, the political and educational history of nineteenth-century Birmingham cannot be understood solely by reference to the lives of Chamberlain and Bright, although they were far better known than their fellow MP, George Dixon. At the core of the town's enduring Liberalism and later Liberal Unionism, was a man of an entirely different disposition, a man well respected if not loved.

Chamberlain and Bright together projected a certain image of Birmingham to the outside world – an image that was not always entirely sympathetic. In 1886, an anonymous author, lurking under the pseudonym as Anoth. R. Shipton (possibly borrowing the allusion to *Mother Shipton's Propheices*) published a

---

51 Ibid., p.137.
52 Ibid., p.370.

sensationalist tract entitled *The Fall of Brum*.[53] It offered a fictionalised account of politics of the day, in which the town and its Liberal caucus were portrayed as threats to the country. None of the characters, however, were modelled on Dixon. He was not melodramatic enough to feature. Instead, beyond the world of fiction, Dixon was seen as a force for good. He was a patient, good humoured and determined educational reformer of considerable standing, and referred to as such across the nation.

The secret of Dixon's more than moderate success was well described by his former colleague George Kenrick in 1909. He identified Dixon's personal qualities as being of paramount importance. He was keen, broadminded, well informed, and scrupulously honourable. At the same time, Kenrick pointed to something extra, which was both enduring and endearing: 'a simplicity in his [Dixon's] character that was very charming, and he frequently told stories at his own expense, into the enjoyment of which he thoroughly entered'.[54]

So was Charlotte Brontë correct after all in her youthful criticism of George Dixon as 'a man without a backbone'? Dixon himself later rebutted that criticism head-on. In his own words 'it was always necessary to be making experiments in every branch of life; many of them, perhaps most of them failed, but without experiment there was no life and no progress'.[55] That is, he had the guts to aim for major changes and to persist in the campaign.

Another member of the Kenrick family, Alderman W. Byng Kenrick, expressed very similar sentiments many years later, speaking at the fiftieth anniversary of the George Dixon School:[56]

> The founder himself was a great merchant adventurer, and part of the merchant adventurer's spirit was to be found in the merchants of Birmingham during his period. He was always in favour of making experiments and was perfectly ready to change his original ideas if he thought it desirable.

George Dixon believed in the ultimately transformative power of education. Not only did he campaign for the pioneering legislation of 1870 and many Acts thereafter, but he also applied himself to making the Birmingham School Board work. If ultimately the school boards were superseded by later educational bodies, their work remained foundational. On this subject, Conan Doyle allowed the great detective Sherlock Holmes to express a rare moment of rhapsody. Holmes having observed the 'big, isolated clumps of buildings, rising

---

53 Anoth. R. Shipton [pseudonym], *The Fall of Brum: Dedicated, without Permission, to the Birmingham Caucus* (Birmingham, 1886).
54 Kenrick, 'George Dixon', p. 72.
55 Ibid., p. 69.
56 *Birmingham Post*, 5 March 1934.

above the slates, like brick islands in a lead-coloured sea', Watson identified them as the new Board Schools:

> Lighthouses, my boy! Beacons of the future! Capsules, with hundreds of bright little seeds in each, out of which will spring the wiser, better England of the future.[57]

George Dixon thoroughly concurred and worked to make it happen. Even the storm petrel of British politics Joseph Chamberlain was ultimately generous not just about the policies but also about the personality and values of his quiet colleague, rival, and fellow citizen whose message, like his, had come out of Birmingham. Of George Dixon, Chamberlain recorded that[58]

> [He] now leaves behind him to his children – as a priceless legacy – the reputation of an English gentleman, honourable, simple-minded, straightforward and disinterested.

57 A.C. Conan Doyle, 'The Naval Treaty' (1ˢᵗ pub. *Strand Magazine,* 1893) in *The Memoirs of Sherlock Holmes* (1973 edn.), p. 215.
58 Hayward, 'The Dixon Family', Part 2, p. 356.

APPENDIX 1

Valuator's Report.

THE DIXON INVESTMENT COMPANY, Limited

Quantity of land
How much flat
How much bush
How much ploughable
How much under crop
How much under English grass
By whom occupied
Number of sections and name of district

Name of nearest township and of nearest port or railway station and distance therefrom

Kind and number of stock at present carried
  Sheep   : cattle   : pigs   : horses

GENERAL REPORT

(The Valuator is requested to include in his report nature of road communicating with nearest town, port, or railway station; description of improvements, fencing, etc., and water supply, character of land and quality of soil and subsoil; carrying and productive capacity; description and value of buildings, and insurance thereon; condition and value of stock; to mention whether there are any disadvantages, such as liability to floods, rabbits, manuka, tauwhino, or other noxious weeds or plants; to say whether in his opinion the land is being well managed and used to best advantage; and to give his opinion as to whether the security is perfectly safe and satisfactory both from the point of view of the land and the character and capacity of the Mortgagor).

VALUATION

(The Valuator is requested to give the amount of Government or County Council assessment for taxation; to give, if possible, the net returns from books kept by occupier or manager for at least three years preceding date of present valuation; or to give his own estimate of net income if estate is properly worked; also to give details, if possible, of the gross annual returns from wool, sales of stock, crops and rents (if any), and of annual expenses, such as labour, rates and taxes, etc.. A valuation should be given based on the above returns, and capitalised at 8 per cent., in addition to the valuator's own estimate of value, and if these two valuations do not agree the reason of their difference should be explained).

Bibliography

UNPUBLISHED PRIMARY SOURCES

Alexander Turnbull Library, Wellington, New Zealand: George Dixon letters written home from New Zealand, 1888.

Birmingham Archives and Heritage: Birmingham Chamber of Commerce Minute Book, 1861-5.

Birmingham Archives and Heritage: Birmingham Chamber of Commerce Minute Book, 1865-8.

Birmingham Archives and Heritage: Birmingham Chamber of Commerce Minute Book, 1868-72.

Birmingham Archives and Heritage: Birmingham School Board Minutes.

Birmingham Archives and Heritage: Birmingham School Board Annual Reports.

Birmingham Archives and Heritage: file MS725/8: Dixon papers.

Birmingham Archives and Heritage: file MS2239: material not incorporated in K. Rathbone, *The Dales: Growing Up in a Victorian Family* (Ledbury, 1989).

Birmingham Archives and Heritage, file MS2536: Rabone and Petersen Ltd. papers.

Birmingham Archives and Heritage, file MS/S/80/1: Log Book of the George Dixon Higher Grade School, 1884-1906.

Birmingham University Special Collections: Joseph Chamberlain Papers.

Birmingham University Special Collections: George Dixon Papers.

British Library, files MS43909 and E1766: Gladstone correspondence files.

British Library: Rev. William Gover, 'Day School Education in the Borough of Birmingham: Our Progress, Position and Needs: A Letter to George Dixon, Esq., Mayor' (Unpublished letter, 1867).

Brontë Parsonage Museum: Dixon Papers.

Guildhall Library, file MS14476-1: Association of Chambers of Commerce of the United Kingdom Minute Book.

Institute of Education, London: Birmingham Education Society Annual Reports, 1868-70.

Institute of Education, London: National Education League pamphlets, 1869-71, bound in 4 volumes.

Kew Gardens, Directors' correspondence files, 1868-99.

Liverpool University, File RPXXI.2.8(3): Rathbone Family Autograph Collection.

Lloyds Banking Group Archives: Group archives, 1865-7.

Nelson Provincial Museum, New Zealand: Dixon Investment Company Limited files.

The National Archives, file BT31/36585/21203: Dixon Investment Company Limited statutory returns 1885-1954.

Terrace Station, Hororata, New Zealand: Sir John Hall papers.

West Yorkshire Archives, file WYL962/2/2: Sir James Stansfeld papers.

PRINTED PRIMARY SOURCES PRE-1914
(The place of publication is London, unless otherwise stated).

F. Adams, *History of the Elementary School Contest in England* (1882; in new edn. Brighton, 1973).

W.C. Aitken and G. Lindsey, *British Manufacturing Industries* (1878).

T. Anderton, *A Tale of One City: The New Birmingham* (Birmingham, 1900).

Anon., *Swiss Notes by Five Ladies* (1875).

J. Arch, *The Story of His Life* (1898).

R.A. Armstrong, *Henry William Crosskey* (Birmingham, 1895).

M. Arnold, *Culture and Anarchy* (1869).

M. Arnold, *Last Essays on Church and Religion* (1877).

P. Ashley, *Modern Tariff History* (1910).

W.J. Ashley, *Birmingham Industry and Commerce* (Birmingham, 1913).

J. Austen, *Emma* (1816).

J.A. Bridges, *Reminiscences of a Country Politician* (1906).

C. Brontë, *Shirley* (1849).

J.T. Bunce, *History of the Corporation of Birmingham* (Birmingham, 1885), Vol. 2.

G. Chesney, 'The Battle of Dorking', *Blackwood's Magazine* (1871).

A. Clayden, *The Revolt of the Field* (1874).

A. Clayden, *The England of the Pacific: Or, New Zealand as an English Middle-Class Emigration Field* (1879).

Jesse Collings, *On the State of Education in Birmingham* (Birmingham, 1868).

J. Collings, *Land Reform* (1906).

L. Creswicke, *The Life of the Right Honourable Joseph Chamberlain, Vol. 1* (1904).

W. Cunningham, *The Rise and Decline of the Free Trade Movement* (1904).

A.W.W. Dale, *Life of R.W. Dale* (1898).

A.W.W. Dale, 'George Dawson', in Muirhead (ed.), *Nine Famous Birmingham Men* (Birmingham, 1909).

R.W. Dale, 'The Nonconformists and the Education Policy of the Government', *Contemporary Review* (Sept. 1873).

W.A. Dalley, *The Life Story of W.J. Davis, JP* (Birmingham, 1914).

J. M. Davidson, *Eminent Radicals In and Out of Parliament* (1880).

R.K. Dent, *Old and New Birmingham,* (Birmingham, 1878; repr. 1973), Vol. 3.

R.K. Dent, *Allday's Gossiping Guide to Birmingham* (1893).

R.K. Dent, *The Making of Birmingham: Being a History of the Rise and Growth of the Midland Metropolis* (1894).

S. Dowell, *A History of Taxation and Taxes in England from the Earliest Times to the Present Day* (1884).

O.J. Dunlop, *The Farm Labourer: The Story of a Modern Problem* (1913).

J.J. Findlay, 'The Genesis of the German Clerk', *Fortnightly Review* (1899).

R. Gregory, *Elementary Education* (1895).

J. Hall, *Speeches Delivered out of Parliament* (Christchurch, NZ, 1911).

W. Hasbach, *A History of the English Agricultural Labourer* (1908).

F.G. Heath, *The English Peasantry* (1874).

J.E. Jones, *A Short History of Birmingham* (Birmingham, 1911).

G.H. Kenrick, 'George Dixon: A Lecture', in J.H. Muirhead (ed.), '*Nine Famous Birmingham Men*'.

J.A. Langford, *Kossuth, Mazzini, Urquhart, and the Conferences* (1855).

J.A. Langford, *Modern Birmingham and Its Institutions: A Chronicle of Local Events, from 1841 to 1871* (Birmingham, 1873-7), Vols.1 and 2.

J.A. Langford, *The Old Liberals and the New: A Tract for the Times* (Birmingham, 1886).

M. Leclerc, *L'education des classes moyennes et dirigeantes en Angleterre* (Paris, 1894).

J. Leese, *Denominational Schools: Their Rights and Interests* (1870).

O. Lodge, 'Early History of the University and its Parent Institutions', in J.H. Muirhead (ed.), '*Birmingham Institutions*' (Birmingham, 1911).

J. Lowe, *The Yew-Trees of Great Britain and Ireland* (1897).

H.E. Malden (ed.), *Victoria History of the County of Surrey* (1911), Vol.3.

A.P. Martin, *Life and Letters of the Rt. Hon. Robert Lowe* (1893), Vol. 2.

J. Morley, *The Struggle for National Education* (1873).

R. Palmer, *Memorials: Part 2* (1898).

H. Paul, *A History of Modern England* (1905).

H.B. Philpott, *London at School* (1904).

J. Ralph, 'The Best-Governed City in the World', *Harper's New Monthly Magazine*, 81 (New York, 1890).

E.F. Rathbone, *William Rathbone: A Memoir* (1905).

C.E.B. Reed, *Memoirs of Sir Charles Reed* (1883).

Royal Commission Appointed to Inquire into the Working of the Elementary Education Acts (1886).

G.W.E. Russell (ed.), *Letters of Matthew Arnold, 1848-88* (1904), Vol. 14.

E.G. Sandford, *Frederick Temple: An Appreciation* (1907).

W.L. Sargant, *Essays of a Birmingham Manufacturer* (1872).

Second Report of the Royal Commission Appointed to Inquire into the Working of the Elementary Education Acts, England and Wales (1887).

A. Shadwell, *Industrial Efficiency: A Comparative Study of Industrial Life In England, Germany and America* (1906), Vol. 2.

Anoth. R. Shipton [pseudonym], *The Fall of Brum*, (Birmingham, 1886).

W. Showell, *Dictionary of Birmingham* (Birmingham, 1885).

A. Sidgwick and E.M. Sidgwick, *Henry Sidgwick: A Memoir* (1906).

James Stansfeld, *The Italian Movement and Italian Parties* (1862).

C.J. Stone, *What Happened after the Battle of Dorking* (n.d.).

S. Timmins, *The Resources, Products, and Industrial History of Birmingham and the Midland Hardware District* (1866).

C.A. Vince, *History of the Corporation of Birmingham* (Birmingham, 1902), Vol. 3.

T.H. Ward (ed.), *Matthew Arnold: The Reign of Queen Victoria* (1887), Vol. 2.

E.E. Williams, *Made in Germany* (1896).

A. Williamson, *British Industries and Foreign Competition* (1894).

W. Wilson, *The Life of George Dawson* (Birmingham, 1905).

J. Wodehouse, *Lord Kimberley's Defence of the Government Brothel System at Hong Kong* (1882).
G.H. Wright, *Chronicles of the Birmingham Chamber of Commerce, A.D. 1813-1913* (Birmingham, 1913).

HANSARD
1868, Vols. 190-3.
1869, Vols. 194, 196-8.
1870, Vols. 199-203.
1871, Vols. 204-8.
1872, Vols. 209-212.
1873, Vols. 214-7.
1874, Vols. 218-221.
1875, Vols. 222-5.
1876, Vols. 228-9.
1887, Vol. 312.
1888, Vols. 326-7.
1889, Vols. 333, 338-40.
1891, Vols. 354-5.
1892, Vol. 5.
1893, Vols. 8,11,15.
1894, Vols. 26-7.
1896, Vol. 40.
1897, Vol. 45.

NEWSPAPERS AND JOURNALS (PRE AND POST 1914)
Birmingham Daily Gazette.
Birmingham Daily Post.
Birmingham Faces and Places: An Illustrated Local Magazine (Birmingham, 1893), Vol. 5.
Birmingham Historian.
Birmingham Post.
Bradford Observer.
Country Life.
Daily News.
The Dart.
The Dart and Midland Figaro.
Edgbastonia.
Greenwich and Woolwich Gazette.
Illustrated Police News.
Lyttelton Times.
Monthly Paper.
The Owl.
Reynolds's Newspaper.
School Board Chronicle.
The Press.
The Times.

PRINTED SECONDARY SOURCES POST-1914

J.W. Adamson, *A Short History of Education* (Cambridge, 1919).

J.W. Adamson, *English Education, 1789-1902* (Cambridge, 1930).

D.H. Aldcroft, 'Introduction: British Industry and Foreign Competition, 1875-1914', in D.H. Aldcroft (ed.), *The Development of British Industry and Foreign Competition, 1875-1914 (Toronto, 1968).*

R. Aldrich and P. Gordon, *Dictionary of British Educationists* (1989).

G.C. Allen, *The Industrial Development of Birmingham and the Black Country, 1860-1927* (1929).

R.D. Anderson, *Education and the Scottish People* (Oxford, 1995).

Anon., *Leatherhead Institute: Hall Restoration Project* [Leatherhead, n.d.].

Anon., *Rabone, Petersen and Company Ltd.* (c.1950).

Anon., *Red House Museum: A Guide* (Kirklees, n.d.).

R.L. Archer, *Secondary Education in the Nineteenth Century* (1921).

W.H.G. Armytage, *A.J. Mundella, 1825-97* (1951).

W.H.G. Armytage, Four Hundred Years of English Education (Cambridge, 1970).

W.H.G. Armytage, *The American Influence on English Education* (1967).

W.H.G. Armytage, 'The Education Act 1870', *British Journal of Educational Studies,* 18 (1970).

W.H.G. Armytage, *The German Influence on English Education* (1969).

P. Auspos, 'Radicalism, Pressure Groups, and Party Politics', *Journal of British Studies,* 20 (1980).

H.C. Barnard, *A Short History of English Education from 1760 to 1944* (1947).

G.J. Barnsby, *Birmingham Working People: A History of the Labour Movement in Birmingham, 1650-1914* (1989).

D.W. Bebbington, *The Nonconformist Conscience: Chapel and Politics, 1870-1914* (1982).

J. Bellamy, *'More Precious than Rubies': Mary Taylor: Friend of Charlotte Brontë, Strong-Minded Woman* (Beverley, 2002).

M. Bentley, *Lord Salisbury's World* (2001).

G. Best, *Mid-Victorian Britain* (1971).

V. Bird, *Portrait of Birmingham* (1970).

Birmingham Co-operative Society Ltd., *History of the Birmingham Co-operative Society Limited* (1931).

J. Bowen, *A History of Western Education,* (1981), Vol. 3.

G.R. Boyer and T.J. Hatton, *Did Joseph Arch Raise Agricultural Wages? Rural Trade Unions and the Labour Market in late Nineteenth Century England* (1990).

A. Briggs, *History of Birmingham: Borough and City, 1865-1938* (Oxford, 1952), Vol. 2.

A. Briggs, *Victorian Cities* (1963).

A. Briggs, *Victorian People: A Reassessment of Persons and Themes, 1851-67* (Chicago, 1955).

A. Briggs (ed.), *Chartist Studies* (1962).

J.H.Y. Briggs, 'Elite and Proletariat in Nineteenth-Century Birmingham Non-conformity', in A.P.F. Sell (ed.), *Protestant Nonconformists and the West Midlands of England* (Keele, 1996).

J. Bright, *The Diaries of John Bright* (1930).

H. Browne, *The Rise of British Trade Unions* (1979).

H. Ashwell Cadman, *Gomersal Past and Present* (Leeds, 1930).

D. Cannadine, *Lords and Landlords: the Aristocracy and the Towns* (Leicester, 1980).

D. Cannadine, 'The Bourgeois Experience as Political Culture: The Chamberlains of Birmingham', in M.S. Micale and R.L. Dietle (eds), *Enlightenment, Passion, Modernity: Historical Essays in European Thought and Culture* (Stanford, 2000).

W. [Bill] Cash, *John Bright: Statesman, Orator, Agitator* (2012).

I. Cawood, 'The 1892 General Election and the Eclipse of the Liberal Unionists', *Parliamentary History*, 29 (2010).

I. Cawood, *The Liberal Unionist Party* (2012).

A. Chamberlain, *Down the Years* (1935).

C. Chinn, 'Was Separate Schooling a Means of Class Segregation in late Victorian and Edwardian Birmingham', *Midland History,* 13 (1988).

R.A. Church, *Kenricks in Hardware: A Family Business, 1791-1966* (Newton Abbot, 1969).

R. Church, *The Dynamics of Victorian Business: Problems and Perspectives to the 1870s* (1980).

J.H. Clapham, *An Economic History of Modern Britain: Free Trade and Steel, 1850-86* (Cambridge, 1932), Vol. 2.

J.H. Clapham, *An Economic History of Modern Britain: Free Trade and Steel, 1850-86* (Cambridge, 1938), Vol. 3.

W.F. Connell, *The Educational Thought and Influence of Matthew Arnold* (1950).

J. Corbett, *The Birmingham Trades Council, 1866-1966* (1966).

T.L. Crosby, *Joseph Chamberlain* (2011).

Marjorie Cruickshank, *Church and State in English Education: 1870 to the Present Day* (1963).

S.J. Curtis and M.E.A. Boultwood, An Introductory History of English Education Since 1800 (1960).

N. Daglish, *Education Policy-Making in England and Wales: The Crucible Years, 1895-1991* (1996).

L. Davidoff and C. Hall, *Family Fortunes: Men and Women of the English Middle Class, 1780-1850* (1987).

Dictionary of NZ Biography.

J.P.D. Dunbabin, ' "The Revolt of the Field": The Agricultural Labourers' Movement in the 1870s', *Past and Present*, 26 (1963).

E.J.R. Eaglesham, *From School Board to Local Authority* (1956).

E.J.R. Eaglesham, *The Foundations of Twentieth-Century Education in England* (1967).

R.C.K. Ensor, *England, 1870-1914* (Oxford, 1936).

K. Fielden, 'The Rise and Fall of Free Trade', in C.J. Bartlett (ed.), *Britain Pre-eminent: Studies of British World Influence in the Nineteenth Century* (1969).

M.C. Finn, *After Chartism: Class and Nation in English Radical Politics, 1848-74* (Cambridge, 1974).

W.S. Fowler, *A Study in Radicalism and Dissent: The Life and Times of Henry Joseph Wilson, 1833-1914* (1961).

D. Fraser, *Power and Authority in the Victorian City* (Oxford, 1979).

W.H. Fraser, *Trade Unions and Society: The Struggle for Acceptance, 1850-80* (1974).

O.Z.A. Garcia, *Sugar and Railroads: A Cuban History, 1837-1959* (University of North Carolina Press, 1998).

J. Garner, *By His Own Merits: Sir John Hall, Pioneer, Pastoralist and Premier* (Hororata, 1995)

J.L. Garvin, *The Life of Joseph Chamberlain* (1932), Vol. 1.

D. Gerhold, *Villas and Mansions of Roehampton and Putney Heath* (Wandsworth, 1997).

W. Gérin, *Charlotte Brontë: The Evolution of Genius* (Oxford, 1967).

C. Gill and C.G. Robertson, *A Short History of Birmingham* (Birmingham, 1938).

C. Gill, *History of Birmingham, Manor and Borough to 1865* (Oxford, 1952), Vol. 1.

S. Gunn, *The Public Culture of the Victorian Middle Class: Ritual and Authority and the English Industrial City* (Manchester, 2000).

D.J. Hallam, *The First 200 Years – A Short History of Rabone Chesterman Limited* (Birmingham, 1984).

J.L. Hammond, *James Stansfeld: A Victorian Champion of Sex Equality* (1932).

H.J. Hanham, *Elections and Party Management: Politics in the Time of Disraeli and Gladstone* (1959).

B. Harrison, *Drink and the Victorians* (1971).

G. Hayward, 'The Dixon Family of Cherkley Court, Leatherhead', *Proceedings of the Leatherhead and District Local History Society, Parts 1-3* (1975; 1976; and 1979).

W.O. Henderson, *Britain and Industrial Europe, 1750-1870* (Leicester, 1972).

E.P. Hennock, *Fit and Proper Persons. Ideal and Reality in Nineteenth-Century Urban Government* (1973).

R.J.S. Hoffman, *Great Britain and the German Trade Rivalry, 1875-1914* (Philadelphia, 1933).

P. Hollis (ed.), *Pressure from Without in Early Victorian England* (1974).

R.V. Holt, *The Unitarian Contribution to Social Progress in England* (1938).

E. Hopkins, *The First Manufacturing Town in the World, 1760-1840* (1989).

P. Horn, *Joseph Arch, 1826–1919: The Farm Workers' Leader* (Kineton, 1971).

T. Hunt, *Building Jerusalem: The Rise and Fall of the Victorian City* (2004).

J.S. Hurt, *Elementary Schooling and the Working Classes, 1860-1918* (1979).

A.R. Ilersic and P.F.B. Liddle, *Parliament of Commerce: The Story of the Association of British Chambers of Commerce, 1860-1960* (1960).

R. Jenkins, *Sir Charles Dilke: A Victorian Tragedy* (1958).

E.L. Jones, 'The Agricultural Labour Market in England 1793-1872', *Economic History Review* (1964/5).

L.J. Jones, 'Public Pursuit of Private Profit? Liberal Businessmen and Municipal Politics in Birmingham 1865-1900', *Business History* (1983).

A.M. Kazamias, 'Spencer and the Welfare State', *History of Education Quarterly* (1966).

C. Kennedy: *Business Pioneers – Family, Fortune and Philanthropy: Cadbury, Sainsbury and John Lewis* (2000).

J. Lawson and H. Silver, *A Social History of Education in England* (1973).

Denys P. Leighton, 'Municipal Progress, Democracy and Radical Identity in Birmingham, 1838-86', *Midland History,* 205 (2000).

J.P. Lethbridge, *Victorian Birmingham* (Birmingham, 2002).

G. Lichtheim, *The Origins of Socialism* (1968).

S. Maccoby, *English Radicalism, 1886-1914* (1953), Vol. 2.

H.L. Malchow, *Gentlemen Capitalists: The Social and Political World of the Victorian Businessman* (1991).

S.E. Maltby, *Manchester and the Movement for National Elementary Education, 1800-70* (Manchester, 1918).

J.S. Maclure, *Educational Documents, England and Wales, 1816-1967* (1968).

J.S. Maclure, *One Hundred Years of London Education, 1870-1970* (1970).

A.K. Manchester, *British Pre-eminence in Brazil: Its Rise and Decline* (Chapel Hill, 1933).

A.J. Marcham, 'The Birmingham Education Society and the 1870 Education Act', *Journal of Educational Administration and History*, 8 (1976).

S. Marriner, *Rathbones of Liverpool, 1845-73* (Liverpool, 1961).

P.T. Marsh, *Bargaining on Europe: Britain and the First Common Market, 1860-92* (New Haven, 1999).

P.T. Marsh, *Joseph Chamberlain: Entrepreneur in Politics* (New Haven, 1994).

W.P. McCann, *Popular Education and Socialization in the Nineteenth Century* (1977).

W.P. McCann, 'Trade Unionists, Artisans, and the 1870 Education Act', *British Journal of Educational Studies* (1980).

E. Midwinter, *Nineteenth-Century Education* (1970).

B.R. Mitchell, *Abstract of British Historical Statistics* (Cambridge, 1971).

A. Morton, *Education and the State from 1833* (Kew, 1997).

S. Mukherjee, *A History of Socialist Thought: From the Precursors to the Present* (2000).

J. Murphy, *Church, State and Schools in Britain, 1800-1970* (1971).

J. Murphy, *The Education Act 1870* (Newton Abbot, 1972).

J. Murphy, *The Religious Problem in English Education: The Crucial Experiment* (Liverpool, 1959).

D. Nicholls, *The Lost Prime Minister: A Life of Sir Charles Dilke* (1995).

P.K. O'Brien, 'The Security of the Realm and the Growth of the Economy', in P. Clarke and C. Trebilcock (eds), *Understanding Decline: Perceptions and Realities of British Economic Performance* (Cambridge, 1997).

D. Owen, *English Philanthropy* (Cambridge, Massachusetts, 1964).

P.L. Payne, *British Entrepreneurship in the Nineteenth Century* (1988).

H. Perkin, *The Origins of Modern English Society, 1780-1880* (1969).

A.D.C. Peterson, *A Hundred Years of Education* (1971).

D.C.M. Platt, *Finance, Trade, and Politics in British Foreign Policy, 1815-1914* (Oxford, 1968).

A.C. Price, *A History of the Leeds Grammar School from its Foundation to the End of 1918* (1919).

R. Quinault, 'John Bright and Joseph Chamberlain', *Historical Journal*, 28 (1985).

A. Ramm, 'The Parliamentary Context of Cabinet Government, 1868-74', *English Historical Review* (1984).

K. Rathbone, *The Dales: Growing Up in a Victorian Family* (Ledbury, 1989).

D. Read, *The English Provinces, c.1760–1960* (1964).

E. Rich, *The Education Act 1870: A Study of Public Opinion* (1970).

N.J. Richards, 'Religious Controversy and the School Boards, 1870-1902', *British Journal of Educational Studies*, 18 (1970).

G.T. Rimmington, *The Rise and Fall of Elected School Boards* (Peterborough, 1986).

J. Roach, *Secondary Education in England, 1870-1902: Public Activity and Private Enterprise* (1991).

S. Roberts, 'John Skirrow Wright: The Benefactor Whose Statue was Destroyed', *Birmingham Historian* (2009).

K. Robbins, *John Bright* (1979).

G.W. Roderick and M.D. Stephens, *Education and Industry in the Nineteenth Century: The English Disease?* (1978).

T.B. Rogers, *A Century of Progress, 1831-1931* (Bournville, 1931).

H. Roper, 'Towards an Elementary Education Act for England and Wales, 1865-8', *British Journal of Educational Studies,* 23 (1975).

J. Sage, *The Memoirs concerning Joseph Arch and the Pioneering Days of Trade Unionism among the Agricultural Workers* (1951).

M. Sanderson, *The Universities and British Industry 1850-1970* (1972).

S.B. Saul, *Studies in British Overseas Trade, 1870-1914* (Liverpool, 1960).

R.S. Sayers, *Lloyds Bank in the History of English Banking* (Oxford, 1957).

Bob Scarth, *We'll All be Union Men: The Story of Joseph Arch and his Union* (Coventry, 1998).

G.R. Searle, *Entrepreneurial Politics in Mid-Victorian Britain* (Oxford, 1993).

B. Simon, *Studies in the History of Education, 1780-1870* (1960).

B. Simon, *The Two Nations and the Educational Structure, 1780-1870* (1974).

V. Skipp, *The Making of Victorian Birmingham* (Birmingham, 1983).

J. Slinn, *Ashurst Morris Crisp: A Radical Firm* (1997).

D. Smith, *Conflict and Compromise – Class Formation in English Society, 1830-1914: A Comparative Study of Birmingham and Sheffield* (1982).

F. Smith, *The Life of Sir James Kay-Shuttleworth* (1923).

R.F. Spall, 'Free-Trade Radicals, Education, and Moral Improvement in Early Victorian England', in M. H. Shirley and T.E.A. Larson (eds), *'Splendidly Victorian': Essays in Nineteenth- and Twentieth-Century British History in Honour of W.L. Arnstein* (Aldershot, 2001).

W.B. Stephens, *Education in Britain, 1750-1914* (Basingstoke, 1998).

W.B. Stephens (ed.), *Victoria History of the County of Warwick* (1964), Vol. 7.

J. Stevens, *Mary Taylor, Friend of Charlotte Brontë: Letters from New Zealand and Elsewhere* (Auckland and Oxford, 1972).

W.A.C. Stewart and W.P. McCann, *The Educational Innovators, 1750-1880* (2000), Vol. 1.

W. Stranz, *George Cadbury: An Illustrated Life of George Cadbury, 1839-1922* (Aylesbury, 1973).

A. Sutcliffe, 'The "Midland Metropolis": Birmingham, 1890-1980', in G. Gordon (ed.), *Regional Cities in the UK 1890-1980* (1986).

G. Sutherland, *Ability, Merit and Measurement: Mental Testing and English Education 1880-1940* (Oxford, 1984).

G. Sutherland, 'Education', in F.M.L. Thompson (ed.), *The Cambridge Social History of Britain* (1990), Vol. 3.

G. Sutherland, *Elementary Education in the Nineteenth Century* (1971).

G. Sutherland, *Policy-Making in Elementary Education, 1870-95* (Oxford, 1973).

G. Sutherland (ed.), *Studies in the Growth of Nineteenth-Century Government* (1972).

D.W. Sylvester, *Robert Lowe and Education* (Cambridge, 1974).

R. Szreter, 'The Origins of Full-Time Compulsory Education at Five', *British Journal of Educational Studies,* 13 (1964).

D. Tate, *Birmingham Gunmakers* (Long Beach, California, 1997).

M.J. Turner, *Independent Radicalism in Early Victorian Britain* (Westport, Connecticut, 2004).

C. Upton, *A History of Birmingham* (Chichester, 1993).

J. Vincent, *The Formation of the Liberal Party, 1857-68* (1966).

M. Vlaeminke, *The English Higher Grade Schools: A Lost Opportunity* (2000).

R.A.J. Walling (ed.), *The Diaries of John Bright, with a foreword by Philip Bright* (1930).

L.O. Ward, 'Joseph Chamberlain and the Denominational Schools Question', *Journal of Educational Administration and History,* 5 (1973).

R. Ward, *City-State and Nation: Birmingham's Political History, c.1830-1940* (Chichester, 2005).

D. Wardle, *English Popular Education, 1780-1970* (Cambridge, 1970).

E.G. West, *Education and the Industrial Revolution* (1975).

E.G. West, *Education and the State: A Study in Political Economy* (1965).

J. Whitcut, *Edgbaston High School, 1876-1976* (Edgbaston, 1976).

P. White, *Thomas Huxley, Making the 'Man of Science'* (Cambridge, 2003).

M.J. Wiener, *English Culture and the Decline of the Industrial Spirit* (Cambridge, 1981).

I.A. Williams, *The Firm of Cadbury, 1831-1931* (1931).

J. Winter, *Robert Lowe* (Toronto, 1976).

T.J. Wise and J.A. Symington (eds), *The Brontës: Their Lives, Friendships and Correspondence in Four Volumes,* (Oxford, 1932), Vol. 1.

UNPUBLISHED THESES

C. Kenny, 'The Lady Herringham Collection' (unpub. MA, Royal Holloway and Bedford New College, 1998).

R.C. Raffell, 'The Radical and Nonconformist Influences on the Creation of the Dual System of Universal Elementary Education in England and Wales, 1866-70' (unpub. PhD, University of Hull, 1993).

D. Roland, 'The Struggle for the Education Act and Its Implementation, 1870-3' (unpub. BLitt, Oxford University, 1957). Currently unavailable in both University of Oxford and British Library (2011).

A.F. Taylor, 'Birmingham and the Movement for National Education, 1869-77' (unpub. PhD, University of Leicester, 1960).

A.F. Taylor, 'The History of the Birmingham School Board, 1870–1903' (unpub. MA, University of Birmingham, 1955).

S. Wright, 'The Struggle for Moral Education in English Elementary Schools, 1879-1918' (unpub. PhD, Oxford Brookes University, 2006).

Index